The Cost of Freedom

The Cost of Freedom

Voicing a Movement after Kent State 1970

EDITED BY SUSAN J. ERENRICH

The Kent State University Press
KENT, OHIO

© 2020 by The Kent State University Press, Kent, Ohio 44242
All rights reserved
ISBN 978-1-60635-401-8
Manufactured in the United States of America

No part of this book may be used or reproduced, in any manner whatsoever, without written permission from the Publisher, except in the case of short quotations in critical reviews or articles.

Cataloging information for this title is available at the Library of Congress.

24 23 22 21 20   5 4 3 2 1

Contents

Foreword by Kenneth Hammond   ix
Acknowledgments   xiii
Introduction   xv

PART I: MEMORIES

Anniversary, May 4, 1988
   Piece by Elaine Holstein   3
A Tribute to Arthur Krause: Delivered at Kent State University, May 4, 1989
   Speech by Kendra Lee Hicks Pacifico   6
May 4, 2000, Commemorative Program Speech
   Speech by Barry Levine   11

PART II: PHOTOGRAPHS OF MAY 4, 1970

Guardsmen Beginning Advance on the Commons
   Photo by Chuck Ayers   19
Guardsmen Throwing Tear Gas
   Photo by KSU News Service   20
Prentice Hall Parking Lot
   Photo by KSU News Service   21
Four Students Killed by the Ohio National Guard
   Photo by KSU News Service   22

PART III: EARLIER ACTIVISM BEFORE MAY 4, 1970

Thy Tears Might Cease
   Piece by Anthony Walsh   25
Save the Pooch
   Piece by Robert Stamps   37

PART IV: THE SHOOTINGS: MAY 4, 1970

It's Alright, Ma, I'm Only Dying: An Eyewitness Report from Kent State
   Piece by Constance Nowakowski   47
A Reminiscence Thirty Years Later
   Piece by Rolly Brown   53
A Short Reflection
   Piece by Curtis Lee Pittman (Jeter)   59

PART V: RESPONSES NEAR AND FAR

The Battle of Washington
   Piece by Tom Riddle   65
A Very Young Activist
   Piece by Patricia Moseley   87
May 1970: North and South, Mountains and Deserts—and Blood
   Piece by John Hunter Gray   90

PART VI: HALLOWED GROUND

Kent State: Destruction of Civil Liberties
   Piece by William G. Arthrell   101
Where Were You on May 4, 1970?
   Piece by James Huebner   111

PART VII: LEGAL MANEUVERING AND THE COURTS

The Ruse of the Kent 25 Indictments
   Piece by Roseann "Chic" Canfora   119
May 4, 1988, Speech
   Speech by William Moses Kunstler   128
The Big Chill: The Stifling Effect of the Official Response to the Kent State Killings
   Piece by William Whitaker   132

Eulogy for Galen Keller Lewis
  Delivered by Rev. Barbara Child   141
The Kent State Shootings after Nearly 50 Years: One Lawyer's Remembrance
  Piece by Sanford Jay Rosen   145

PART VIII: TESTIMONIALS BY SOME OF THE WOUNDED STUDENTS

My Life Was Forever Changed
  Piece by Dean Kahler   157
Speech on May 4, 1984
  Speech by Tom Grace   162
May 4 Recollections
  Piece by John Cleary   168
Russell and Me: Surviving Kent State
  Piece by Joseph Lewis   174

PART IX: TROUBADOURS OF CONSCIENCE

The Kent State Massacre
  Piece and Song by Barbara Dane   189
Twenty Years Later
  Piece and Song by Holly Near   193
Kent
  Song by Greg Artzner and Terry Leonino (Magpie)   197
An Eyewitness Recollection Thirty Years after the Shootings
  Piece by Terry Leonino   200
You Carried Us: For Professor Glenn W. Frank (1928–93)
  Song by Greg Artzner and Terry Leonino (Magpie)   203

PART X: ANNUAL RITUALS AND HISTORIC MARKERS

The Candlelight Walk and Vigil
  Piece by Jerry M. Lewis   207
Parking Lot Dedication Remarks
  Piece by Carole A. Barbato   217
Preserving the Site and Story of the May 4, 1970, Kent State Shootings
  Piece by Laura L. Davis   221

PART XI: LASTING LEGACIES

Why Is It So Cold in Northern Ohio?
   Piece by Mark Rudd   261

The Greater Kent State Era, 1968–70: Personal Transformations and Legacies of Student Rebellions and State Repression
   Piece by Darlene Clark Hine   265

Simple Themes and Complex Realities in the Spring of 1970
   Piece by Tom Dietz   275

Message from a May 4 Baby: (P)reflections on the Fiftieth Commemoration of May 4, 1970
   Piece by Idris Kabir Syed   279

Appendix: May 4, 1970, the Struggle for History and the Internet
   Piece by Michael Pacifico   298

Index   309

Foreword

Find the Cost of Freedom

KENNETH HAMMOND

Kenneth Hammond attended Kent State University beginning in fall 1967. He joined Students for a Democratic Society (SDS) in 1968 and wrote the SDS weekly column in the Daily Kent Stater *through spring 1969. In May 1970, he took part in the demonstrations at Kent and was one of the Kent 25 indicted by the Ohio grand jury. He teaches history at New Mexico State University.*

While growing up in the eastern suburbs of Cleveland in the 1950s and 1960s, the town of Kent and Kent State University were part of my consciousness. My father liked to take us for Sunday drives, which often had as their turnaround point a late lunch or early dinner at the Robin Hood Inn in Kent, at the corner of Main and Depeyster, right across from the university's Prentice Gate. When I was in high school, taking part in the annual science fair, the regional competitions were held in the old gym at Kent State University, so I became familiar with the rolling hills and ivy-covered halls of the campus. When the time came for college, I had aspirations to go to schools in Washington, DC, or in upstate New York, but like many families, mine could not afford the high tuition costs, so I made my way once more down the thirty-five miles to Kent State to begin classes in the fall of 1967.

I entered Kent State with an already active interest in politics. I had spent the summer between high school graduation and the beginning of the fall semester volunteering for the campaign of Carl Stokes, who became the first black mayor of a northern city with his election to mayor of Cleveland that November. I was also very much aware of the war in Vietnam, where my older brother was flying missions off the USS *Yorktown* in the South China Sea. I had grown up in a home where political affairs were not a common topic of discussion, but some stimulating high school teachers and my own rather scattered and random reading had begun to raise questions in my mind about the ways power and privilege worked in our society. I was raised in a liberal Methodist church and had been drawn into some early activity with civil rights when my high school was desegregated during my senior year. And like many American families in those years, we often had dinner while watching the evening news on TV, which brought images of war, urban unrest, protests, and demonstrations from across our country and in other parts of the world into our living room. Arriving at Kent State, I was eager to begin my studies and found the freedom of college life exciting and energizing.

My freshman year was one of great transition and increasing awareness. Some of this took place in the classrooms at Kent State, where I took courses in political thought and history and began to read more critically and systematically. But much more was the result of encounters with other students, many of whom would become comrades in the radical movement at KSU over the next few years. Conversations about Vietnam, racism, poverty, police violence, and the connections between the many issues facing our country and the world were amazingly stimulating. I became aware of the weekly vigils of Kent State's Committee to End the War in Vietnam, which were held outside the old Student Center on Wednesdays at noon, and by the spring of 1968, I had stepped across the divide and joined those who were silently protesting. I began to read Marx and other radical thinkers, and to search for the connections between the ideas and experiences I read about, and the things I observed in the world and the community around me.

In March 1968 I saw a poster announcing a meeting to form a chapter of Students for a Democratic Society (SDS) at Kent State. I went to the meeting and was swept into the rising storm of activism that was coming to KSU. SDS became the focus of my life for the next year and a half as I consolidated my ideas about politics and economics and became dedicated to the radical transformation of American society and the wider world. The friendships and bonds of support and loyalty forged in SDS would be sorely tested in the struggles ahead, but we were a community of radical activists sharing a vision of a just and equitable world, to the creation of which we dedicated ourselves. This dedication was shared with other activists outside SDS as well, as the accounts included in part III of this book recall.

From the fall of 1968 through the spring of 1969 the movement at Kent State increased dramatically. Weekly SDS meetings regularly drew the attendance of two hundred or more students. We held rallies, showed films, hosted speakers, and took part in marches and demonstrations both on campus and in the community. By the spring of 1969 rallies often had a thousand or more participating students. A set of demands, designed to highlight the links between the university and the injustices and exploitation in the wider society, were developed and presented to the administration. Confrontations took place between protesting students and university authorities. In April, at the Music and Speech building, students protesting against repressive disciplinary hearings were trapped and had nowhere to escape the police, so they were arrested in a crackdown, which resulted in SDS losing its campus charter; fifty-nine students faced charges of trespassing, and a few were arrested on more serious counts.

In the wake of the repression of SDS at Kent State, the national organization self-destructed in June. Theoretical divisions over the nature of the political situation in the country and the proper strategic and tactical way forward led to the collapse of SDS and to a reduction in radical activism at Kent. The antiwar movement was growing, with hundreds of thousands of people marching in the great semiannual demonstrations in Washington. Militants of the Black Panther Party were struggling against racist police in cities across the country. But at Kent State many young people chose to step back from political engagement to concentrate on their studies, and perhaps to give Nixon a chance to put his "secret plan for peace" into practice. There was still political activism at KSU in the winter of 1969–70, but the level of participation was greatly reduced and the mood was sometimes one of despair.

All of this changed dramatically the night of April 30, 1970, when Nixon announced the invasion of Cambodia. It was instantly clear that far from a plan for peace, he had actually been planning for more war. Students and others at Kent State, along with millions across the country, were outraged and infuriated. Hundreds of students rallied at noon the next day on the Commons, launching protests that would continue through the weekend, demanding that the university condemn the invasion of Cambodia and the expansion and continuation of the war. A rally was called for noon on the following Monday to receive the university's response.

The events of May 1–4, 1970, are recounted in parts II, IV, and VIII of this volume and need not be revisited in detail here. Students vented their rage and frustration, while activists scrambled to give some direction and coherence to the passions being played out in the streets. State and national politicians fanned the flames of repression, armed soldiers occupied the university, and when students assembled on their grassy campus in the noonday sun on Monday, May 4, forces of the state responded with lethal violence. I had spoken from the brick housing of the Victory Bell at noon, trying to call for a student strike, but was drowned out by the bullhorns of the National Guard and then driven over Blanket Hill by the tear gas and bayonets of the troops. Minutes later, when the shooting stopped, I and the rest of the crowd stood up, shocked and forever marked by the death and injury around us.

The search for justice after May 4 has been a harsh and bitter one, as part VII makes clear. The State of Ohio responded by indicting twenty-five students, young people, and faculty for getting in the way of the bullets. No soldier who fired into the assembled students, no commander of the Guard, no political officials of the state or federal government ever took responsibility for his or her actions, and none was ever held responsible by legal authorities. The shootings at Kent State have been characterized as a tragedy by the university and by most mainstream voices, as if some ineluctable drama had been played out with no one really to blame. But in fact, as the contributors to this volume make clear, the events represent a clear example of the willingness of those with power to use whatever means they deemed necessary to protect and preserve their own privileges and interests.

Fifty years later, those of us who lived through these events have begun to pass from the scene. Each reunion brings together fewer of us, though among those who gather there still burns a passionate devotion to both our own history and to the ideals for which we struggled. And today, young people who dream of a better world are speaking of radical change, of the need for fundamental transformation in political and economic life, perhaps more clearly than at any time since the years that preceded the event at Kent State. This is a time to remember, and the essays, images, poems, and other contributions brought together here by Susie Erenrich, especially in parts I, VI, and IX, are a treasure trove of material that must not be lost or forgotten. Each of the voices heard in these pages is a precious legacy of a time that we must not allow to fade away or be distorted. As parts X and XI make clear, the memory and legacy of those days remains contested. We still demand justice for Kent State, 1970. But even more, these voices call upon us and all those who have marched with us, as well as those who will march on into the future, to carry forward the struggles for justice and equality, to bring the spirit of Kent State to the work that remains to be done in building a better world.

Acknowledgments

Words can never sufficiently express my appreciation to my Kent State family, many of whom are participants in the creation of this book. They lovingly and patiently waited for decades for this project to finally take shape. Without their memories, expertise, and commitment, this venture would not have been possible.

A special shout-out to two members of my Kent State family, who went above and beyond the call of duty—Tom Grace, who meticulously reviewed and critiqued the original 650-page manuscript, and Ken Hammond, who graciously accepted my invitation to pen the foreword for this book. Both men generously invested time and effort in this undertaking to ensure its success.

Brad McKelvey, my best friend and longtime companion, was always by my side. For thirty-five years, he has been my rock. Brad encouraged me through all the trials and tribulations in creating this text, humored me during the various stages of this adventure, provided affable remedies as I sifted through stacks of content-related material, and listened intently during each critical juncture.

I am grateful to the Kent State University Press for recognizing the importance of covering this turbulent time in American history. It takes courage to publish an anthology about shootings that happened in your own home.

Last, but certainly not least, I want to thank my mom and dad. Wherever you are, this moment is for you. I miss you. I love you.

Susie Erenrich signing copies of *Kent & Jackson State 1970–1990* (Source: Brad McKelvey)

Introduction

Susan Erenrich is a professor at American University. She was a founding member of the May 4 Task Force and is the founder and executive director of the Cultural Center for Social Change.

May 4, 2018, was a gray, overcast day with intermittent rain. At noon, folks were slowly congregating inside the Kent State University campus ballroom. Another year had passed. The crowd was a bit smaller, a bit grayer, and quite a bit older. Nevertheless, they came. They reunited with friends, strolled down memory lane, and critically examined the history that they helped to shape.

At 12:24 P.M., a restrained hush filled the room. Then a peaceful stillness. It seemed like the world came to a complete halt—at least for a few seconds. Mourners carrying lanterns solemnly entered the scene. A moment of silence for the dead. It was time for the annual commemorative program to begin. Speaker after speaker took the stage. They paid tribute to the departed and encouraged us all never to forget. Forty-eight years had passed, but for many inside the auditorium, it felt like yesterday.

The keynote address was delivered by William C. Hine, PhD. Hine, a retired history professor from South Carolina State University, was unfortunate enough to be present at Orangeburg and Kent State when the various shootings took place. The year 2018 marked the fiftieth anniversary of the shooting at Orangeburg, which is why he was invited to participate in the dedicatory activities by the May 4 Task Force.

For readers not familiar with the incident, on the night of February 8, 1968, law enforcement officers fired upon student protesters on the campus of South Carolina State College at Orangeburg. When the volley of bullets stopped, three young men were dead—Delano Middleton, Henry Smith, and Samuel Hammond Jr. At least twenty-seven others were wounded. Sparked by a series of events set in motion by the continuing crusade for equality and justice, nonviolent young demonstrators took to the streets. In this case, the facilities of a segregated local bowling alley were at the center of the conflict. After days of campaigning against the establishment, which was a holdover from the Jim Crow South, a harrowing confrontation between students and the state ensued.

The events at Orangeburg received sparse news coverage in the national media, and most of that was frivolous, perfunctory, and inaccurate. Unlike the white students at Kent State University who were gunned down two years later and captured the attention of the world, the Orangeburg dead and wounded were black. No one wanted to hear their story.

The room was quiet during Dr. Hine's testimonial. For many observers, it was the first time they had heard of the tragedy.

Earlier that afternoon, onlookers also heard about the shootings that took place on the Jackson State College campus ten days after the event at Kent State. Shortly past midnight on May 15, 1970, the Mississippi Highway Patrol and local law enforcement officers opened fire on the Jackson State college campus. Two hundred-thirty bullets riddled that institution in a matter of thirty seconds, claiming the lives of Phillip Gibbs, a twenty-one-year-old prelaw student from Ripley, Mississippi, and James Earl Green, a senior at Jim Hill High School in Jackson. Countless others were wounded by the fusillade, and others were traumatized. The students shot at Jackson State have been memorialized at every commemoration.

The 2018 gathering was significant for another reason. After forty-eight years, a portion of Kent State University's main campus had finally taken its place alongside some of the nation's most consequential locations, like the 1864 Sand Creek Massacre, Pearl Harbor, and the Edmund Pettus Bridge in Selma, Alabama.

Seventeen acres where the fateful events of May 4, 1970, took place were designated a historic landmark. An official ceremony was slated for 3:30 P.M. Several of the day's speakers commented on the magnitude of the moment.

Prior to the start of the remembrance, I had strategically positioned myself at the back of the ballroom. It was the best place to flag down longtime acquaintances and friends. I happened to glance at my watch and noticed it was almost 2:00. The program, usually scheduled for just a few hours, apparently was going to continue. Nobody seemed to notice or care. It wasn't as if our carriage would turn into a pumpkin and our riches would turn to rags. Two o'clock, however, was the witching hour—the demarcation line when the ceremony would stop and folks would get back to business as usual.

But it was never really business as usual on the Kent State University campus. Not since May 4, 1970, when the Ohio National Guard opened fire on unarmed students, killing four and wounding nine others. Forty-eight years before, on that dreadful day in May, it took only thirteen seconds and sixty-seven rounds from M1 rifles to end the lives of Allison Krause, Jeffrey Miller, Sandra Scheuer, and William Schroeder. It took only thirteen seconds and sixty-seven rounds from M1 rifles to wound Dean Kahler, Joe Lewis, Jim Russell, Robby Stamps, Scott MacKenzie, John Cleary, Tom Grace, Alan Canfora, and Douglas Wrentmore. And it took only thirteen seconds and sixty-seven rounds from M1 rifles to forever change the course of history.

My personal journey began in 1975, when I was a freshman at Kent State University. I joined the May 4 Task Force, a new student group on campus, and became familiar with the names of the students shot at KSU and Jackson State. I marched around the campus on more occasions than I would like to remember, chanting, LONG LIVE THE SPIRIT OF KENT AND JACKSON STATE.

But at the time, I never really understood what it meant. I wasn't a history major and even if I had been, I would have only been introduced to a Eurocentric view of the world, opposed to the people's scholarship that has guided my life since my undergraduate days at Kent State. It took fifteen years and an invitation to edit an anthology for the twentieth anniversary of the Kent State and Jackson State shootings for the story to sink in.

Three decades have passed since the release of that first anthology, *Kent & Jackson State 1970–1990,* and much has changed. As we mark this fiftieth anniversary milestone, I am proud to present readers with *The Cost of Freedom: Voicing a Movement after Kent State 1970.*

The submissions are of varying lengths and forms. Each author chose a particular topic of interest and writing style. The only criterion was to cover some aspect of the May 4 Movement and the half-century crusade for truth and justice.

There are eleven major parts, each of which deals with a particular motif and is strategically placed within the framework of the book. For example, the publication opens with "Memories." These are heartfelt testimonials written by some of the family members and loved ones—those who have lost the most and, in some cases, have said the least. Several of the wounded students also provide thoughtful remembrances about varying aspects of their experience. These eyewitness accounts are given an appropriate space in the anthology. There is a part for the lawyers and one for early activism on the Kent State University campus. Also included are pieces on the shootings and the long aftermath. In addition, annual rituals and historic markers have a distinct place in the book, as do some of the troubadours of conscience. A portion of the anthology covers the 1977 battle over hallowed ground. And last, but certainly not least, lasting legacies and the meaning of the May 4, 1970, shootings are at the end of the book. All in all, the compilation comes together in a colorful composite that celebrates the role each of the contributors played in the May 4 Movement's campaign for justice.

Readers should also bear in mind that this book is a collection of primary source material. Every piece was written by someone who participated in some aspect of the May 4 Movement, which makes it vastly different from other books on the subject. All too often the experiences of ordinary citizens are interpreted by third parties. By the time a narrative of a particular incident appears, the lifeblood of what actually occurred is diluted, or is reconstructed years later by academics, who are far removed from the entire picture. This doesn't mean that *The Cost of Freedom* is not scholarly. Quite the contrary. Many of the writers hold advanced degrees from accredited institutions. Because they are stakeholders, however, they are able to fill in gaps and shed light on the topic with firsthand knowledge that isn't necessarily available when conducting more traditional forms of inquiry.

Despite the collection's breadth, I am saddened that it is not all-inclusive. It is impossible to incorporate every person who was directly or indirectly touched by the May 4, 1970, calamity and its impact into a single volume. The voices presented here, however, represent a half century of struggle by homegrown activists, who were on the scene during significant moments of the movement for truth and due process.

Fifty years is a long time. Many of the survivors of the May 4 Movement are aging gracefully now. Many are deceased. With each death a bit of the American past is buried deep below the ground. This book was an attempt to seize and preserve as much of the history as possible while folks were still around to tell their stories.

Now it is time to invite the reader to commemorate this consequential milestone and to share this valuable work with generations to come.

PART I

Memories

Left to right: John Adams, Joan Baez, Sarah Scheuer, and Martin Scheuer (Source: John Rowe)

John Rowe attended Kent State University as an undergraduate and graduate student from 1970 to 1980. He was a founding member of the May 4 Task Force, and an active member of the May 4 Steering Committee and the Kent State May 4 Center. His pictures captured all the major May 4 events for decades. John died in 2018 at the age of sixty-eight.

Anniversary, May 4, 1988

ELAINE HOLSTEIN

Elaine Holstein's son, Jeffrey Miller, was one of the students killed on May 4, 1970, on the Kent State University campus. She worked to preserve his memory and to memorialize his death until her passing on May 26, 2018. This piece was written in 1988.

At a few minutes past noon on May 4, I will once again observe an anniversary—an anniversary that marks not only the most tragic event of my life but also one of the most disgraceful episodes in American history. This May 4 will be the eighteenth anniversary of the shootings on the campus of Kent State University and the death of my son, Jeff Miller, by Ohio National Guard rifle fire.

Eighteen years! That's almost as long a time as Jeff's entire life. He had turned twenty just a month before he decided to attend the protest rally that ended in his death and the deaths of Allison Krause, Sandy Scheuer, and Bill Schroeder, and the wounding of nine of their fellow students. One of them, Dean Kahler, will spend the rest of his life in a wheelchair, paralyzed from the waist down.

That Jeff chose to attend that demonstration came as no surprise to me. Anyone who knew him in those days would have been shocked if he had decided to sit that one out. There were markers along the way that led him inexorably to that campus protest.

At the age of eight, Jeff wrote an article expressing his concern for the plight of black Americans. I learned of this only when I received a call from

Ebony magazine, which assumed he was black and assured me he was bound to be "a future leader of the black community."

Shortly before his sixteenth birthday, Jeff composed a poem he called "Where Does It End?" in which he expressed the horror he felt about "the War Without a Purpose."

Was Jeff a radical? He told me, grinning, that though he might be taken for a "hippie radical" in the Middle West, back home on Long Island he'd probably be seen as a reactionary.

So when Jeff called me that morning and told me he planned to attend a rally to protest the "incursion" of U.S. military forces into Cambodia, I merely expressed my doubts as to the effectiveness of still another demonstration.

"Don't worry, Mom," he said. "I may get arrested, but I won't get my head busted." I laughed and assured him I wasn't worried.

The bullet that ended Jeff's life also destroyed the person I had been—a naïve, politically unaware woman. Until that spring of 1970, I would have stated with absolute assurance that Americans have the right to dissent, publicly, from the policies pursued by their Government. The Constitution says so. Isn't that what makes this country—this democracy—different from those totalitarian states whose methods we deplore?

And even if the dissent got noisy and disruptive, was it conceivable that an arm of the Government would shoot at random into a crowd of unarmed students? With live ammunition? No way! Arrests? Perhaps. Tear gas? Probably. Antiwar protests had become a way of life, and on my television set I had seen them dealt with routinely in various nonlethal ways.

The myth of a benign America where dissent was broadly tolerated was one casualty of the shootings at Kent State. Another was my assumption that *everyone* shared my belief that we were engaged in a no-win situation in Vietnam and had to get out. As the body counts mounted and the footage of napalmed babies became a nightly television staple, I was certain that no one could want the war to go on. The hate mail that began arriving at my home after Jeff died showed me how wrong I was.

We were enmeshed in legal battles for nine years. The families of the slain students, along with the wounded boys and their parents, believed that once the facts were heard in a court of law, it would become clear that the governor of Ohio and the troops he called in had used inappropriate and excessive force to quell what had begun as a peaceful protest. We couldn't undo what had been done, but we wanted to make sure it would never be done again.

Our 1975 trial ended in defeat after fifteen weeks in Federal Court. We won a retrial on appeal, and returned to Cleveland with high hopes of prevailing, but before the trial got under way we were urged by both the judge and our lawyers to accept an out-of-court settlement. The proposal angered us; the case wasn't about *money*. We wanted to clear our children's names and to win a judicial ruling that the governor and the National Guard were responsible for the deaths and injuries. The defendants offered to issue an apology. The wording was debated for days, and the final result was an innocuous document, stating that, "in retrospect, the tragedy . . . should not have occurred" and that "better ways must be found to deal with such confrontations."

Reluctantly, we accepted the settlement when we were told this might be the only way that Dean would get at least some of the funds to meet his lifelong medical expenses. He was awarded $350,000, the parents of each of the dead students received $15,000, and the remainder, in varying amounts, was divided among the wounded. Lawyers' fees amounted to $50,000, and $25,000 was allotted to expenses, for a total of $675,000.

Since then we have lived through Watergate and Richard Nixon's resignation, crises in the Middle East and in Central America, and the Iran-contra affair. To most people, Kent State is just one of those traumatic events that occurred during a tumultuous time.

To me, it's the one experience I will never recover from. It's also the one gap in my communication with my older son, Russ: Neither of us dares to talk about what happened at Kent State for fear that we'll open floodgates of emotion that we can't deal with.

Whenever there is another death in the family, we mourn not only the elderly parent or grandparent or aunt who has passed away; we also experience again the loss of Jeff.

This piece appeared in *Kent & Jackson State 1970–1990*, edited by Susie Erenrich. It was reprinted by permission of *The Progressive Inc.* © 1988.

A Tribute to Arthur Krause

Delivered at Kent State University, May 4, 1989

KENDRA LEE HICKS PACIFICO

Kendra Lee Hicks Pacifico has been part of the extended May 4 Family since 1982. At that time, she played the role of Allison Krause in a production of Kent State: A Requiem *at the University of North Carolina at Greensboro and at the 30th annual May 4 Commemoration at Kent State. She moved to Kent in 1988 and has become instrumental in organizing the annual May 3 candlelight vigils. This piece was written in 1990.*

I am here before you to pay tribute to a man—Arthur Krause, the father of Allison Beth Krause, a student slain in a parking lot on the Kent State University Campus on May 4, 1970.

Most of us here know him as the most prominent leader in the quest for justice for the murders that took place here in 1970, a man whose efforts enable us to gather here today.

When I questioned those who knew him well, I heard these descriptive words mentioned: "strong," "stubborn," "vital," "larger than life," "warm and generous," "fierce." I heard phrases like "the iron man of the Kent State family," "he was relentless in his quest for justice," "I felt lucky that I had the benefit of his friendship," "we are richer for having known him." I feel fortunate to have met him.

America first heard from Arthur the day after the shootings. When speaking with television newsmen, he expressed the sentiments of the horribly shocked citizens of this country: "Have we come to such a state in this country that a young girl has to be shot because she disagrees with the action of her government?"

We stopped and listened to him. And we heard from him again. For the next four years, Arthur continually asked for justice. He wanted someone held accountable for the death of his daughter. He called for congressional hearings and federal investigations into the shootings. He appealed for the right to a day in court. He pushed through the Ohio District Court, the US District Court, the US Court of Appeals, and finally to the US Supreme Court, all the while trying to break down the wall of Ohio's sovereign immunity law—the law that said defendants could not be sued without first giving their consent to such an action. But he would never back down. As Martin Scheuer, the father of Sandy Scheuer, once told me, "Arthur was a man of principle."

In the first year of the struggle, Arthur was joined by Peter Davies, an ordinary citizen from Staten Island, New York, who had been appalled at the shootings and he himself had spent months researching the shootings, looking for clues to explain why the National Guard had fired:

> For almost a year . . . we tilted at windmills alone, but without his dynamic strength I could not have stayed the course. Arthur's quest was never idealistic. He was always a realist in dealing with the Nixon administration, and despite his grief and anger, whenever we accomplished something that seemed to me a big step forward, he would laugh and say, "that and ten cents'll get us a cup of coffee." We had more cups of coffee than I care to remember.

Elaine Holstein, the mother of slain Jeff Miller, described Arthur as "totally indispensable." She writes, "Indispensable—because my life in those years after our children were killed and we struggled to find some semblance of justice—would have been far more hellish without the Rock of Gibraltar that was Art Krause."

In 1971, Arthur and Peter were joined by Rev. John Adams of the United Methodist Church. This addition to the team had a very positive effect. As Sanford Jay Rosen, attorney for the families in the final settlement, observes: "Two people, Arthur Krause and John Adams, are most responsible for the measure of justice the Kent State victims and their families have received. Arthur brought anger and passion to the cause. John brought hope and compassion. Without these two, all would have been for naught."

Arthur's passion was so deep due to the fact that he knew what lay at the root of the problem. As he recalled his life, he said, "I was like everyone else, and then this happened to us." In recalling other episodes of extreme violence in our country before May of 1970, he said:

> I feel a great sense of guilt because I realized what was going on but didn't do a damn thing about it. Like most Americans these days, we sit on the fence and depend on the lawyer, the church, and the government to do whatever should be done, but if the government doesn't have the right people on the job, nothing will be done . . . and we, the people, have to make the government good. Apathy will not be part of my make-up anymore. Apathy is what caused Kent State.

In 1975, Arthur's four years of persistence paid off. The victims' families were given their day in court. Vindication should have been forthcoming. It was not. Elaine Holstein recounts:

> It turned out to be many, many days—some of the most painful days of my life. As we sat in the courtroom and heard our lovely children vilified by the defendants and their lawyers . . . I found myself increasingly seeking out Art, to become healed by his unshakeable determination and common sense and—most importantly—his humor. Even under the horrendous circumstances that brought us together . . . Art's brilliant and sometimes bitter wit would break the tension and lift the oppressive burden we all carried and we would feel the blessed relief of laughter that enabled . . . all of us to survive those terrible months.

When the verdict was announced in favor of the National Guardsmen, it was Arthur who announced that the trial proved that the Constitution had been destroyed.

While the families waited during the appeal process, the Kent State administration once again showed its insensitivity to the history of May 4, 1970. After the construction of the gymnasium annex on Blanket Hill, which destroyed part of the site of the shootings, Arthur Krause vowed never to step foot on the Kent State campus again.

In 1979, when the other families and victims decided on an out-of-court settlement for the murder of their children, it was Arthur who held out on giving in to that decision the longest. While some may have attributed this to his usual stubbornness, others attributed it to the devoted love he had for his daughter Allison. As one of the lawyers put it, "He doesn't want to give in to a settlement because it means he'll have to give up Allison."

Arthur Krause (Source: John Rowe)

Dean Kahler, shot on May 4, 1970, spoke truthfully when he told me "the sense of loss Arthur felt for his daughter was very prevalent when you were around him. He never really fully recuperated from her death. It was the focal point of his life and he was determined to get justice." Tom Grace, also wounded in 1970, observes: "Without Arthur's drive, his fortitude, his unmovable presence, the drive for justice may well have stalled. Our quest is not finished. Yet, Arthur's efforts have allowed us, in some small measure, to answer yes to the question that Doris Krause asked nineteen years ago: "Do we say that there is justice, Allison?"

While Arthur's years in the battlefield of the United States' court system came to an end, the pain of the loss of his daughter did not. And his bitterness toward the Kent State administration did not fade either. Arthur told me this past summer that he was still waiting for an official notification of Allison's death. I am sure that he was conscious of this when he told the *Ravenna Record Courier* in 1986 that the Kent State administration was "a worthless organization."

Arthur's last years were spent enduring the emotional roller coaster of the May 4 Memorial building process. And he did not keep his emotions to himself. Alan Canfora, another student wounded in 1970, told me of some of his last conversations with Arthur: "As Arthur suffered the pain of his terminal illness, he poignantly described his continued frustrations as a result of the cover-up of his daughter's murder and the continued failure of Kent State University to create a lasting memorial tribute in memory of his daughter Allison."

It's a shame that Arthur could not have observed the final vindication of his daughter's death. But, as pointed out earlier, he was very pragmatic. Arthur told me last July, "Anybody that would believe that Kent State University would make any attempt to meet the desires of the Kent State families must also believe in the tooth fairy."

What does Arthur Krause's death mean? It's too soon to know the broader ramifications in the struggle to remember May 4, 1970. On a more personal level, Sandy Rosen says it best: "He marked our lives, so that we are richer for having known him and much poorer now that he is gone." Speaking for myself and all the others who have fought against the whitewashing of the facts of May 4, I feel like I've lost my father.

So how do we really pay tribute to such a man as Arthur Krause? Words are not enough.

We could start by emulating his passion for justice. We can remove the apathy from our own lives. We can build a proper memorial to the memory of Allison, Bill, Jeff, and Sandy—one that is fitting to the magnitude of the event. We can heed Arthur's own advice, "If you don't stand up for your own rights, they will be taken away from you just like they were from Allison." You can love your own children as Arthur loved his.

This piece originally appeared in *Kent & Jackson State 1970–1990,* edited by Susie Erenrich.

May 4, 2000, Commemorative Program Speech

BARRY LEVINE

Barry Levine's girlfriend, Allison Krause, was killed by the Ohio National Guard on the Kent State University campus on May 4, 1970. This piece was written in 2000.

Good afternoon. I don't know how many of you are aware of this. Allison was planning on being here today. But, unfortunately, because of a prior engagement, she was unable to make it. So she sent me instead.

You see, thirty years ago on this very spot where we stand, Allison Krause was engaged in exercising her right of free speech. And apparently, something that was said that day was so threatening to some people that they decided . . . some even say conspired . . . to deny her the right to be here today and to deny us the pleasure of having her here today.

Now, I think we should make no mistake about it. What happened here thirty years ago had very little to do with rocks and bottles and snipers. It had everything to do with the right of free speech and the right of assembly and the suppression of those rights.

About a week after the shooting, Richard Nixon made a public statement in which he said, "When dissent turns to violence it invites tragedy." And I would like to suggest today what he probably meant to say is that when a government interferes with the free flow of ideas and when a government suppresses the right of its citizens to speak freely and to assemble peacefully, that government invites tragedy and in so doing it takes responsibility for any violence that might ensue.

I didn't come here today to lecture you about the politics of 1970. I'm sure that before the day is over, you are going to hear more on that subject than you care to hear, but you're not going to hear it from me. Instead, I came here today to just take a few moments and share a few thoughts with you about this girl Allison Krause. I thought it would be appropriate on this day in particular and on this spot in particular to talk a little bit about what she was like when she was a student here and sat on this hill where you sit and walked these paths where you now stand.

And I was just told when I got here that this speaking schedule is a little bit tight and I should keep my comments brief. So the one or two stories that I had planned to tell you, I'm sorry to say, are going to have to wait for another time. [Shouts of NO! NO! NO! by the audience—Barry chuckles.]

What I would like to do is take a moment to let you know that if Allison were here today, she would thank all of you for being here, for sitting and for listening, those of you who organize for organizing, and those who are here just participating. She would thank you for just being here. Your very presence here makes a very important statement, a statement that needs to be made this year and in following years: "That the world should never forget what happened here thirty years ago."

But I've got to tell you that if she was here, she would also be reminding us of something else. And that is that we should not become too smug about these ceremonies and about these memorials and about these markers that have been erected. They are all very nice and they're very much appreciated.

But if we're here to remember those things, we need to also remember a few other things and that's the voice that I hear in my ear, of Allison telling me that Barry, "Remember that there's a man here today who hasn't walked for thirty years and, as far as I know, thirty years later, no one has taken responsibility for that." And there are eight other men here today. [Applause] There are eight other men here today whose physical wounds may have healed, but clearly, they'll be carrying emotional scars for the rest of their lives. And as far as I know, to this date, thirty years later, no one has been held accountable for that!

And then there's Bill Schroeder and there's Sandy Scheuer and Jeffrey Miller and Allison Krause. Four young people whose lives ended much, much, much too soon. And we all know that their tragic loss of life was unnecessary. It was unwarranted and it was inexcusable.

But the fact remains that thirty years later [a child wanders onto the stage and distracts Barry], the very men who took their lives actually have been excused. So if we're going to stand here today and we're going to ask the world to remember and never to forget the tragedy that occurred on

May 4, 1970, I think we damn well better ask the world to remember and to never forget the tragedy that has occurred since that date. And the tragedy that has occurred since that date is the fact that nobody has been held accountable for what happened here thirty years ago.

They say that time heals all wounds and thirty years is a long time. Memories fade and wounds do heal. But this wound will never heal completely. Nor do I think that we should allow it to heal completely until somebody stands up and is held accountable for the blood that spilled on this campus.

If any of you are having difficulty who to nominate for that honor, I'd like to help you. In closing, I'd like to read you something that was written in honor of Allison and in her memory. It's a poem. It's based on a previous work by one of Allison's favorite contemporary American poets, Robert Zimmerman. It's called "Who Killed Allison?", but when you hear it, you should know that it could have just as easily be called "Who Killed Allison and Who Killed Bill and Who Killed Sandy and Who Killed Jeff?" When you hear it, I'd like you to keep that in mind. I would like to read it for you now so that maybe you can hear her voice speaking out from this campus one last time.

Who Killed Allison? Why? What Had She Done?

Not us says the **Kent Townsfolk**.
Those rotten students thought this was some kind of joke
Marchin and yellin, and singing those songs,
Why wasn't she in class where she belonged?
Her parents shoulda learned her better.
Those stinkin kids don't appreciate what they've got
If it had been up to us, they would have all been shot.
You can say what you want, and say what you must
Just don't point your fingers at us
We're not the ones who made her fall
No, you can't blame us at all.

Who Killed Allison? Why? What Had She Done?

Not us says the **University**
That girl was here to get a degree
To inquire, to learn, to reflect, and debate.
It wasn't her place to demonstrate—against the State
If she had something to say,
She should have said it clear

In a paper, or in the classroom, where free speech is dear.
And no one can hear, and no one can hear.
Sure she was an honor student, but she should have known better
Than to stand up and speak out in public, where did that get her?
There is a time and a place for freedom of speech
She should have known that because that's what we teach
Here at Kent State University.
But please, don't point your finger at us
We are not the ones that made her fall,
No, you can't blame us at all.

Who Killed Allison? Why? What Had She Done?

Not me says the **Mayor of Kent**
If only those kids knew what it had meant
To burn down ROTC—they left me no choice
They were all chanting "End the war" in one loud voice
I had to call the Guard—it was hard, it was hard,
But I tell you, we needed Law and Order
And anyway, she wasn't my daughter
It's a shame she had to die that day
But when you throw rocks, well, that's just the American way.
I feel bad, I do, but I didn't pull that trigger
It wasn't me that made her fall
No, you can't blame me at all.

Who Killed Allison? Why? What Had She Done?

Not me says **Tricky Dick**
I listened to my advisors, take your pick
Haldeman, Ehrlichman, Mitchell and Dean
Agnew, and Colson, they all knew the scene
Those college kids were bums—they needed a lesson
So I put out the word around this great land
To stop those damn hoodlums any way that you can
And Rhodes, he heard me, thank g-d for that
He knew exactly what to do with that group of brats
But you can't pin it on me, don't you see?
It wasn't me that made her fall
No, you can't blame me at all.

Who Killed Allison? Why? What Had She Done?

Not me says **Governor Rhodes**
The man who made this whole thing explode
Yes, I'm the son of a bitch who pounded the table
And ranted and raved until everyone was able
To hear me call those students Brown Shirts,
The worst element that we harbor in America today
But that was my job, to incite the Guard, and I did it OK
If those kids wanted a riot to create,
They picked the wrong town, they picked the wrong state.
There will be no riots in the State of Ohio, not on my watch, not on this date
Look, the Guard got my meaning, the Guard got my drift
They did what they had to—they laid 'em out stiff.
It's a shame it had to be that way, but who's to know and who's to say

It might have been different had it not been Election Day.
So what are you going to do? Sue me?
I'm not the one that made the call
And I'm not the one that made her fall
So fuck you, you can't blame me at all.

Who Killed Allison? Why? What Had She Done?

Not us says the **National Guard**
Who chased those kids across the yard,
And through the fields so thick with gas
With our bayonets fixed, it became certain, there was no doubt
We would teach those little bastards what Law and Order was all about
Yes, we're the ones that climbed the hill and turned in our tracks
And aimed our rifles dead center in her back
But if we didn't act, she would have overrun us for sure,
There were snipers, she had rocks, and those curses that we endured.
We had no choice, we had to act—it was her life or ours
Yes we shot her in cold blood, it's true, it's true,
But that is what we were told to do
Don't say "murder," don't say "kill"

We Were Only Following Orders, It Was God's Will.

PART II

Photographs of May 4, 1970

Chuck Ayers drew cartoons for the Daily Kent Stater *and the* Akron Beacon Journal *while he was a KSU student. In 2000, Ayers and Tom Batiuk created a* Crankshaft *comic strip thirtieth-anniversary story arc about the KSU shootings, the originals of which are now part of the May 4 Collection.*

Guardsmen beginning their advance on the Commons (Source: Chuck Ayers)

Guardsmen throwing tear gas (Source: Kent State University News Service)

Prentice Hall parking lot (Source: Kent State University News Service)

Four students killed by the Ohio National Guard (Source: Kent State University News Service)

PART III

*Earlier Activism before
May 4, 1970*

Thy Tears Might Cease

ANTHONY WALSH

A criminal defense attorney in private practice, Anthony "Tony" Walsh died unexpectedly on March 12, 2005. He worked with Legal Aid while in law school and was politically active all his life, including defending students who were arrested after the Kent State shootings, Ohio University students arrested for protesting, and inmates who were charged after the Attica riots of 1971. This piece was written in 2000.

Dear Susie,

Here at last is the article I promised you. What a beast it was to write! I had resisted for thirty years to write about what I went through. Being naturally depressive for an Irishman, I had a great deal of trouble and angst going through this.

One thing I rediscovered was the sheer volume of work and the things we were involved in through the sixties and the seventies. We never seemed to stop running. How I answered the academic demands of University life I will never know.

So here it is. The sheer emotion that went into writing this article cannot be expressed. A very persistent person will have to beat me repeatedly on the head with a heavy object to get me to expand it into a full book. I can, too.

All the best,
Tony Walsh

. . .

I have borne a crushing burden of rage and pain and grief for thirty years. It follows me like the furies, snarling and unrelenting. It is at its worst in the spring of every year when the searing memory returns. It is the unquenchable rage against the State of Ohio for the shootings of May 4, 1970, on the campus of the university about which I cared so much. It is the pain of seeing my life and the lives of so many others utterly changed by those hideous thirteen seconds of gunfire. It is the unspeakable grief I will always have as a graduate of Kent State who participated in so much of what happened on that campus in the 1960s, and who witnessed all that has happened since May 4, 1970. Even now, after thirty years, it is the central defining moment of my life as a lawyer.

Who among us could predict that the work we did during the 1960s would lead to the desecration that occurred on May 4, 1970? It was a sacrilege during which Ohio National Guardsmen, egged on by a contemptible governor and a bully of an adjutant general, killed four students and wounded nine others. By doing so they forever changed higher education in this state. Nothing in our experience on the campus of Kent State during the 1960s could prepare us for the savagery of May 4, 1970. Nothing!

Those of us who lived through those events fought for years to have a memorial erected on the site of the shootings. Instead, in 1977, seven years after the shootings, the trustees announced that they would build a new gymnasium on the site of the shootings. To do so would obliterate part of Blanket Hill. They knew that. The gymnasium was planned for a plot of land on the south side of Summit Street. They didn't care. The new gymnasium was a brutish and unfeeling insult to the dead and wounded and their families.

In the early 1980s, the Mildred Andrews Fund of Cleveland donated $100,000 to place a George Segal sculpture of Abraham and Isaac on the site of the shootings. A craven and fearful board of trustees rejected it. A full twenty years after the shootings, they put a nice liberal memorial in place and planted a garden. It was to be a place of quiet contemplation. No noise, please! Just be sweet, quiet, and peaceful, my dears. Even so, thirty years later, the memorial does not diminish the rage, lessen the pain, and does not take away the grief.

In the 1960s we were motivated not so much by rage or pain or grief as by the altruism that was the heritage bequeathed to us by our immigrant, working-class, Depression-shattered parents. We wanted simply to take four years in the springtime of our lives to go to college and learn about the meaning of history and science and art. We sought, most of all, to find the answers to the questions that have driven humankind since the dawn of time. What is good? What is true? And, most important of all, What is beautiful?

We attended the lectures, read the texts, and wrote down our triumphs of scholarship. We sought out the treasures of the libraries and bookstores and made them our own. We talked at, argued against, and disputed with our professors and companions. We laughed loudly with the joy of our discoveries. We wept with and loved one another without shame. We took our drink with enthusiasm and did our penance for it. We brawled with every passion of the day. We were big with the surprise of our awakening to the promise held out to those of our generation who were the first in history to attend college. We fought fiercely for enlightenment and meaning.

In all this, we knew we were "young and young once only." We examined and came to understand those transcendent ideas that are the foundation of goodness, the strength that is born of truth, and the grace and compassion of beauty, all of which will be our legacy to our children.

I remember fondly those years before May 4, 1970. I long for the purity of experience that was the legacy of public higher education in those days. My special memory is for the Honors College Program, which began after my first year of commuting. In those years, I gloried in the struggle to add something to Kent State to replace what I took away with me. Kent State will be with me for a lifetime.

In August 1966, I left that golden heyday behind and carried with me the two things I wanted most in life—to hold Mary Walsh's loving grace in one hand and, in the other, to hold the first college degree ever won by a member of my family.

In the years that followed, law school, work, and politics took up my time. There was plenty to do. The war in Southeast Asia was devouring the best and the brightest of our neighbors. The government drafted the children of the working class by the millions and sent them to Vietnam. The lucky ones had student deferments, or joined the Peace Corps, or said they smoked a lot of dope—"You can smoke all the dope you want in Saigon, kid"—or declared that they were gay. Even more fortunate were those who had wealthy and influential parents. They could join the National Guard because Daddy had the connections. They could win deferments because Daddy knew someone important and powerful in Washington who, in turn, knew someone even more important and powerful who could keep them out of Southeast Asia all together. Then the draft lottery happened.

No one could buy good fortune then. Even law students lost their deferments. Before those of wealth and power could fix the oversight, half of the class that entered the law school at Case Western Reserve University in September 1969 was drafted. Either less well-connected young men were drafted or they enlisted in a safe branch of the armed services. The most courageous among them left the country, some never to return.

I was doubly fortunate. I pushed my draft number. I was an orphan and had no powerful connections. On my eighteenth birthday, in 1958, my draft notice arrived. For two years and nine months, nothing happened. The most exciting moment came one day while I was on guard duty in a German forest. A lieutenant colonel, who did not know the password, drove up to my post. He tried to bluff his way through. That scam didn't work. He got downright nasty about a private who wanted to take his gun away and march him to see the major general. Of course, I had smelled a trick. It sounded like the colonel was pulling a security check. I also knew a bully when I saw one. Therefore, I did what any self-respecting Irish kid with a loaded gun would do. I threatened to shoot him. The major general was very pleased that the colonel was not successful. It was the most fun an army grunt could have with a loaded gun in his hands. It was the first and last time that I ever pointed a weapon at anyone. My time in the service was a lot less deadly than actual combat because there were no wars to fight, no hostages to rescue, and no students to shoot.

On August 10, 1961, I left the army, just ten short days before the enlistment of every US service member was extended for a year. The buildup in Southeast Asia was about to begin. The pesky communists of North and South Vietnam, who had fought for decades to free themselves from the blessings of French colonialism, now wanted to do away with the artificial partition of their country, and, in 1961, to free themselves from the clammy hands of American capitalism.

Young Americans poured into Vietnam to fight, to bleed, and to die in the jungles and rice paddies, and to destroy villages to save them. Many of them came home in body bags. Many returned with limbs missing. Too many came home with emotional scars, crippled by seeing and doing things that no one should have to see and do. Some, like Kenny Woodrum from the west side of Cleveland, even went back to Vietnam a second time because he had acquired a heroin habit the first time, and Vietnam was where the good dope was. Too many men like Kenny Woodrum now walk the streets of our cities, haunted by memories of the bloodshed and by the ghosts of the dead that will not leave them alone. They visit the Vietnam Memorial in Washington, DC, to ask why and to beg forgiveness, to plead for the meaning of it all, and to weep and grieve for those who died.

When the buildup began, veterans like myself together with nonveterans spoke up and organized against the war. We also marched, picketed, and argued. We picked up the Kenny Woodrums from the sidewalks of Cleveland and got them into drug rehab. We were doing penance for those who jeered and taunted them when they returned home.

To oppose the war in Vietnam was not an easy or popular thing to do at Kent State. The students were mostly the sons and daughters of factory workers, farmers, and small-business owners. Many commuted from towns and cities throughout northeast Ohio. Many who wanted to join our picket in front of Bowman Hall could not do so because they had to answer to angry parents whose labor gave them the wherewithal to go to college in the first place. Anything that jeopardized that degree from Kent State was forbidden.

The picket was lonely and cold most of the days. There was no fun in it most of the time. Nevertheless, we stuck with it. We passed out leaflets. We marched anytime and anywhere we could. Our main activity at Kent was to stand for an hour or so in silent witness in front of Bowman Hall every Wednesday at noon. Others by the hundreds would come by to encourage us or to jeer. They occasionally threw fruit. However, they gave that up when we stood our ground and ate the fruit. It was delicious, most of the time.

Even the FBI sent agents from the Akron field office to take our photographs. We estimated that enough photos were taken to completely paper the walls in J. Edgar Hoover's bedroom so that he and Clyde Tolson could have someone to loath while they drifted off to sleep. We held clandestine meetings in Hargreaves's basement. Roy Inglee, Barbara Brock, Ron Wittmaack, Al Diamondstein, Beverly Kristen, and others pitched in to design posters and print flyers. It was a farcical giggle right out of the anticommunist screeds of the 1940s and 1950s that we were required to read in grade school. We always registered each demonstration with the university. We always got the posters stamped before we put them up. We had no problem with that. Except on one occasion. We put up a poster that we knew would not be approved. It was a gory depiction of little children roasted by napalm and fleeing in terror toward the camera. We did not put up many posters like that in the months that followed. It was just too heartrending.

We were required to have a faculty adviser. The main function of the adviser, we insisted, was to get lost. This was especially so when we plotted our activities in our dark and secret Bolshevik basement. The adviser disappeared willingly. Several faculty members, including our adviser, risked the wrath of the deans to join our picket lines. Dolores Noll, Edward McGehee, Doris Franklin, Sid and Clara Jackson and their children, and several other faculty members, mostly young, were in the thick of it. The same people were there when we demonstrated against the denial of the basic rights of students to speak out, to publish, and to demonstrate. They were there when we fought for approval for a chapter of the Congress on Racial Equality on campus. They were there when we railed against curfew hours for women, the in-loco-parentis rule, the idiotic hazing of first-year students, and especially the hated dress codes, which seemed to apply only to women. We even held a sit-in in the office of President Robert White to save a literary magazine, named COLLAGE, that the chairman of the journalism school did not like. We published the magazine. We got into student government. We printed our leaflets on university mimeographs. Moreover, we used university paper to do so. We even stole some of it.

We made a lot of trouble. In addition, we pissed off many people. We were doing these things long before Mario Savio and the students at Berkeley thought of doing so. This does not mean that the students at Kent State were more hip or more sophisticated than the students at Berkeley. They were just in a different time zone.

When the war in Vietnam escalated in 1964, and later when it spread to the rest of Indochina, we were ready. When we held teach-ins and invited speakers to Kent State, the campus police, at the behest of the FBI, usually sent Leroy Peach to cover the event and report back. Leroy Peach was a big gentle bear of a cop, and we made him as welcome and as comfortable as the small seats in Lecture Hall A of Bowman Hall would allow. Later, at Case Western Reserve University, when we found the University Circle Police at our meetings, usually hiding with tape recorders in the projection booth of Strosacker Auditorium, we threw them out.

We marched in Cleveland, in Washington, DC, and wherever there was activity. Others joined us as they came to Kent State. Howie Emmer, Jerry Persky, Mark Real, Sue Gibson, Sus Marie Hipp, Jim Lincoln, Bobby Franklin, and many others carried on as we graduated. They continued to make trouble—more so and in many different ways than we did before them. As I neared graduation, we were holding large rallies on the Commons at the Victory Bell. We were no longer a small group of diehards. The work was paying off.

As the war dragged on and got uglier, so did many of the demonstrations. At the demonstration at the Democratic National Convention in Chicago in 1968, the call to "Bring the War Home" was answered in a full club-swinging, police-state fashion. The Democratic Party and its new middle-class liberal supporters were baptized in a brutal political fashion that day.

America woke up fast in those days, but not in the way contemplated by John Wayne. The Weather Underground, which grew out of the Kent State

Chapter of the Students for a Democratic Society, became the bête noir of the entire country. Wherever they took action, the fight was on. Confront and fight was their mode of operation. It was as ugly as the war that was tearing this country apart. The middle class had now joined the working class in the struggle against the war in Vietnam, and against racism and poverty in the country.

The COINTELPRO (Counter Intelligence Program) of the FBI was fully implemented by 1968. Clandestine military intelligence units sent teams of agents into every large American city to spy, to watch, to steal files of contributors to leftist peace groups, and, most of all, to provoke activists into committing crimes so that they could be made to spend their time and money on defending themselves in criminal proceedings instead of on their political work.

The most exciting event on the Kent State campus before 1970 was the protest of the Music and Speech building. The university community was getting closer to the brink. Many of the student participants were arrested, expelled, and banned from campus. For some of them, there was no appeal. They continued to engage the university from off campus. Some moved away to do political work in Cleveland and other cities. Some became part of the Weather Underground faction of SDS. The war did come home to the streets of America.

At the same time, the Black Panther Party grew into a national organization. They fought and died in raids by local police departments working with the FBI and the clandestine military intelligence units. Several times, American cities erupted in riots and rage over the murder of Martin Luther King Jr. and others not so famous. They went to trial and into prison in greater numbers than other groups. Always, they were represented in court by volunteer lawyers from the National Lawyers Guild and others who were just as highly motivated.

Priests and ministers raided draft offices and went joyfully into prison. Thousands of Quakers, pacifists, ministers, nuns, priests, union workers, students, assorted independent radical crazies, the Young Socialist Alliance and Socialist Workers Party from Kent, and many others marched against AT&T, the largest war profiteer at the time, which was meeting at the Convention Center in Cleveland one day in 1968. Even the Yippies were there. The Cleveland Mounted Police, on orders from the subversive squad of the Cleveland Police Department, moved around the Hanna Fountains on the Mall to arrest anyone associated with the SDS contingent, who were carrying black flags of anarchy. A loudmouthed law student from Case Western Reserve got them to desist by predicting a hell of a brawl if they persisted in riding through the crowd. The police moved their horses away.

The contradictions between our nation's ideals and its actual practice in nearly every sphere heightened enormously during the late 1960s. The debacle at the Chicago Convention shattered the Democratic Party. The Republican Party was now completely in thrall to its right wing and about to embark on its ridiculous adventure with Richard Nixon and Spiro Agnew as its national leaders.

In Cleveland, Ohio, the Ohio National Guard went in to quell the Glenville uprising on July 23, 1968. Before it was over, more than a dozen police and black residents were dead. As in 1970, the adjutant general of the Ohio National Guard was Sylvester Del Corso, who was quoted as saying that the "only way to treat a rioter was to stand him up on the sidewalk and shoot him." As the events of the next two years showed, General Del Corso would get the go-ahead from Governor Rhodes.

On April 30, 1970, Richard Nixon ordered the invasion of Cambodia. The nation erupted in rage again. Americans everywhere hit the streets with demonstrations. Students took action on the campuses. The war at home was fully engaged. The students at Kent State marched downtown and trashed windows. They made a general mess of things. The police responded with tear gas, cleared the streets, and drove the students back to the campus. There was no way to stop it. Then the ROTC building burned. The game was on.

Governor Rhodes sent in the National Guard, with his general in charge. Only a week earlier, Major General Del Corso had sent his guard units to escort scab truck drivers during a region-wide strike by Teamsters. Enraged Teamsters fired shots. However, the Guardsmen were forbidden to fire back. By the time they got to the city of Kent, they wanted blood. When Governor Rhodes arrived in Kent, Ohio, he held a news conference and informed everyone that the Guard was taking over. Mayor Leroy Satrom of Kent and President Robert White of Kent State had been silenced. Rhodes described the protesting students as "brownshirts" and "the worst kind of Americans." Coming from the governor, that insult is a badge of honor that we still wear with great pride.

The Guard banned all demonstrations and assemblies on campus. Even so, the "worst kind of Americans" did not stop. They continued to gather through the weekend in defiance of the governor. They were still there on campus on the morning of May 4. The students were loud and defiant. The Guardsmen faced them in a sullen rage.

On the campus of Case Western Reserve University, the community was out in force for a demonstration on the Case Quadrangle. Other law students and I always attended the demonstrations to take part and observe. This was our ongoing commitment to the upheaval around us. Shortly after

12:30, Irene Tenenbaum, the law school registrar, sent a message to me at the demonstration. National Guardsmen had just shot student demonstrators at Kent State. In that instant my life changed utterly.

I organized two carloads of law students to drive immediately to KSU to do what we could for the dead and wounded students, and to provide some legal first aid. As we drove through the main intersection in Streetsboro, we saw that the police had already begun to seal off the approaches to Kent, Ohio. We drove east through Brady Lake and entered Kent along Main Street. We stopped at an apartment on Water Street that I knew was something of a coordinating office for the student demonstrators. No one was there.

We then went up to the campus, where we learned that affairs of the day were being coordinated out of the Administration building and Wills Gymnasium. Guardsmen, administrators, and newspeople were in disarray. No one seemed to be in charge. The Portage County prosecutor had already asked for an order from the Court of Common Pleas to shut down the university and send the students home. The power-hustling vice president of Kent State, Ronald Roskens, was seen walking along the upper seats of the Gym holding sheaves of paper and looking important but totally lost. I moved around the building to see if I could gather information. As I entered a stairwell in a neighboring classroom building, I came upon a Guardsman carrying a rifle, wearing a helmet, and sporting a large wet stain on the front of his trousers. He was just a kid, really. The savagery of the day had caused him to wet his pants. I gave him a few cigarettes, wished him well, and moved on.

Having nothing further to learn in Wills Gym, we drove to the hospital in Ravenna to see what we could learn. It turned out to be nothing. No information was coming from any official source—not from the university, not from the hospital, certainly not from the police, and not at all from the National Guard. The authorities had already clamped down on information. One dean at Wills Gym, who knew me well, said, "All we need now is you and a bunch of law students poking around." The Guard clamped down on news releases and press conferences.

I watched as Dorothy Fuldheim walked through the hallways in a fog of grief. The soft strength of her face had become a tight white mask of conflicting emotions. She appeared ready to explode.

We could do nothing more. If we could not get information, our presence would only be interference. I did not want that. The wake was going badly enough.

We then drove to the apartment on Water Street to see if anyone had returned. As I approached the building, Natalie Finn came running down the stairs to tell me with great excitement that there were men with guns in the second-floor apartment. They were afraid at that point and asked to return to Cleveland. I was not ready to leave. I had something to do. Nate Backus, Natalie Finn, and I went up the stairs. As I entered the apartment, a man I did not recognize came from the room facing Water Street and pointed a submachine gun at me. I said, "Who the hell are you?" He did not answer, but looked toward the rear room. I turned and, to my amusement, there stood Arnold Schwartzmiller, the Kent State police chief, also holding a gun. I knew Arnie Schwartzmiller when I was an undergraduate. I told him to tell the other man who I was and to put that damned gun down before he hurt someone. The plainclothes police officer lowered his gun as well, and the moment ended peacefully.

No one wanted to stay a moment longer. We returned to Cleveland. I learned later that while we were in Kent, a roundup had begun. Police had fanned out through the city of Kent and arrested as many activists as they could find. It was obvious to me and to many others that an arrest list had been prepared well in advance of the shootings. It was like the lists of members of leftist unions and organizations that were prepared in the early 1950s by the FBI under the McCarran Act. Students fled their homes to avoid arrest. Campus residents were forced out immediately. They were thrown out, actually. Whoever was in charge allowed the students to return days later to retrieve their belongings. Many arrived in Cleveland and Oberlin like refugees. There they found temporary shelter in churches, private homes, and campus buildings.

Many students and townspeople developed their film at Campus Camera. They never saw their film again. Shortly after the shootings, local police and FBI agents approached the willing owner and confiscated everything. A valuable record of what happened on May 4, 1970, was lost forever.

I went home and sat alone for a long time that night, trying to dispel the sadness and to sort out my emotions. I was in a state of shock that I had never experienced before. I did not sleep that night.

For May 5, 1970, I had volunteered to watch a polling place for the election. I planned to stay all day. For me, it would be a day of rest and recovery. The polling place was at 114th Street and Woodland Avenue in Cleveland in a barbershop in an Italian neighborhood. I was prepared for a tough day. I was a stranger who was there to watch the poll for the candidate who was not favored by the people of that neighborhood. The shootings at Kent were on their minds. The usual tough-minded comment about "shooting all of them" was made by one of the men. I held my tongue until the noon news began on the television. Then the comment was made again, by a different man this time. I said, "They did shoot all of them. But they only hit thirteen. The rest were missed." One man said, "Those kids shouldn't have been there if they didn't want to get shot." I didn't really press the point. Later, however, when Dorothy Fuldheim gave her now-famous tearful report, the men and women present in the barbershop came to understand the grief and pain of the parents whose children were slain and wounded. These were like kids they knew. They were from all nationalities and mostly from working-class families—kids very much like their own. "Sure, some of them were only going to class. Maybe they shouldn't have been shot." That remark was a small victory for me. When the poll closed, the gall and wormwood had receded into a quiet grieving sadness.

While I continued to work for my law degree, my wife and I volunteered to work on the Federal Court case brought by the American Civil Liberties Union (ACLU). David Scribner from New York came in with us at the behest of William Kunstler. Ben Sherer volunteered for the Ohio ACLU. Later in 1970, Judge William K. Thomas ordered the infamous Portage County Grand Jury Report sealed. That was only half of the loaf. Judge Thomas would not dismiss the indictments against the twenty-five men and women who were indicted, the Kent 25.

The legal team then turned to the defense of the criminal cases. The Kent Legal Defense Fund had mounted a mighty effort to support the defense. The people who worked for the Fund were all volunteers. There were many of them: students, faculty, and townspeople who came to wish us well. They pasted, typed, collected money, and shared their food and their laughter. Beyond that, they gave to us the greatest gift of all—their strength. Sometimes they worked sixteen hours a day. Among the many, the volunteer I remember most is Roseann Canfora, the magnificent "Chickie." All of them were the quiet heroes of that year.

We knew that the charges of riot, for the burning of the ROTC building, would rise or fall on the question of identification. The first two cases heard were pleas to a lesser charge. Later, on a day I shall never forget, a hearing was called for all the defendants to appear in Portage County Courthouse. Something important was about to happen. The legal team had an idea about the reason for the hearing.

On that morning, the legal team took their seats and the special prosecutor rose to speak. "The State of Ohio moves," he said softly, "to dismiss the remaining cases against the following named defendants." He then called out the names. One by one, they rose from their seats. The judge then said, "The motion of the special prosecutor is granted. The cases against the defendants are dismissed." It was a moment of pure experience for me and for everyone in the courtroom. The defendants and spectators erupted in joy. They had won. Few events in the years since that day can match that moment.

What this all means for us, at this remove of thirty years, is hard to say. The hurt is still there in many of us. We are still haunted by the memory. Its meaning is elusive, to say the least. For me, it is an ongoing effort to pin down the responsibility for what happened. The peace and repose that I seek still eludes me. The dead have been buried. The wounds have healed. I recall a remark made by Daniel Moynihan at the obsequies for Robert Kennedy in the Rotunda of the National Capitol in Washington. "You are not Irish unless you know your heart is meant to be broken." Maybe that is how my heartbreak will heal and I can come to rest.

The shootings at Kent State on May 4, 1970, is now a major event in American history. Our innocence bled out of the bodies of the dead and wounded students onto the hill above the Commons that day. Our lives and the world around us changed utterly in the spring sunshine. We would never be the same. The violence at Kent State on May 4, 1970, and at Jackson State ten days later, sears the soul to this very day.

The Huguenots, who languished in the dungeons of Lyons after the Edict of Nantes, scratched a slogan on the walls of their cells. RESISTEZ! TOUJOUR RESISTEZ! When we face bullies and goons, even the ones wearing uniforms, the command of the Huguenots calls out to us down the centuries. RESIST! ALWAYS RESIST!

In facing the future, I am reminded of lines from a poem:

When comes time that grieving is all in our keeping
And the spirits that watch us stop by this way,
Let them cry out as we do on this saddest of mornings,
May love's joy abide us the rest of our days.

May 4, 2000

Save the Pooch

ROBERT STAMPS

Robert Stamps was shot by the Ohio National Guard on May 4, 1970, at Kent State University. Until his death, on June 11, 2008, he was an outspoken critic and an active member of the May 4 Family. This piece was written in 1990.

It was the first hot spell of the year in Ohio, and in Kent, a small college town at the tip of the Bible Belt, our spirits, weighted down so heavily from winter snow, were soaring. Before day's end they would climb higher still.

We anticipated a huge, excitable crowd, what with all the threatening phone calls and hate mail we had received. The war at home had hibernated for the winter, and now it was awakening like a hungry, angry bear.

My only pair of wide bell-bottom jeans stayed safely hidden in the closet of my dormitory room. In the dark ages before the capitalists discovered that a hefty return could come from the counterculture, I had strained to find a pair, coming across them of all places in the Army-Navy store six miles down the road in Ravenna, the conservative county seat.

For this special day I would dress like a gentleman, forsaking my boots for shiny dress shoes and my blue jeans jacket for a sport coat I had bought in downtown Kent at the used clothing store for three bucks. Ah, and I remembered to shave.

"There are plenty of fascists running around in blue jeans," Allie had lectured the group. "Let's not give the media the opportunity to label us as dirty hippies or revolutionaries."

The fully developed and yet hastily conceived conspiracy was born two weeks before, in a council, outside the dorms under the still leafless spring trees. We sat in the darkness to conceal our identities, far from the stray microphone of a narc, the camera of a G-man, or the notebook of a campus cop.

An odd dozen we were—black, white, girl, boy, Eastern Seaboard liberal and homegrown Cleveland working-class radical. We passed radical politics around like a sweet doobie, and we had comradeship to share. Still, we were a brigade of nonconformists, and no one flashed an SDS card or the Chairman's little red book. Precious little dogma, considering the tenets of the times.

To the best of my knowledge, neither was anyone the beneficiary of smuggled monies sent north by Fidel Castro to foment revolution, as was alleged in Washington. America got an A-plus for scapegoating. Fidel's grant would have been consumed by record albums, assorted intoxicants, and other staples of equal revolutionary merit anyway, not weapons or mimeograph machines. This was social change with a backbeat.

But if social unrest was our avocation, it was reflected as well in our studies. There were no marketing majors in this clan. Future yuppies, perhaps, business tycoons, no.

Sarah and Sam were lovers. In their senior year, in a flower-child ceremony, they would marry. Later, in the 1970s, they would divorce.

And Lars Christensen, the Errol Flynn of campus agitators, rented a room like the rest of us, upstairs in Tri-Towers. He was never there.

I lived in Tri-Towers as well, in a single room with a mattress on the floor and just enough space for a stereo and a refrigerator. My door, like others, stayed unlocked. Mi casa was su casa.

Built only three years before, the modern style of Tri-Towers thumbed its nose at the common dormitories and campus buildings within its view. In fine dialectical fashion, its costly rooms were hideouts for the radical elite of the university. The ground floor connected the three air-conditioned residences in a space station–like arrangement. In the center was a lounge, complete with rehearsal rooms with pianos, television rooms, study rooms, and a large, uncluttered, circular meeting room nicknamed The Pit, with a thick, Lenin-red carpet. That spring, The Pit would become the headquarters for the Kent People's Army.

Intrigue is not best considered in the barracks, however, so we snuck out into the spring evening unannounced to make our plans.

Lars, the future history teacher, began: "It seems to me," he said, "that we should give up on trying to organize anything this spring. It is April already, and not much is going down. Nothing exciting on this campus since the Moratorium last fall. Can we stop kidding each other that we can get this campus hopping by June? Organizing is a slow, painful process. The mood around this campus is one of apathy. I'm tired of handing out leaflets all day in front of the Student Union for rallies that no one shows up for."

The smooth young man with the red beard waited patiently for Lars to finish. He disagreed with Lars, but needed Lar's speech nevertheless as a preamble to his own. He spoke so quietly that I strained to hear him.

"Students around this school are sheepish," he said, as if he were beginning a lecture. "Even the ones who want to get politically involved. They need direction. They need leadership. They need an event to rally around. They will come out by the thousands."

As I was about to offer an idea, he began again: "Do you all remember last year, when Rebel Davis was passing out flyers that contained the famous four-letter word outside the Union?"

We remembered. The cops had arrested him on the spot and hauled him off to jail.

"When the administration refused to make his suspension hearing public, what happened? Three hundred students took over the building in protest. Over one hundred of them were arrested.

"The next day, eight thousand students ringed the campus in support. EIGHT THOUSAND. And one week before that, any one of you would have given me that apathy speech."

Lodi, an Ohio biker nicknamed for his hometown, took exception.

"Well, the administration is a lot smarter now, and they ain't into provoking people like they used to. You know damn well they leaned hard on those students who took over the Music and Speech building. Some of 'em are on probation, and some of 'em ain't around no more to do any complainin'."

He pointed his finger at the group each time he raised his voice. We felt his eloquence.

"Students are runnin' scared round this campus, and most of 'em don't want to get thrown out on their butts over some protest that don't make a damn bit of difference. It just gives Agnew the excuse to call us bums."

"His new word is radiclibs," Lars said, and we all laughed nervously.

The woman from Toledo sat with her legs crossed. Her long brown hair was parted down the middle. She looked at no one in particular when she spoke. "Here is the plan," she began.

There was a professor on campus in whose class I had the good luck to enroll. In those turbulent years when QUESTION AUTHORITY became a theme song, he downplayed his PhD and asked his students to call him Jonathan. His casual nature, however, did not stem from any deference to the fashion of the times or from a disbelief in the enormity of his influence over young people. He took great pride in what he did, but he felt it his task first and foremost to convey a sense of mistrust and even of scorn toward established institutions, and if he would give anything at all to his students, it would be to introduce them to critical thinking. This he did with a mountain of statistics, all committed to memory, and a persuasive manner in his speech.

And so at 11:00 one morning I left my Spanish American Literature class, which was always benign as a sheep, and crossed the street in my fringed leather jacket to Social Problems. On any given day, it could be the gospel according to C. Wright Mills or Eldridge Cleaver.

I was to be the bearer of what I considered to be a crucial message for the class, and my own experience at public speaking was limited. I shook in my boots all through the lecture until Jonathan gave me the floor.

Standing in front of a large class in a larger auditorium, I stuck my hands in my pockets and I cut loose.

"This being a Social Problems class and all, and the fact that we've been talking a lot about the war and things, I am very pleased to announce that for your edification and amusement, next Tuesday at noon, in front of the Student Union, a group of concerned students will napalm a dog to demonstrate scientifically the effects of this incendiary on a living organism. Everyone is invited, there is no admission charge, and we look forward to seeing all of you there."

A few rows down, in the middle, a girl moaned, "Oh God."

A vet in the back with a green army jacket bolted for the door and shouted, "You're sick!" He pushed the door open and disappeared.

Later in the day my phone rang. "This is Jonathan, your sociology prof. Is anyone else in your room right now?"

"No".

"I've just gotten a phone call, a call from a man who identified himself as a police informant. He claims to be enrolled in Social Problems, but he wouldn't give me his name or tell me for whom he works."

"Do you believe him?"

"Perhaps not, but I wanted to tell you what he told me. He claims that possession of napalm is a federal offense, and that all of you will be arrested next Tuesday and charged with federal crimes if you go ahead with your demonstration. I have reservations about having an informant in my class, but I think you and your people need to be extremely careful."

I thanked him.

"Where do you have the napalm?"

"Can't tell you that, Jonathan."

"Whose dog are you going to use?"

I said nothing.

"Can you at least raise bail money so we can go down to the Ravenna jail and get you out?"

"Thank you, Jonathan. It has all been arranged."

"I don't know how you could say that. Bail could be set extremely high."

"Incarceration would only increase the publicity. See you in class."

The five iron that stuck its head through my door announced the arrival of Mickey, a member of the campus golf team and the resident mediator of the sixth floor of Leebrick Hall, the single-room dorm for Tri-Towers. It was his role to intercede in the recurring hubbubs that broke out between the doves and the hawks in the sixth-floor lounge. Each floor had its own den in front of the elevators, and daily, after dinner, the debates began. Vietnam, marijuana, ROTC on campus. Each side considered the other ignorant, naive, and hoodwinked. When push came to shove, as it sometimes did, Mickey would be right there with his golf club diplomacy.

"All weekend long there has been talk around the dorm about this napalm thing. You a part of that?"

"Yes, yes, I am."

"I don't want to tell you what to do, but some of the other guys on the golf team plan on showing up, and they're not too pleased with the whole idea, to say the least."

He tapped his club on the floor.

"You would be smart if you didn't show up," he told me and left my room without fixing his gaze on mine.

Monday's sultriness lingered into the evening. Touring the campus with Lars, we handed out the remaining leaflets among the other dorms, retreating before having to answer any hostile interrogations.

Lars had been elected master of ceremonies for Tuesday's demonstration.

"You ready for tomorrow?" I asked him.

"If you mean have I done my homework, then the answer is yes," he said. "I know what I'm going to say. But the rumors I've heard about the governor's office being there, and the police—what if they arrest us before we even have a—"

"A chance to make our statement."

"Right. What happens then?"

The Student Union was a Hyde Park of sorts. Its entrance was a stage for moralizing Christians, for Yippies, and for the brownnosers from student government. For the spectator it was always a treat.

Having much preparation in front of me, I cut Jonathan's class Tuesday morning and stopped by the campus police station to pick up the bullhorn we had reserved. In my dorm room I finished dressing, pirating a tie from a business major down the hall. Polished and alert, we all gathered in The Pit, linked arms, and headed straight for the Union.

We talked and laughed along the way, but our hearts were in our throats and we could think of nothing else but whatever awaited us. First, I noticed the police ringing the crowd—motionless, erect, with big sunglasses and wooden batons. They looked like movie extras from *Billy Jack*.

An old lady pushed a leaflet in my hands. Representing the ASPCA, she carried hundreds more under her arm. A stone's throw from her stood a deputy with an empty leash in his hand.

Quickly, Lars switched on the bullhorn. It would not work. And so raising his voice instead, which created much more drama anyway, he began:

"Napalm is a grayish, tough jelly that once ignited may reach two thousand degrees centigrade. The flaming gel becomes sticky and adheres quite well to human or animal flesh."

The crowd was becoming angry, and people were beginning to hoot. At the back of the crowd I saw golf clubs gleaming in the sun.

"Napalm burns with an orange flame and generates a huge amount of smoke. One bomb can plaster gobs of stuff over an area the size of a football field."

Lars's voice was beginning to crack.

"Officials of the company that accepted the contract to manufacture napalm stated that they did so in part because they felt that 'good, simple citizenship' required that they supply their government and military with the goods that they need when they have the technology and have been chosen by the government as a supplier."

(At the 1966 price of fourteen cents a pound, the company would receive over $42 million for the three hundred million pounds of polystyrene converted to napalm.)

Lars had lost all traces of objectivity.

"Inhuman acts done against any civilian population constitute a crime against humanity, according to the Nuremberg principles."

He put his notes and bullhorn on the ground. His white-on-white dress shirt was untucked and he was so disturbed it hurt to look at him.

"How many of you have come today to see a dog napalmed?"

The people booed.

"And how many of you are prepared to use physical force to stop us?"

Robby Stamps and Bill Arthrell (Source: John Rowe)

The people cheered. Like a conductor, Lars silenced them with his waving arms, took a deep breath, and lowered his voice.

"I have some news for you. I have some real news for all of you, my friends. There is no napalm. There is no dog. There never was. The way we see it, you have all done the right thing by coming here today, and we applaud you. But we need for you to know that halfway around the world, napalm falls daily on your brothers and sisters, and we don't seem to hear their screams. What do we all know of the anguish of yellow people in Vietnam?"

Lars scanned the crowd. "There is someone here today from the Society for the Prevention of Cruelty to Animals. Fine. What about a Society for the Prevention of Cruelty to People?"

Lars had a last breath in him. "Thanks to all of you for effort. We hope to see you at other rallies on campus."

The silence in the air was for us golden. After a minute perhaps, someone in the crowd began the applause, which spread outward like a ripple in a pond, and the clapping embarrassed us with its endlessness and its sanction.

We twelve walked slowly back to Tri-Towers, speaking very little. Before Vietnam moved from television to textbook, Lars would see the inside of a jail cell no less than twenty times. My path would take me elsewhere, but, like him, my life's priorities had been cemented on a warm spring afternoon by a hound who never even existed.

This piece originally appeared in *Kent & Jackson State 1970–1990,* edited by Susie Erenrich.

PART IV

The Shootings: May 4, 1970

It's Alright, Ma, I'm Only Dying

An Eyewitness Report from Kent State

CONSTANCE NOWAKOWSKI

Constance Nowakowski was a senior at Kent State University and an eyewitness to the May 4, 1970, shootings on campus. Her account appeared in Harry, a Baltimore Underground Newspaper *on May 14, 1970.*

Friday (Mayday) was the day following Nixon's speech. Friday was the day that Kent State, an unknown and uninvolved small-town university near Cleveland, had its first big protest demonstration since the November Moratorium. (Winters are quite rough in Ohio.) Exactly one year before, Kent State SDSers took over the Music and Speech building in a Vietnam protest, and all our radicals—about thirty—were arrested and imprisoned. This left the campus virtually without any activists. They were freed just in time for this demonstration, but unfortunately could not participate because of their parole rules.

Some graduate students, a couple of professors, and a group of not normally active undergraduates buried a copy of the US Constitution in a silent and peaceful ceremony on the grass of the Commons, where they traditionally hold archery and baseball games, ROTC drills, and peace demonstrations.

Friday night in the downtown area along Bar Row has everyone as clientele: freaks, radicals, bikers, the Fraternal Order of Eagles, the Kent Moose Club, fraternity members, and regular students. Another demonstration was held that looked more like a block party: booze and a bonfire—good clean revolutionary fun. Grass and opium were being smoked on the streets and the bikers from Ravenna, Ohio, passed out blotter acid until the police came and a bottle was thrown at their car. The crowd became excited then. It seemed as if the police were going to just let the thing wear itself out. The bars closed, but the kids still sat around turning on, cursing Nixon, and recruiting drunks and women to the Cause. The riot cops came upon the scene, beat some heads, and we split the area, heading for campus, breaking windows on the way. A girl running next to me was clubbed. Then I was caught behind the line of rushing riot cops, so I snuck through bushes and backyards, where I ran into a kid freaking on acid. We made our way to campus, rejoining the group, and sat down in protest only to be dispersed by tear gas.

On Saturday the mayor of Kent declared a nighttime curfew, and made a few statements to the local newspaper. Many were angered at the beatings, and the fight against police brutality caught on. Fourteen had been arrested. That night about three hundred kids gathered on the Commons. We set a small American flag afire and carried it to the ROTC building, broke a window, and threw it in. Cheers of victory went up from the crowd. The building was an eyesore—a frame barrack-type structure located at the head of the Commons in the center of the campus. The papers reported $50,000 damage to supplies and files housed there. Firemen attempted to control the fire, but the hoses were cut and confiscated. Riot police beat a few heads and teargassed a little. We happened to be near a waiting Red Cross truck. A cop went up to it, reached in, and took out a box of mace. I yelled, "Hey, man, the Red Cross is ratting on us. I thought they were here to help us." He retorted, waving a rifle, "Yeah, you'll get help—helped right into the can."

The city of Kent is normally very conservative, but this was becoming more than just an incidental case of brutality; it was turning into a major crisis and students were quickly being radicalized. The number of activists increased progressively all weekend.

After burning ROTC, we burned a small wooden shack that housed Phys Ed bows and arrows because it was the only small burnable thing around and we wanted to give the pigs more shit. We then circled (the crowd numbered about four hundred now) around to front campus, where we saw a parade of approximately five hundred Guardsmen with armored personnel carriers, jeeps carrying guns, and whatever. It is difficult to describe the emotional reaction to their ominous arrival: it was certainly one of panic and massive paranoia. Imaginary Vietnams and World War IIs went through my head. The National Guard immediately set to work breaking up the crowd; thirty-three were arrested before they could make it home. Later that night, I was standing on my street corner watching the flames rise a distance away from the ROTC fire. Several people, some residents of the same street, were curious also, and a small group silently gathered there. We stood just watching until Guardsmen, apparently hiding in nearby bushes, suddenly rushed at us with bayonets fixed. We ran for our homes.

At this point I polarized—instant radicalization. I had always been a demonstrator, but I had never been activated until then. Many of us who were never before aware became so that weekend. It took a personal nightmare and a physical threat to my own person to awaken me to the realization that action is not for someone else to do, that everyone is oppressed and everyone must conquer it. I had always protested for the war to end, but didn't believe in bringing it home. Now I saw and felt that it was already here, and had been for a long time.

Sunday was a beautiful day for a revolution. Everyone gathered as usual on the grass all over campus—disgusted, but determined to be real good love-and-peace freaks one more time. We talked to the pigs, turned on, etc. There was even a semiofficial guided tour of the ROTC building for parents and university guests, including Governor Rhodes. The Guard had their armored personnel carriers set up all over campus at what they thought were strategic points. Thirty or forty of them spent all day guarding the rubble. Students stared at them from the other side of the rope, some out of curiosity, some just to make them uptight. Guardsmen with guns patrolled the campus and the town. There were strange feelings, but no hassles. This is when Allison Krause, one of the shooting victims, put a daisy in the barrel of a Guardsman's rifle and told him that flowers were better than bullets. I asked a Guardsman if his gun was loaded. He said he didn't know. "Are you going to use it?" He said if he had to.

The Guard was pissed off at being there. They had been on duty for a couple of weeks now because of the Teamsters' strike in Cleveland. They weren't used to military routine, they had little training in riot control, and one cat said he'd been in for only three weeks, avoiding the draft. A brother came home that afternoon and reported that he had been called aside by a young Guardsman who said, "Psst . . . I'm on your side. I'm in college."

Governor Rhodes was behind their presence there. He was running for a Senate seat in Ohio and thought that by putting down campus radicals, he could pull in the winning votes. The elections were held two days after the shootings and he lost.

Sunday night we again broke curfew and also martial law, which by this time was in force not only in Kent, but in all surrounding towns. Gas stations, liquor stores, and other businesses had been closed all day and would remain so. Pigs patrolled the streets: there were nearly a thousand Guardsmen in the area, and also every available policeman from as far as forty miles away. The number of protesters had grown from eight hundred to nine hundred.

We started marching from the most outlying dormitories and apartment complexes to front campus, protesting the military occupation, the beatings, the tear-gassing, and the arrests of more than a hundred brothers and sisters. The enemy surrounded a group of about three hundred at the main gate of campus. Helicopters flew low and hovered, keeping high beams on the trapped demonstrators, who sat down and refused to go anywhere. They were gassed, but they did not move. They threw tear gas canisters back at the Guard. There was a tremendous feeling of unity. This is where a boy was bayoneted in the face. Another boy was bayoneted in the foot and laid for an hour on a nearby sorority lawn before help came. On this night also a girl was badly wounded as she was bayoneted in the abdomen when coming out of her dormitory after curfew.

I was in the group with a first-aid kit, but they would not let me through to the trapped students. The whole first-aid scene was very bad. We, as well as others throughout the area, opened our house as a first-aid center. One cat and one chick painted a red cross on a white truck, got an authorization from the health center, and tried to get through enemy lines to help, but they were arrested.

The only thing that could be heard was the sound of the eight or so helicopters and the crowd that was behind the lines surrounding the sitdown group singing "We Shall Overcome" and "Give Peace a Chance." The Guard held the small group in their circle for three or four hours, finally pepper-gassing them, then arresting as many as they could catch. About sixty arrests were made that night. Several were injured on our side, none on theirs. Kent City police and campus police arrested a couple of kids to protect them from the Guard. The helicopters flew all night long.

Monday classes were held, though we were still under martial law. There was a rumor that the pigs had orders to shoot to kill. It was also rumored that there would be a rally on the Commons at noon to call for a strike and protest the pigs on campus. There was. About two thousand students, faculty, newsmen, photographers, and undercover agents were gathering in the area. The faculty backed us and became one with us. Our faithful university president, after having lunch with Governor Rhodes in Kent on Sunday, split for Iowa. We gathered on the hill overlooking the Commons, while the enemy center was still at the ROTC rubble. They were armed with mace, M1s, mortars, and tear gas. Pepper gas was being flown around in the helicopters. Each pig had his own mace and tear gas on his belt. We had nothing, except for wet rags in Baggies that someone passed around to use in case of tear gas. None of us felt fear any longer. The only thing that mattered was to be freed, and if you couldn't be free, what was the fun about living under military rule?

A jeep emerged from their sanctuary, and they said over a loudspeaker, "You have orders to disperse immediately. This area is under martial law. There can be no gatherings." We chanted, "Fuck you" and "Pigs go home," and continued our rally. They threw tear gas. We threw it back. No one ran. We were sick of running. About seventy-five Guardsmen charged up the hill, fully armed, and another battalion circled to the side. We split, walking to another hill on the back of the Commons behind the Journalism building. They followed, finding themselves outnumbered. They got uptight. We threw any available stick or stone—no rocks. There were no rocks in that grassy area.

All of a sudden, a Guardsman gave a signal, swinging his arm down. His fist was clenched. Then they were on their knees, firing into the group, a group of nothing but name-callers, onlookers, demonstrators, and stone-throwers. They fired directly into them, not at the ground nor at the sky nor at the top of a building. Some Guardsmen didn't fire.

We were shocked and stunned—at the noise mostly—most of us thought they shot blanks. The only thing you could hear was the volley of shots—and then total silence, except for some screams and moans. The enemy split back down the hill to their sanctuary, leaving dead kids, wounded kids, scared kids, and blood. We tried to stop them. We were immobilized. We couldn't believe it. Bedlam. Kids and profs were screaming and crying, forming circles around the bodies to give them air—and to keep the crowd—some still disbelieving—away. We waited for the ambulances to come and take them away. There were nine wounded and four dead (it appeared that they died instantly—at least the girl who got hit in the jugular vein did). The boy with his foot shot was the last to be taken away. There was not a Red Cross truck in sight, only privately owned ambulances.

There were groups of people standing at the bottom of the hill—the building blocked their view of the shooting. I ran down, shouting what had happened. I don't know if they believed it. If they did, they were so stunned that they didn't move. Somebody on the hill, a boy, dipped the black flag into the blood and the crowd took it down the hill to show the pigs. The sense of unity that overtook us was our only weapon. Crowds of people joined together—we were crazed with anger. The pigs were crazed with fear. One had a heart attack and one was treated for shock—the only casualties for them all weekend. One young Guardsman was yelling that he didn't know his gun was loaded. A chick ran up to the line of Guardsmen and said, "I hope you're happy. Smile, you fucking murderers." A Guard gave her a shit-faced grin. A freak knelt

Dr. Glenn Frank (Source: Kent State University News Service)

before them, saying nothing. The huge crowd sat before them angry and shocked. They still had their guns poised. Finally, their leader, General Del Corso, got them to put the rifles at "parade rest." But still we sat there crying for justice, wanting to know which Guardsmen were the murderers. Indescribable tensions were mounting on both sides. Several people were trying to speak to us. Some kids got scared and left. They were trying to calm us so that there would be no more bloodshed. We didn't care. Professors and newsmen finally persuaded us to get up and slowly walk away because the Guard sent a message that if we didn't leave immediately, they would use any measure necessary to clear the area. Their thing was that the place was still under martial law and there were to be no gatherings. One boy who refused to go had to be carried off the field by fellow students. The word had spread all over campus by this time, and it is impossible to describe the emotion that was registered on faces as we slowly walked away, being forced by inches from the area by highway patrolmen (a Guardsman would have gotten killed).

A Reminiscence Thirty Years Later

ROLLY BROWN

Rolly Brown attended Kent State University from 1967–1971 and was an eyewitness to the May 4, 1970, shootings on campus. This piece was written in 2000.

For many years after May 4, 1970, I refused to speak about the events of those four days. The fact that I was a student at Kent State would come up in conversation, questions would be asked, and I would change the subject or simply say, "I'd rather not talk about it." I didn't want to demean the profundity of the experience.

So what was profound about it? At the time, I felt it was a profoundly pure act of civil disobedience, based on the most humanistic and idealistic precepts. Over time, that feeling has remained, and I'd pit it against the common media portrayal of the 1960s, which features goofy-looking kids in bell-bottoms and paisley shirts dancing mindlessly in what seems an attempt to be fashionable. While we did our share of mindless dancing, and we may have looked goofy by today's standards (although not too many of us actually wore those paisley shirts), it is a huge disservice to truth and history to ignore the level of serious thought that went into and emerged from the student movements of the 1960s. Evidently, it still serves the public relations agenda of our government today to trivialize these movements.

As for the four young people who lost their lives at Kent State, they may have been poor victims of capricious circumstance, and I don't believe they represented the most political or sentient aspect of the student movement at KSU, but their hearts were in the right place. And I believe today, as I did then, that their unintentional martyrdom put an end to the war in Vietnam. That is not, as it may sound, such a grandiose claim. Consider this: Until the shootings at Kent State, the general perception, in the media and in the public eye, was that the people of America were mainly, if not totally, behind the government in its military involvement in Vietnam. Within a week of the shootings, the largest antiwar march of the era was mounted in Washington—I remember watching it on TV from the hospital room of one of the shooting victims—and from that point on, the general perception was that Vietnam was a huge mistake, and that the government would strive to get us out of there as soon as possible.

My own involvement in the happenings of that weekend was not as part of any organization. I wasn't in SDS or any other organized group, although I did have strong political opinions. In fact, when the radical ideologues would come to the dorms and want to "break into small groups and rap it down," I often found myself playing devil's advocate to what I felt was an unrealistic and rigid dogma.

What I recount here is, I must admit, a memory of thirty years ago, so some details may be hazy or even incorrect, but probably more true than most of the lies reported in the media. Also, I've chosen not to use the names of any cohorts in what might be construed an illegal action, so the term *we* means *me and whatever friends happened to be along*. On Friday, May 1, I attended a rally on the campus that was a response to the bombing of Cambodia by the Nixon regime. It was a beautiful warm spring day, and we dropped mescaline to heighten the experience. There was a reasonably large crowd, but it should be noted that Kent, Ohio, was not a hotbed of left-wing activity, and the greater student population was as hostile to student radicals as the government was.

That evening, I was playing guitar with Alex Bevan, a local singer/songwriter, in a club on Main Street in downtown Kent. From the makeshift stage, we could see over the half curtains and out to the street. The audience could not. There was a lot of activity on the street. On our breaks, we walked over to Water Street, where a bunch of "hippies," for want of a better word, had gathered in front of Orville's, the one bar in town, which had a sort of hip clientele. They were dancing in the street and blocking traffic. Meanwhile, most of the student body in town were partying as usual in a totally nonpolitical fashion in the several subterranean bars along Water Street.

Alex and I had begun what was probably our third set when we saw, from our vantage point on stage, that the street scene was turning into a riot of sorts. Students were swarming along the streets, and windows were getting broken. We did a quick "That's all, folks!" and headed outside to see what was up. By this time, the police had realized they were outnumbered, and had called for a tactical crew from the county. It was at this moment that Kent State became radicalized. Before the bars closed, the rioting was carried on by a fairly small and very politically minded minority, but as midnight drew near and the tactical police descended upon Water Street, the bars closed up and the great majority of apolitical students emerged from the subterranean drinking establishments, only to be attacked with indiscriminate police brutality. The police drove the students back toward campus through an area that included many frat houses. Thus, even those fraternity brothers who had stayed home that evening were radicalized when they witnessed the spectacle of their innocent right-wing friends being bludgeoned on the lawns of their domiciles. In two hours, the police did more to promote student radicalism in Kent than the student radicals had done in two years, and the lines were drawn. It was no longer "frat boys versus hippies." It was "students versus cops."

My memories of Saturday and Sunday are fairly sketchy. There was a lot of excitement and discussion among the people I knew who still lived in Tri-Towers, which was the dorm complex most associated with long-hair types, and also in various group houses of my acquaintance. On Saturday night, I witnessed the burning of the ROTC building on the campus. It was exciting, and the sense of mob destructiveness and student unity hung heavy in the air, but it should be remembered that the ROTC building was basically a large wooden shack that had been erected in the 1940s as a temporary structure and had somehow, educational budgeting being what it was, remained standing, along with the similarly constructed Kent State Art Department, for twenty years longer than originally intended.

I think it was Saturday when the soldiers arrived in force, and the command was issued for students not to congregate on campus. Of course, everyone immediately congregated. On Sunday evening, I was part of a group on the front campus when armed soldiers started marching in a formation to sweep the area clean. With a friend, I escaped across Main Street into a residential area, hoping to avoid arrest. There were helicopters with arc lights patrolling low over this neighborhood, and we thought we were in pretty deep trouble until some nice young women called from their porch and allowed us in to spend the night in their living room. (Thanks again, ladies, wherever and whoever you are!)

On May 4, the word went out that there would be an impromptu rally on the Commons at 11:00 or noon. We arrived early, and, when the time came, we decided to ring the bell, which was lodged in a small brick wall on the Commons. The bell brought people out, and the stage was set for the tragedy to follow—soldiers on one side, students on the other, the rubble that had been the ROTC building sitting alongside. Someone from the military read the riot act over an electric megaphone. The students responded with boos and bravado. Then there were tear gas canisters, which some brave students managed to throw back at the soldiers. The air was thick with the stuff.

At one point, essentially blinded, I retreated to Dunbar Hall, where I was washing the tear gas out of my eyes at a water fountain when we heard the shots. Once we knew what had happened, there was a mixture of disbelief, outrage, and fear. The rest of that day was pretty much a blur. The school was officially closed, students were automatically evicted from both on-campus and off-campus housing and ordered to evacuate the area, and we mostly grabbed our stuff and ran. In Ravenna, we were stopped by vigilantes and held at gunpoint while they searched our car.

Finally, we made it back to Cleveland, where I became involved over the next couple of weeks as cochair of a group called Kent in Exile, which was given space to operate on the Case Western Reserve campus near University Circle. Our purpose was to provide a place for displaced Kent State students (many of whom were from the Cleveland area) to reconnect and process the events that we'd been involved in, and, as such, we held several meetings to that end. I also spoke at rallies at Cleveland State and at Oberlin. I remember nothing of what I said. I'm quite sure it was very critical of the government and of the war in Vietnam, and also that it emphasized that the rioting was not without purpose, but that the demonstrations were a protest against the immoral actions of a militarized government run amok, i.e., the bombing of Cambodia. This, of course, was true and not so true. On one hand, you could say that most of the students couldn't have cared less about Cambodia and were responding to the police brutality. On the other hand, you could recognize that brutality as a much closer-to-home manifestation of what our government was doing in Cambodia. The great majority of Kent State students may have been oblivious to the United States government's politics of force on the morning of May 1, 1970, but I assure you that they were profoundly aware of this issue by the evening of May 4.

For me, that felt like the end of my college education. Oh, I spent the summer in the city of Kent, and took a course or two during the fall and winter quarters, but I was already gone. A group of us left for Cape Cod in the spring, and I worked in various jobs, musical and otherwise, for the next ten years. It would be another quarter century before I got a college degree. The events of May 4 made the rest of my college experience seem incredibly meaningless and divorced from real life. There was no single reason to bother finishing.

I've thought a lot over the years about the personalities who made up the "Left" at Kent State. As is the case in any political movement or faction, there were various kinds of political people at KSU. Some were temporary true believers. Others were deep thinkers. Some were just trying to get laid, or to attain notoriety. For some people it was just a whim, but for many, it was the beginning (or middle) of a lifelong dedication to humanism and/or nonviolence. Today, when I hear an interview on the radio with some former 1960s leftists who are now Reagan-esque Republicans, and whose message seems to be, "See, all of us former radicals now realize that we were just young and foolish back then!" I can hear immediately that they were among the fanatical and mindless "true believers," and that their allegiances were never based on deep conviction.

In 1985, there was a reunion in Kent, Ohio. It wasn't held at a vanilla monument, and it wasn't sanctioned by any university organization. It wasn't even held on campus, but at a little park in town. No one gave any speeches or sang any songs of protest. It arose by word of mouth, and included a number of people (maybe twenty-five or thirty) who had lived in Tri-Towers between 1968 and 1970. It was a large circle of old friends, who had traveled from all over the country, and it was interesting to learn where our paths had led us after that spring afternoon in 1970.

Here are some of the things I noticed: A curious number of these folks had ended up marrying the person they were with at the rally on May 4. The great majority of us had careers in the human service sector. Few, if any, worked in the corporate or government areas. Many owned their own small businesses or worked as subcontractors of some sort. I don't believe that anyone there had really undergone any polar reversal of their former political views. No investment bankers. No Wall Street types. No political aspirants.

It is my belief that those of us who "survived" Kent will rarely put our faith in a large organizational structure of any kind. We largely see ourselves as working around the system, but not in the system. We're very skeptical of anything we read in the newspaper. We believe in a power structure that works from the bottom up rather than from the top down. Maybe we were just always the sort of people who didn't want to take orders from anyone. Maybe we got that way in college. Maybe we got that way after seeing the results of the top-down style of the Ohio National Guard in May 1970.

For me, I'll never be able to make sense of these events. Not Kent State. Not Vietnam. Not the Cultural Revolution in China, or the Cold War here in the West. There simply is no sense to be made! It's not a political issue. It's a humanitarian one. I mourn the deaths of Jeff and Sandy, whom I knew,

Rolly Brown with Magpie (Source: Brad McKelvey)

and William and Allison, whom I didn't know. And of those who perished in Vietnam as well. How could you not mourn the deaths of so many who died so young?

For me, I've decided that all I can manage is to try and make sense of my own life, to find a way of living (and making a living) that is life-affirming, and to try not to be part of the senselessness. I suspect that many of the people who lived through Kent State feel somewhat the same.

Brad McKelvey has been photographing the May 4 commemorations since 1990. He serves as an advisor, confidant, and archivist for projects of the Cultural Center for Social Change.

A Short Reflection

CURTIS LEE PITTMAN (JETER)

On May 4, 1970, Curtis Pittman was a member of Black United Students (BUS). The organization advised all its members to stay away from the noon rally scheduled to take place on the Commons on the Kent State University campus. He graduated from Kent State in 1978. This piece was written in 2001.

It was Sunday, May 3, 1970. My teammates on the track team and I were returning from Bowling Green State University. We had just finished competing against BGSU that weekend. When we arrived, all the things we had read in the newspapers or seen on television were becoming a reality. Kent State looked like a military base. I saw many guys in military fatigues with weapons, radios with antennae twenty feet long swinging on their backs. Not only was it a fantastic sight, it also had me worried. Just a few days before we left for Bowling Green, I attended a Black United Students meeting, which had anticipated such a gathering by the National Guard. A warning was coined by Fargo (Ibrahim Al-Kafiz): "a comprehension of the past has two advantages in the present, it makes us aware of how different people have been in other ages and accordingly enlarges our awareness of the possibilities of human experience and at the same time it impresses upon us those tendencies in human beings which have not changed and which accordingly are unlikely to change at least in the near future." He warned all black students to refrain from exposing ourselves on campus for we are always the first targets should there be trouble. I had no idea that the prediction would become partially true. (The next year Dick Gregory called those killed the "new nigger.")

Curtis Pittman (Source: John Rowe)

Being an athlete was cause for double jeopardy. Our coaches stressed staying out of trouble. The Athletic Department wanted us to be apolitical. And my fellow students wanted answers. As a Black United Student leader, I felt responsible for providing answers.

The next day, which was May 4 (my day of infamy), I made it a point to attend my morning classes because of the scheduled rally on the Commons that noon. I had one class at 12:05 P.M. It was Ms. Flemming's Sociology class. I enjoyed that class because we were discussing the Vietnam War and Cambodia. Days before, Cambodia had been invaded by US troops. Class time was also spent discussing affirmative action, apartheid, and the demise of the War on Poverty. I was late. I had to travel from Twin Towers to White Hall, which was the Education building. This meant going past Taylor Hall, where the rally was in full swing. I made it over the hill to Ritchie Hall, the old Student Union. Then I heard a popping noise and a lot of screaming. From my vantage point, I could still see the unforgettable scene—the military pointing their rifles at the people on top of the hill. I was mesmerized. I didn't realize what was taking place until I smelled tear gas. I took off for my class to inform and warn the others. I was unable to return because of the Guard, so I found a haven at the Institute of African American Affairs (IAAA). IAAA and BUS paved the way for our safe exodus from campus, like they did in 1968 when students went on strike.

It's difficult to put my feelings from that time into words. I pray that the events of May 4, 1970, will never be forgotten and never happen again.

PART V

Responses Near and Far

The Battle of Washington

TOM RIDDLE

In 1970, Tom Riddle was an undergraduate student at Kent State University; he graduated in 1974. He wrote this story as an assignment for a creative writing class that he took around 1972. In late 1999, he scanned the faded mimeographed copy of the story into editable text.

INTRODUCTION

It is only with the utmost reluctance and the constant prodding of my teenage son that I have decided to publish this story.

This is how the story came to me. I was driving from Philadelphia to Cleveland to cover a convention, and on my way I stopped in Warren, Ohio, to visit a friend I hadn't seen in many years. The side trip proved futile. But I thought that as long as I had gotten off the interstate, I would see a little of Ohio and not get directly back on the highway. Everything was going fine until I got to Kent.

In downtown Kent I had the misfortune of being stopped by a train for over an hour. When the train finally passed, my Monte Carlo would not start. With the help of a passerby I pushed my car to a nearby parking lot. I then tried to procure the services of a garage to start the car. However, there was no reputable garage open at 2:00 A.M. on Friday in Kent, Ohio. I was in despair, stuck in a small Ohio town with no place to go until the next morning.

I explained my plight to the gentleman who helped me push my car; he directed me to an all-night café.

The café was just a short walk from my car and the night was cold, so I heeded the gentleman's advice. I approached the café and realized that it was not at all like the places I frequent in Philadelphia, but I wasn't getting any warmer. Inside the cook was reading a comic book and a girl was sitting at the end of the long single bar. The cook didn't look up from his comic book when I entered and the girl did not bother to lift her head, which was buried in her knees.

Finally, I managed to distract the cook from his book just long enough for him to pour me a cup of coffee. Still, I needed someone to talk to, having left all reading material in the office and feeling quite distraught. I thought I would try my luck with the girl. After all, I am a man with two teenage children and I felt myself competent to establish rapport and somehow pass the time. I moved toward the end of the bar. No luck. She would not so much as lift her head from her knees. I decided that I would have to be more aggressive.

"Rather cold tonight, wouldn't you say?" I said in the friendliest tone I could muster.

That did it. The body groaned, threw the long sandy blonde hair back over her shoulders, stood up, and stretched. I saw that I had made an error in judgment, for it definitely was not a female I had awakened. He stretched, yawned, pulled his hair from his eyes and said, "What'd you say, man?"

I tried not to show my surprise, but frankly I was dumbstruck. I looked again; yes, he definitely was a male. He stood no more than five foot seven, was thin, and had on blue denim trousers that were as battered as the flannel shirt he wore. He looked at me with large blue eyes and a baby face that looked no more than twenty years old.

I quickly recovered my composure and said, "I commented that it is rather cold outside this morning."

By this time he had sat down again. I noticed that his eyes were bloodshot, and he smelled a bit of alcohol.

"Yeah, I guess so," he said, waking up a little more.

I had gotten his attention and after I volunteered to buy him a cup of coffee, he told me a little of himself. His name was Jeff Griffiths, but most people called him Grif. He had been a student at Kent State University since the fall of 1970.

I told Grif that I was a journalist and would be very interested if he would give me an in-depth account of what happened on the Kent State campus when four young students died in a clash with the National Guard. He refused. He said that he had given up trying to explain what happened then, but if I would buy him another cup of coffee, he would relate another experience—that of May 3, 1971.

So I bought him another cup of coffee and nonchalantly turned on the tape recorder that I carry inside my briefcase. The story lasted until dawn, during which I was obliged to repeatedly give Grif dimes to play what he called "movement music" on the jukebox. During the story he would sometimes dance around, all the while talking; other times he would simply stare blurry-eyed out the window, reminiscing with a tinge of emotion.

—R. J.

THE BATTLE OF WASHINGTON

PART I

Nearly a hundred people were at the meeting. The man in charge was some guy named Tiny. He was a big fat man with a cowboy hat and a suede leather coat. He looked like a big cowboy and someone who knew what he was doing. He was so big he was imposing; he was the biggest thing in the room.

"Well, people," he said, "as you know, the People's Coalition for Peace and Justice has called a demonstration in Washington this weekend. So what I thought we might do is ride down in vans. Two big U-Haul vans could take forty people each down to Washington. We'll leave tomorrow about 12:30 P.M. with some weed and wine, drive down to Washington and camp in this park that the government has set up for us there. We get there Friday night, party Saturday—there's a big rock concert Saturday night. Sunday we present our demands to the government with a march on the White House, and Monday we march on Washington. Tuesday we'll be back in Kent for the memorial service. The May Day people have asked that the demonstrations be peaceful and that if you are a violence freak, you stay home."

"I figure that it should cost us about eight dollars apiece." He went on for a while taking his cowboy hat off and putting his foot up on the table answering questions about what to bring and if he thought anyone would get arrested. Tiny described a serious but fun-filled weekend in Washington.

After the meeting I ran into my best friend, Jesse Rodriguez Gonzales. He was Mexican by birth and a dope- and fuck-head by life—very macho. In high school he had gotten an award for being the dirtiest football player on the team. He has long black hair and the dark eyes that only a Mexican can have. I tried to talk him into going

"Jess, come to Washington with me. We'll have a fine time. It will be decent—seeing a concert, the city, and getting high. Everyone will be there."

"Ah, no man, like I've told you before, I'm just not into that trip."

Jesse, unlike me, believes that nonviolence never got anybody anywhere. Jesse couldn't get into marching around Washington singing, "Give Peace a Chance." But I persisted and eventually talked him into going to Washington.

I went back to my room and called my old friend Cathy. She said she'd go, so I told her to bring something to sleep in and all the money she could get her hands on. But I assured her that I didn't plan on being arrested.

Friday, April 30, 1971, was a beautiful spring day in Kent. With my blue air-force coat over my shoulder and my toothbrush and a few other things in the plastic KSU bags they give you at the bookstore, I made my way to the Student Union. There was Jesse Gonzales in faded blue jeans and a muscle shirt with a star in the middle of it showing off his muscles. I talked to Jess for a while and in walked Cathy. I was glad Cathy was going. She was a quiet but nevertheless strong and beautiful woman. She wore a long, black coat that looked like it was once the overcoat to a tuxedo that Rudolf Valentino might have worn; I liked it. After introducing her to Jesse, the three of us went outside to look at the truck.

There isn't much you can say about a U-Haul van. It looks like a big shoebox fastened to a semi. I went around to the back of the truck and looked inside; it was dark and deep. The floors, walls, and ceiling were lined with plywood. Someone asked me if I knew it was illegal to ride in the back of a U-Haul van. I didn't. He added that there wasn't any ventilation in there once the door was pulled down, and that plywood wasn't the softest thing around. I didn't pay any attention to him.

To get a seat we moved to the back of the van. Soon there were more than forty people in the truck. With everybody's sleeping bags and coats there wasn't much room; some people didn't even have a wall to lean on. Everybody was arranging his or her stuff so as to get comfortable for the long ride ahead. People were joking. I introduced myself to the people sitting around me, organized my stuff, and got ready to leave.

We were sitting there and this student leader came over to wish us a good trip. He was Jerry Persky, president of the Yippies. A real hippie-dippie. He had a beard and talked in hip jargon. He said he was going to stay in Kent and keep the movement alive. He passed around the hat. Some people put money into it; I gave him a quarter.

After sitting a while, Tiny told us, "Well, people, in my calculations I neglected to figure in money for gas." Around went the hat. I put a quarter in. After another long wait the door was pulled down; the engine boomed, there was a jerk, and everybody cheered. We were off to Washington.

There was no way to get comfortable. I tried in vain to anticipate bumps and jerks, and sometimes it was necessary to stand up just to try and alleviate the pain in the butt that came from sitting on that plywood. I didn't care, though. I was having a good time. Somebody in the truck had some weed, so we all got stoned. The bumps weren't quite so bad after that.

The hours slowly went by. I tried to sleep, only to be awakened as my body hit a large bump. Finally, Tiny decided that we needed a rest, so he stopped at a truck stop. I stretched my aching limbs, and everybody got out of the truck complaining about their aches and pains. Half the people on that truck smoked and there was no ventilation. It felt very good to get some fresh air.

We appeared to be in the mountains of Pennsylvania. The hills were green and rolling as the night approached. I went into the restaurant of the truck stop—it was the first place I had ever seen that had ultraviolet lights on the toilet seats to kill crabs. Because there were nearly eighty of us, we took over the place. The hostesses were swamped. Later I learned that many of the KSU people had ordered things and walked out without paying for them, saying that the truck stop was making a contribution to the antiwar movement.

Back on the road, it was dark, and the inside of the truck was like a cave. All I could see was the red glow of a cigarette or the flame of a match. The truck began swerving across the road. At first people started to play like they were on a roller coaster, and soon everybody was screaming like ten-year-olds, but the van kept going on like that and we got tired playing roller coaster. The word got passed up to the back of the van to open the door a little bit and see if we were still in the mountains.

The people near the door reported that, in fact, we were on a level interstate. The fresh air felt so good to us that we decided to risk arrest and leave the door open. Every time a car passed, even the area furthest from the door managed to get some light.

The swerving continued; I began to wonder what the hell was going on.

Soon everyone in the truck started to get tired of the insane swerving. One person was getting sick and I got a headache. We started banging on the truck. Finally, Tiny stopped and the kid who was sick got out and threw up. We started again and this time the bumps didn't come for a while, but then Tiny started swerving the truck again. I was starting to think that maybe Tiny wasn't such a good driver. Soon everybody started screaming, but we weren't playing anymore. We were scared. I prepared to die. I thought, "This is it. I won't even make it to the demonstration. The headlines will read—40 KENT STATE STUDENTS KILLED IN U-HAUL TRUCK TIP-OVER." Cathy and I held on to each other as we slid around the truck. After we got tired of sliding around sitting down, we stood up and watched our belongings slide around the floor. It was horrible.

After what seemed an eternity of bouncing around the truck with forty other people, a guy up front reported seeing a sign saying that Washington was near. We were at a red light and Tiny slammed on the brakes. Everybody got thrown together only to get thrown together the other way when the light changed again. Once inside the city we stopped for gas. We all wanted to kill Tiny. We definitely did not want him to drive anymore.

"Ah, come on. I was just having a little fun," Tiny blabbered.

"A little fun? You almost got us killed and you say you're having a little fun?" said someone who was trying to take control from Tiny, but Tiny wasn't seeing it that way.

"This is my truck; it's in my name, and I'm responsible, so I'm driving." Tiny didn't understand that he was talking to people who had been sitting on a plywood floor for ten hours bouncing around like basketballs. He didn't understand that we hated him. But he wouldn't surrender the keys.

We all piled back into the truck. Hopefully, we were almost there. Tiny floored the truck in reverse. Crash! I thought Tiny had run the truck through a plate-glass window, but it turned out that it was only a phone booth. Tiny had destroyed the phone booth.

After what seemed like another eternity, we reached West Potomac Park, Washington, DC. We had made it. I would live to see the demonstration. The door was lifted all the way up and I could see out into the park—it reminded me of a scene from the movie *Woodstock*. People were everywhere, camped out in tents, in vans, or on the ground. Flashlights were shining into the truck. People were jumping on to welcome us to the city. I remember a group of black men chanting, "Power to the people" and "Today's pig, tomorrow's bacon."

People were singing, yelling, "Hey, Kent people!" "Hello, you motherfuckers!" People jumped off the truck as we moved through the park. It was a revolutionary party. It was the biggest gathering I had ever been to and it might have been the biggest gathering of the New Left ever. To see it you would have thought we could have stopped the war. The park overflowed with people—a veritable haven of young leftists.

On either side of the road were campgrounds—the Carolina, the Connecticut, the Rhode Island, and finally the Ohio camp. We were there in record time: Kent to Washington in twelve hours—a ride that normally takes five. But what the hell, we were there. Cathy, Jesse, and I gathered our stuff and piled out of the truck.

I set my junk down on the ground, walked off to the bushes, and threw up.

"You all right?" Cathy asked.

"Yeah, but that was just the preamble." I threw up again.

There is nothing like vomiting to make you feel better quick. I almost forgot the fact that I hadn't had anything to eat since breakfast, that I had a terrible headache, and that I was dead tired. So we went exploring. Jesse, Cathy, and I wandered around in the cold night by the banks of the Potomac. We were all amazed by the number of people there. They say that if you have enough people, you can do anything. All we wanted to do was end a war. It wasn't as if we wanted to do something really radical like start a war or kill somebody. We just wanted peace.

It was too dark to see much, so we headed back to the Ohio camp to sleep. I stretched out in my air-force coat, Cathy in her Rudolph Valentino coat, and Jesse in his tiny sleeping bag.

PART II

I awoke Saturday to learn that Tiny had been doing LSD while driving the truck. The lives of forty people were in his hands and he was tripping his brains out. I vowed never to ride with him again. I also learned that two of my good friends had made it to Washington—Tom Grace and his girlfriend Roseann (Chicken) Canfora. Tom was one of the few people I knew who had the intellect and charisma to be called a revolutionary leader. In three years he had come from being a worker for Hubert Humphrey to joining the SDS and becoming a leader of the antiwar movement at Kent State. Tom had also had the misfortune of having part of his foot shot off by the National Guard on May 4, 1970. He still limped. His girlfriend Chicken was a crazy motherfucker. In the course of five years she had gone from being a cheerleader to becoming a member of the SDS. Last year she had watched her brother get shot through the wrist. After the May 4 shootings, Chicken ran through the apathetic classrooms hysterically screaming, "They've killed students, the fucking National Guard has killed students!" only to be told that she was interrupting a class and would she please leave.

From about noon through the rest of the day Jesse, Tom, Chicken, Cathy, and I rocked and rolled with about two hundred thousand other people at the concert in West Potomac Park. It was great. Everyone got wrecked. Some strategy meetings were planned, but they had to be postponed because we were all too stoned. The day flew by in the excitement of the concert.

PART III

Before the sun came up the next day, I heard people talking. Chicken kicked me. "Grif, wake up. Grif, the motherfucking pigs are throwing us out."

I got up in time to see a police helicopter flying over us taking pictures. I pretended that my finger was a gun and shot at it. I felt a little like the Vietnamese woman who threw her hoe up in the air and brought down a US helicopter, but mostly I was angry at the pigs. It figures that as soon as you get something together and are almost ready for the most aggressive antiwar activities in the nation's history, the pigs will try to wreck it.

I heard a distant amplified voice. "You are hereby ordered to evacuate West Potomac Park. Your continued presence past 12 noon will constitute grounds for arrest." Nixon had gotten scared. There were too many of us to let us stay in the park, so he'd decided to disperse us and send us home. We were dicked by Dick.

Tents came down, sleeping bags rolled up, and cars drove away. People were cursing Nixon. Some said that it was hopeless and that nothing further could be done. A lot of people in cars left. I didn't know what to do. The KSU people got together for a meeting. Everybody was irritable and cold, standing on one foot and then the other, and campfire smoke filled the air. Many people wanted to go home.

They were tired of playing revolutionaries. The concert was over, the fun had passed. We were all straight for once, since it was so early in the morning. Everyone was just standing around mumbling when Bill Arthrell, one of the Kent 25, spoke. "I say we stay. Look, people, we didn't come here for a rock concert. We came here to protest the war. The way I see it, if we leave now, we've wasted our time and our money. Tomorrow is May Day and I want to be here."

Tom Grace then came in to help out Arthrell. "I know that some of you people are tired and it looks like the pigs aren't going to stop at anything to try to turn us away. But I say we stay here. Let's not give Nixon the moral victory of a peaceful May Day. The Vietnamese people have been struggling against the Americans for ten years with more problems than we've got, so I think you all should be able to stay until Monday." What else could be said after that? We would stay at least long enough to see what was going on. We thought that maybe the organizers of May Day might have canceled the protest because so many people had left.

Back in the truck we found our usual places and sat down for what seemed like a short and pleasant drive around Washington to a place called American University. The truck parked in a lot outside the university. Nobody had ever seen the place before; we walked around for a while and ended up in front of the Student Union, which was closed. I talked to a student there. He told me that anytime there is a demonstration in Washington, the demonstrators think they can stay at American University, and that the students were getting tired of having their school used as a cheap hotel by vagrant demonstrators.

Nevertheless, a few minutes after we arrived, a free food kitchen was set up and they began giving out paper cups filled with some sort of hot cereal. I was hungry and it tasted good. By this time all of the Kent State tribe had found their way to the Union and were standing around in the drive in front of the Union or stretching out on the grass. Jesse, Cathy, and I were sitting on a curb eating our breakfast.

I felt frustrated. "They've won," I said. "There's nothing to do now but go home. Nixon has done what for him was a superior strategic move. He broke our camp and made it impossible for us to plan our strategy. We've lost. Just look around and you can see that our morale has been broken. We're tired and probably most of the other people have gone home."

I said it and I wasn't ashamed of it. I was tired, dirty, and broken. You figure that there were maybe two hundred thousand unarmed college kids in Washington Saturday night who were determined to shut down a city of two million. Then figure that the city is headed by a man who, among other things, is insane and will stop at nothing to maintain power. And then figure that this man has the biggest and best intelligence network in the world and a near infinite supply of money and men at his disposal. Then figure what the odds of success are when the insane man who heads the city decides to split up the two hundred thousand college kids. I was willing to play ball with odds like me, plus two hundred thousand hippies against the city of Washington, but when it came to odds like me, plus less than two hundred thousand scattered and broken hippies against the city of Washington, I thought that maybe it was time to go home and come back some other time.

I was a coward—that's what it basically boiled down to. Jesse also wanted to go home. He was willing to call a spade a spade.

"Grif, it's like you said. Our presence here was enough. We've said our part; now it's time to split."

The Student Union opened and somebody announced that there had been an emergency meeting with the president of the university. He said we could stay in the Student Union tonight. Meanwhile, word had filtered from the office of the organizers of May Day that the plan was the same—we were going to shut down the city. After that I didn't hear any more talk of leaving.

We went into the Union and more people from different parts of Ohio and around the country started appearing. The Union became a sort of revolutionary headquarters. I got more to eat and sat down to get my head together. There had been over two hundred thousand people at the rock concert last night. Nixon got scared, so he had decided to call out the cavalry and get the Indians moving in the morning. People had scattered throughout the city—in churches and homes, but mostly at Georgetown University and other schools around Washington. Today someone was going to come over from May Day headquarters and tell us about the planned strategy for tomorrow. Tomorrow, Monday, we would try to close down the city and after that be back in Kent State for the memorial service on Tuesday. KSU seemed very far away.

It wasn't long before word got around that the people from the May Day office who were going to teach us nonviolent tactics and what to do tomorrow had arrived. I still hadn't made up my mind about tomorrow, but I thought hearing what they had to say would be a good idea.

The meeting was near our van. I was surprised at the number of people who were there. The spokesman from the May Day office looked about thirty-five or so. He had long, thin, blond hair and spoke in such a way that we wanted to hear him.

"Tomorrow," he began, "the people from Oho will shut down the Theodore Roosevelt Bridge. The bridge is the main artery into the city. We feel it is essential that the bridge be closed to show our determination. We also feel that if we are to be effective, we must close the bridge nonviolently. This means that we have got to be willing to risk arrest, tear gas, and harassment from the police.

"I have come here to demonstrate some of the methods that we have found effective in the past for accomplishing what we call nonviolent direct action. We feel that when you resort to violence, you put yourself on the same plane as your enemy. If we use violence in accomplishing our goals, we are no better than Nixon is when he bombs North Vietnam. Also, any violent tactics give the police and Nixon the excuse they need to write us off as crazies. Violence also has the effect of isolating the American people from our cause. We have been peaceful in our efforts to close down various government offices in the last week. If people prefer violence at times, we're asking that you stay home.

"Now, if I can have some volunteers, I will demonstrate how to effectively shut down a bridge."

He stepped down from the truck and grabbed some people who were standing at the front of the crowd—arranging them across an imaginary road. Instructing them to get down on their hands and knees, he then put a second line of people behind the first.

"This is how you'll be on the bridge. Walk out in two lines, face the traffic and get down on your hands and knees. As soon as these people are out in the street, other people will come out in the street behind them and so on until you are all out in the street. While this is going on, a few people can leaflet the cars that have stopped. We want you to ask the people if they will please park for peace. Most of the people are sympathetic with us in our efforts to end the war; we feel that if we can explain ourselves to them, they will cooperate with us.

"The police will probably arrive within a few minutes to try and clear the intersection. When this happens, they always pick up the people in the front line first. At this time, other people should come up and take the place of the people the police arrest.

"When the police come, remember that they are probably just as much against the war as you are and that they are just doing their job. I urge you not to call them pigs or any other names that dehumanize people. I believe we can convert some police to our side with our nonviolent direct action. At this point, are there any questions?"

A couple of people in the back had been saying bullshit to the speaker all along and now one of them shouted, "Yeah, what about alternative strategy?" What they meant by that was "What are we going to do with your nonviolence when the pigs start busting heads?"

The man at the front wasn't fazed by the question. "I have been arrested twice in the last week. Both times I got out of jail that night after paying a fine. Remember that the Washington police are the best trained in the country. Many of them are college graduates and I have found them to be respectful people. Both times I was arrested, it was for blocking the entrance to a public building. The first time I went limp when they picked me up. I was carried into the paddy wagon and had the additional charge of resisting arrest. The second time I was arrested I walked with the arresting officer to the bus. Both times the police did not strike me or harm me in any way.

"The police may use tear gas. If they do, I suggest you carry a wet handkerchief and put it over your mouth. Whatever you do, don't wear contacts or jewelry, and make sure that your hair is tied back.

"If you're in a group and you see the police running toward you, WALK. If you run, the slower people will be caught by the police and possibly trampled. If you are caught running, you'll be arrested for resisting arrest, which in many cases is more serious than what they could arrest you for otherwise. Urge people to walk. If you stay together as a group, your chances of the police leaving you alone are much better."

He stopped and was apparently thinking of some concluding remark when the man in the back of the crowd again yelled, "What about alternative strategy?" This time the speaker ignored the question.

I noticed that the people from Kent State who were normally cynical when it came to anything called nonviolence were just standing there with their mouths open. Perhaps they had never seen a professional nonviolent revolutionary before or maybe they thought this thing was bigger than they were.

The speaker asked again if there were any more questions. Someone asked him to say something about the target area.

"Theodore Roosevelt Bridge is a four-lane main thoroughfare into Washington. We are asking that you be there about 5:30, so you arrive before the heavy morning traffic. Another wave should come in about 6:30 to support the first wave of people.

"One more thing, people: I urge you again to be nonviolent. Gandhi invented nonviolence in India; he called it Satyagraha, which means truth-force. If we are to succeed, we are all going to have to be Satyagrahas. Truth-force can work. I have seen it work in the civil rights movement and in the antiwar movement. I knew Martin Luther King. I was his disciple. He taught me to believe in people and in nonviolence.

"Good luck tomorrow. Peace."

He jumped down from the truck and the crowd dispersed. On the way back to the Union, I admitted that he had impressed me. He seemed to believe in what he said. I had seen too many people like that rabble-rouser at the back of the crowd who have big mouths, but when it comes to doing something, they don't amount to a pile of shit.

By this time, it was late afternoon. I wanted to see the news to find out what the Dick had planned for Monday. The first thing on the tube was the story of the park. The chief of police of Washington said that West Potomac Park was a health hazard and that the area was overflowing with illegal drugs. Rennie Davis, one of the May Day organizers, then came on the tube to say that there were no drugs in the park and that the whole thing was a government harassment and a violation of the park permit. The TV showed the police clearing the park that morning. About two hundred demonstrators had opted not to leave the park with everyone else. They sat in the center of the park and sang as the police lifted them up and hauled them away.

After the commercial the announcer said, "Police spokesmen said that they are prepared for anything the demonstrators do." Those words were etched in my mind as I saw that the fourteen hundred–man Washington National Guard was on the alert and as I saw that ten thousand army and marine troops were being flown into the city. The TV showed troops getting out of an airborne transport with a duffel bag in one hand and a gun in the other.

It is hard for me to describe the feeling in my stomach when I saw those army and marine troops getting off those planes. It wasn't fair that they were allowed to carry guns and we weren't. Hadn't they heard of nonviolent direct action? What about the first amendment? What about George Washington? What about my mother? What about Nixon's mother? Wasn't she supposed to be a Quaker?

This latest event definitely changed the odds a bit. Before it was the demonstrators against the city of Washington. Now it was the demonstrators against the city of Washington, the US Army, the Marines, and the National Guard. And they had guns! I thought of the words of an old Cheyenne Indian before his people were wiped out by the US Cavalry: "It is a good day to die."

We spent a long time over a hamburger and a Coke trying to talk about anything except the next day. It was the calm before the storm. We talked about Cathy's drunken stepfather and my neurotic mother, but it wasn't easy. I remembered that on the Kent State campus on May 4 there was only a fraction of the number of military who would be on the streets tomorrow and that the KSU rally where the four kids were killed was a legal rally!

We found a nice corner of a hallway to spend the night. Trying to find a place wasn't easy—the Union was stuffed with wall-to-wall people. The party atmosphere from the night before was gone now. People were lying on the floor talking quietly or having last-minute strategy meetings. Lying on my air-force coat, I was nearly asleep when Jesse nudged me and whispered, "Grif, what are we going to do tomorrow?"

"Jess, what do ya mean 'what are we going to do tomorrow'? We'll get up with everybody else, go downtown, get arrested, and go to jail. Got any better ideas?"

"Yeah," Jesse said, "I got a feeling that tomorrow is going to be pretty fucked up. We could take a bus out of the city and hitch home. What do ya say?"

"Look, Jess," I said, "to tell you the truth I can't afford to be arrested, but I do think that as long as we've come this far, we might as well go downtown and see what we can do. There may be people hurt who will need help. Maybe we can leaflet or talk to people in cars or—"

Jesse interrupted me. "Grif, don't you see? I could get into some ACTION. But tomorrow these people are going to go downtown singing 'Peace, brother, peace' and get wiped out by the pigs."

"Jess, listen. Trust me. Come with us tomorrow."

"All right, I'll come with you, but if I don't like it, I'm going to split."

PART IV

Later that night somebody turned on the lights in the hall. Rolling over, I said to the guy standing above me, "We're going in the second wave."

"Look, man," he yelled, "the more people down there, the better our chances are. Do the Vietnamese sleep when there's a bombing raid?"

I sat up. "OK, OK, you talked me into it."

We all got up, and I went outside to see how cold it was and if it was still dark. It was cold and dark. The door shut and locked behind me, so I had to walk around the building to the front door. I was amazed. There were people outside sleeping in the cold like they were on a beach on a summer night. I tried to wake one body, but it was too asleep to respond.

Back inside I put my things together in the KSU bag. Cathy, Jesse, Chicken, Tom, and I made our plans. Chicken and Tom were to go first with some of their friends who knew the way. Then Jesse was to follow a block behind Chicken with a friend of his. Cathy and I were to follow Jesse. The day before we had been told to follow this strategy; supposedly it would attract less attention to us and if somebody was ripped off on the way, the rest could still make it to the bridge. Different groups took different routes.

We said good-bye and wished each other well. Tom Grace was nervous for once. "Well, Grif, I hope you don't get ripped off. I'm sure I'm going to get arrested. I can't run because of my leg. I just hope I can do something before they get me."

So we went out into the dark, cold Washington morning. I was singing movement songs to quiet my nerves. The stars were still out and the streetlights on as we walked through the closely packed neighborhoods.

It was a long time before we came to a business district. As soon as we saw businesses, we saw cops. Cops everywhere. We lost Jesse—he started making all sorts of turns and we lost him. The police looked funny standing in the early morning light in their Day-Glo vests and shiny boots. It was too early for them to put on their helmets; they just stood there trying to keep warm. A cop happened to be on a corner where we were waiting for a light to change. He looked like a friendly guy, so I struck up a conversation with him. "Good morning, Officer," I said. "What are you doing this early in the morning?"

"Oh," he said, "I thought I'd come out for a little fresh air. By the way, what are you doing out this early in the morning?"

"Oh. Me, I just thought I'd do a little early morning sightseeing. You know how the crowds are these days. If you want to see anything, you have to get up early. Can you by any chance tell me the way to the Theodore Roosevelt Bridge?"

"Why certainly. Just continue straight ahead until you come to the light and then turn right. Can't miss it."

"OK. Thank you very much, Officer. Have a nice day."

We walked on. I noticed that other people were talking to the Law. Some were even having serious conversations with them about the war and the demonstration.

We must have been getting close to our target because the street was filling up with people, all of whom seemed to be walking to the same place. An old lady stopped me and asked me to tell her the way to Dupont Circle. I didn't know, but someone nearby did. The woman then gave us the clenched-fist sign, said, "Right on!" and hurried away.

It wasn't long before we were walking down a hill beside a main thoroughfare with about twenty other people. There were some government buildings around, but mostly just grass and a big sidewalk. At the bottom of the hill were about thirty helmeted policemen swinging billy clubs and running in formation toward us. I looked up to the top of the hill to see if maybe there was some rock-throwing or something going on up there; there was nothing. The cops were after us. Didn't they understand that we had just gotten there and that we hadn't even done anything yet?

The group started running, but not me. I didn't panic, I was no fool. "Cathy, don't run," I said. "If we walk, they'll think we're completely innocent and leave us alone. Don't you remember what the guy said yesterday?"

Cathy paused. "Jeff, they've got billy clubs in their hands. I don't think they're messing around."

"Well, on second thought," I said, "I've got a better idea. Let's run!"

Everybody ran. Cathy and I tried to split off from the main group, but we kept running just the same. When we were sure we had lost them, we slowed down. By that time, we were near Pennsylvania Avenue. Below us was an entrance ramp onto Pennsylvania Avenue. I saw a kid pull a temporary barricade into the road. "Cathy," I said, "there are the heroes of our generation." We ran down the culvert out into the street. By now about ten cars were stopped on the entrance ramp.

People were throwing trash barrels out in the street, and one guy was slashing the tires of a cop car while the cop talked in the microphone on the other side of the car. I walked out into the street and said, "Park for peace" to a station wagon filled with businessmen. One of them rolled down his window and yelled out, "Come over here, kid, so I can kill you!" Other people in cars were honking their horns and shouting obscenities at the demonstrators. The natives were giving us really bad vibes. Soon the police arrived en masse and chased us down Pennsylvania Avenue, catching a few of us and putting them in trucks.

We regrouped and this time moved out into Pennsylvania Avenue proper and blocked traffic for a minute or so until the police charged again. A policeman would single out a particular demonstrator and then charge after him, running him down with his billy club or tackling him. Occasionally a demonstrator would outrun a policeman. One demonstrator, being chased across a big lawn, was cheered on by everybody on the other side of the street. He eventually outran the cop.

The police were getting pretty hostile. A group of them came upon a businessman who just happened to be walking to work. They sprayed him with mace. He was shouting, "But wait, you can't do that to me! I'm just going to work." But it was no use. They sprayed him in the eyes, and he cried out in pain. It was becoming clear that today would be a case of the police against everybody else. They were having a good time hassling people.

I just kept moving down Pennsylvania Avenue.

A group of demonstrators who must have come from a small school were sitting together in front of an entrance to a government building singing "Give Peace a Chance." The police were just watching them for a while when one of them started singing a song of his own. It must have been one of those they teach in pig school. It went something like this: "This is the way we spray the freaks, spray the freaks, spray the freaks. This is the way we spray the freaks, so early in the morning," The most sickening thing about it was that he was smiling. He was enjoying spraying the liquid pain of mace at the kids sitting there singing their song. But they weren't singing long before they were crying from the sting of mace on their bodies.

We kept running down Pennsylvania Avenue.

Up ahead was a large group of young people who weren't doing anything except walking down the sidewalk. A few of them went out into the street, but the rest wouldn't follow. One of the women in the street was Nancy, from Jerry Rubin's *DO IT*. I knew her because she had come to Kent State after the killings. Anyway, she was shouting at the people on the sidewalk. "People, what did we come here for? Come on, people, what did we come here for?" She was crying; she had a white tear-gas handkerchief around her throat. Maybe she had just been gassed or maybe a policeman had hit her. Her screaming paid off. People started to heave litter barrels out into the street to block traffic. It was cool because Washington has lightweight rubber trash barrels that you can heave up on top of people's cars.

The pigs were having a hell of a time. This was about the time they realized that if they were going to stop us, they would have to arrest us all. We were winning. The traffic was moving too slowly for the authorities not to arrest us all. Not all the credit should be given to the street people, though. Some demonstrators were driving around in cars and stalling them at intersections. The pigs got wise to the people in cars after a while, which just added to the confusion and tied up the traffic even further. A few drivers simply abandoned their cars and left them for the police to worry about.

The police and military concentration was getting dense. Up ahead was the White House. It looked like the 7th Cavalry had been called out to protect the fort from the Indians. There were so many cops and soldiers that no one could even get within a block of the White House. Still, we had to keep moving, so we walked to Ellipse Road, which is a block in front of the White House. A pig car that was waiting to get out into the street gunned his engine as we walked in front of him. I jumped and looked at him. The pig stuck his head out the window of his car and yelled, "Hey, you smart-ass motherfucker, come here and I'll kick your ass!" I was scared shitless and thought that he was serious. I turned to him and said, "Peace," while giving him the peace sign, and kept on walking. I guess he was too lazy to get out of his car.

Back on Pennsylvania Avenue, we walked toward the Capitol simply because there seemed to be no other way to go.

Between the White House and the Capitol are all sorts of government offices. Each one was lined with police, National Guardsmen, marines or army men. The servicemen mostly played statue; it was the Washington police who were the aggressive bastards. People were getting ripped off all around us. One woman being hauled off by the pigs was screaming, "Officer, I have a permit to leaflet this area! You can't arrest me!" I then formulated a theory: never underestimate how far the authorities will go to maintain power. Never give the people in power any credit for obeying the law except when it profits them. When the police want to break the law, I can assure you that the Constitution doesn't mean shit.

By this time my heart needed a chance to slow down, so Cathy and I wandered away from the government buildings and, after a while, ended up in a ghetto, complete with porno theaters and pawnshops. A businessman stuck his head out the door of his office and yelled at us, "Sons of bitches!" After that we sat down on a curb for a moment only to have a police car drive up and tell us to keep moving; we jumped up and started to walk back to the heart of the city.

On the way we kept seeing caravans of soldiers. One truck was open, and when it stopped for a red light, a black man yelled at us, "I agree with you, but if I was you, I'd get the hell out of the city!" I gave him the peace sign and he was off.

Back in the main part of town we were walking across a square that stretched for a block in front of a government building. At the end of the block a policeman stepped in front of us and pointed his gun, ordering us to go back. I tried pleading with him, "But we were just passing through!"

He wasn't moved. "Nobody gets through," he said.

So this was it. The pigs had finally caught us. I thought that maybe we could walk down the street from the corner, but the pigs were sweeping people up that street also. I told Cathy that I would try to get in touch with her back at the university as soon as I got out of jail. We made sure the legal aid numbers were written on our arms and that we both had a dime to make a phone call. I told her I was sorry I got her into this mess. There was one possible escape, however, and that was to go back the way we had come and hope that the police didn't head us off. So we hurried to the other end of the plaza in hopes of crossing the street before the police completed their sweep. It looked like they were going to push everybody together from two sides. At the end of the block the police were coming toward us from our side and from our rear, but the light was green and there were too many cars to try running across the street. The pigs were getting closer. That was the longest light in history, but at exactly the last second, the light changed and we dashed across the street.

After we were down the street half a block or so, I turned around to see people I should have been with being loaded onto a bus and taken to jail.

It was getting to be late morning and the morning edition of the paper was on the newsstands. I didn't feel like buying a paper, but I looked at the headline "MAY DAY FAILS—CITY STAYS OPEN." There was some other stuff about traffic running smoothly by 9:30 or something. They said we had failed, but I didn't think so. Maybe we didn't stop it, but we sure as hell slowed it down.

By this time things were pretty much over. The major street action, at least where I was, had ended. The sirens could still be heard, but the streets were starting to clear as the police succeeded in rounding everybody up until they thought there weren't enough of us left to make any difference.

Cathy and I moved away from the government buildings to the business district and hunted around an hour or so for a bus stop. Finally, we saw a kid who looked like he was waiting for a bus. He told us a bus would be there in five minutes.

I sat by the window of the almost-empty bus and looked out at the tremendous number of people who were guarding the buildings and parks from the hippies. Little green men every ten feet, with guns in their hands, were standing at ease looking out into the street. At Dupont Circle the bus slowed down as we drove around the park inside the traffic circle. The park was surrounded by little green men. I put my middle finger against the window. One of the green men wrapped his middle finger around the barrel of his gun to acknowledge my salute and another gave me the peace sign.

After one transfer and more desolation out the window, we made it to the university. There were a few people there, but nobody knew anything about the fate of Chicken, Jesse, or Tom Grace. Everybody had a story to tell, though. The infamous Tiny, with the help of another kid, had pretended that a policeman was a battering ram and tried to knock down a tree with him. Tiny said that he had wrestled with another pig and that the cop had bashed him in the leg. Tiny was limping. One girl had made it to her target, gotten busted, and was out already. Other people had seen their friends get busted. Everybody had seen tear gas, mace, or a billy club. Many people were in some sort of shock. I remember one kid kept saying, "This is so fucked up, this is so fucked up." I asked him why and without any hesitation he told me, "Do you know what the Black Panthers would say about this? Do you know what they'd say about today's demonstration? They'd say it's bullshit, pure bullshit. What these people with their nonviolent demonstrations are doing is putting their lives in the hands of the pigs. Dig? Like what they're saying is, 'Mr. Pig and Mr. Nixon, we're going to demonstrate without guns, without clubs, non-violently, but you can carry guns and clubs and we're asking you please not to hurt us.' You see? The hippies put their lives in the hands of the pigs, and you see what happened when they did? The pigs got no respect. This nonviolence is bullshit because you can't trust the pigs with your life. The Black Panthers would never do anything like today's demonstration. They'd carry their guns and keep their lives in their own hands."

I was getting pretty worried about Chicken, Jesse, and Tom. I was sure that Jesse had gotten into a fight with a policeman, that Chicken had probably gotten mad enough to attack a policeman herself, and Tom couldn't even run.

I went off to a dorm to heat up a can of beans. The afternoon news was on the TV. They said the police were not even sure how many people they'd ripped off. Some congressman went on the tube to say that the demonstrators weren't ecologically minded because they tipped over some trash barrels. I wondered what the fuck that jerk was talking about. The shit was falling from the sky, falling from the sky.

A few minutes later Jesse and Chicken came in. I hugged Jesse, then Chicken, and then both of them at the same time. We danced around and shouted obscenities about the police and Nixon. They hadn't seen Tom Grace. I tried to get Chicken to tell me what happened to her, but all she could do was curse the police. "Grif, those cocksuckers, I hate pigs! Motherfucker, I never saw so many pigs. All I did was block traffic and run from pigs. You should have seen—the pigs were just picking people off the street and hitting them over the head." Chicken went on like that for a while before I decided to wait until some later date to find out what really had happened.

Jesse was a little more coherent in his story. "It was so tremendous. I had such a good time throwing rocks and tear-gas canisters back at the pigs. I threw a rock through a pig car window—you should have seen—it was a real long beautiful shot right through the window. Wow! Then you know those big garbage bins like they use to haul garbage away from apartment complexes? Bill Arthrell and I took those, pushed them down hills and out in the streets, and we set one on fire. And you know what else? Listen to this! We tipped over a garbage truck! Yes! Tipped the motherfucker over. We got the help of some other people; everyone heaved and over it went. I got gassed, but it was OK. Grif, I had such a decent time."

It turned out that only a few of the Kent State people had been busted and that Tom Grace was at the police station trying to get them out.

There was nothing to do now but sit around and wait for the rest of our tribe to get back. Jesse, Cathy, and I went off to the corner of the Union where we had slept the night before. I fell asleep for a while only to wake and hear more war stories. Someone said that over at Georgetown University there had been really heavy fighting—the pigs gassed the campus and a pig was shot as he chased a kid up the stairs of a dormitory. Another kid was out of jail and he told what a comedy it was. The pigs had more people than they could handle, so they had turned a stadium into a jail and everybody was doing weed right in the jail.

We were sure from what everybody had said that the Indians had beaten the cavalry. Maybe we didn't stop the city, but the people of the nation had gotten the message of what we were trying to say and how desperate we were in saying it. The children of America had to become the outlaws of America even to be heard.

It was 10:00 that night before most of the Kent State people came back and we could get back on the trucks to try to make it back to KSU for the May 4 memorial service. Cathy and I found our seats on the floor of the truck, but there wasn't enough room for Jesse, so he got on the other truck. Before getting on the truck I made sure that Tiny wasn't driving.

On the way out of town we stopped at the jail to try to free the rest of our people. The police wouldn't let any of us out of the truck. We waited an hour, then people started asking the driver to start heading home. Tom Grace came over to the truck to talk to us. I couldn't see him—I could only hear his worn-out and hoarse voice move through the dark quiet truck. "People, I know you're tired and you want to go home, but your brothers and sisters are in jail and we're going to wait until we get them out. Don't you think I want to get back to Kent? I was shot on May 4. I want to get back more than any of you. But we can't leave people behind; just wait a little longer and we'll have your brothers and sisters out of jail." Nobody said anything more about leaving after that. We just waited.

Tom Grace must have given the police a good sob story because soon the truck filled up with people from jail and we were on our way back to Ohio.

I was amazed at how comfortable a U-Haul van can be when the driver isn't doing LSD. I actually was able to sleep for a couple of hours, but most of the time I watched the red glow of a cigarette and the stray car lights. There was a holy aura about that truck. It seemed we had been on a holy pilgrimage—only this was a sort of backward pilgrimage. On a normal pilgrimage you go to a place to have your faith rejuvenated, but on this one the people went and had their faith destroyed. If there was anybody on that truck who believed in the government or Nixon when we left, they didn't now.

I woke up once and saw a gray light under the door. It was dawn already. Somebody said that we were still in Pennsylvania, but that we should be home by noon. I went back to sleep. When I woke again, we were in Ohio and I was too excited to go back to sleep. Most people were awake and wondering if anything had happened at Kent State—supposedly the campus was to be deluged by outside agitators of some sort. The administrators had said that the school would shut down if anything happened again.

The U-Haul pulled into Kent at 11:30 A.M., a half hour before the memorial service was scheduled to start. The truck parked near the Commons where the memorial service was to be. The door rolled open and the sun flashed in. I picked up the battered KSU bag, and Cathy and I climbed out of the truck. I walked up to the Union and there was Jerry Persky, the Yippie leader, trying to sell some sort of Yippie newspaper. He looked a little too clean and smiley for his own good, standing there spouting revolutionary bullshit when he had stayed at KSU and not gone to Washington. He tried to sell me a newspaper for a quarter. I gave him a look like I was going to kill him, and he gave me one for free.

Nothing had happened at Kent State. There were more reporters than students at the events the administration had planned. Everything had gone just like the board of trustees had hoped. From what I heard, not one outside agitator had come to KSU.

At noon I walked to the Commons. There were seven thousand people there. Some folksinger was singing a song about peace. Up on the stage were some campus police and the school president, Robert I. White. Everybody was on that stage except the people who should have been there. Some police and plainclothes men were walking around with walkie-talkies, looking at the crowd. One of them came over to look at me; I gave him the finger.

So the ceremony went off like clockwork. A priest said that all the kids the Guard had killed were now in heaven, and a rabbi said they had died for peace. A student said they died because of the war. I thought it was all bullshit. Robert I. White had not even publicly condemned the National Guard for killing four of his students, and here he was leading the memorial service. What the fuck was going on?

The last speaker said that students should sit in front of the ROTC building as a gesture of contempt for the military on campus. I wanted to go. Jesse said he was leaving. And then Cathy met some friends and we parted. Alone now, I decided that maybe I too had had enough. I found Tom and Chicken and said good-bye. They begged me to stay, but I couldn't. The desolation of seeing America close up was more than I could handle. I walked away from the ROTC building and tried to find my way home.

The story done, Grif thanked me for the coffee, put on his long blue coat, and walked out of the café. That was the last I have seen him.

After I returned to my native Philadelphia, I tried to find out how much of Grif's story was true. There were seventy-two hundred people arrested in the streets of Washington, DC, on Monday, May 3, 1971. Of these, only four hundred arrests stood up in court. Speaking shortly after the demonstration, at a convention of peace officers, Attorney General John Mitchell likened the demonstrators to Hitler's Brownshirts "who roamed the streets of Germany in the 1920s bullying people, shouting down those who disagreed . . . and denying other people their civil rights."

Further research found that all the people Grif mentioned in his story were students at Kent State University, and that Roseann (Chicken) Canfora and William Arthrell were indicted with twenty-three other people for activities connected with May 4, 1970. They were later acquitted.

Judging from these facts and from the way Grif told his story, I have concluded that it is safe to assume the other details in the story are true.

This story was written by me, Tom Riddle, as an assignment for a creative writing class that I took in probably 1972. Of the people mentioned in the story, Jesse Gonzales is the only person who read a working draft. His comment was that I, the character named Jeff in this story, had an excellent memory. In late 1999, I scanned the faded mimeographed copy of the story into an IBM computer and used the amazing OmniPage 9.0 to turn the scan into editable text. Rereading it now, I see how exciting it was to be twenty years old in 1971.

A Very Young Activist

PATRICIA MOSELEY

Patricia Moseley attended the Woodstock Music Festival in 1969. Two years later she was on the streets of DC protesting against the Vietnam War following the shootings at Kent State University. She died on July 3, 2013, after a lengthy but valiant battle with amyloidosis, at her home in Washington, DC. This piece was written in 2001.

We rounded the corner at C Street. I was pushing Scott in the stroller and my husband had the other two by the hand when five National Guardsmen confronted us, shouting "Get back!" before they even saw us.

May 2, 1971, was a beautiful day. Maybe it seemed a little more beautiful because of such a pleasant surprise. That huge, fervent crowd supported ending a god-awful war. We'd lived in Washington only since December. We were still amazed just walking by the Supreme Court and the Capitol. And now half a million people were confronting all that power. Peacefully. But angrily. You could see it in their faces. Here's the difference, I thought. Less than two years ago, at Woodstock, the faces were happy. Blissful, actually. These faces today were angry—no, stern. Stern but scared. It felt good to be part of it.

A rush of emotion from every corner—not just from those of us opposing the war, but also those marching for women's rights, gay rights. A lot of people talked about related issues like racial equality. Even welfare rights. What I thought about most was the generation gap. We were different in lots of ways, but we were pretty much the same generation. This argument had started in the 1950s.

We got up early that day, and we dressed "respectably." It was my husband's idea—they'll take you seriously if they can see you're not a lunatic. I didn't really agree, but that's OK, just so long as all five of us are there to show our conviction against this war. We listened oh so earnestly to John Kerry and Coretta Scott King. We sang along with Pete Seeger. We spent a lot of time explaining what was going on to our six-year-old. (Especially the veterans in uniform marching against the war—that confused her.) I felt grown up. I'd spent a lot of years looking for a world with no rules, but now I wanted a world with changed rules, changed by me and the rest of us who cared so desperately.

On that day, being a citizen meant being an activist. What a terrific lesson for kids, my kids. It was a dream come true for someone who came of age in the 1950s.

The soldiers had gas masks on, but we decided to keep walking anyway. There was no logic to the command. "Keep back" from what? Walking on a public sidewalk? I started to explain that we were just returning to our car when something landed on the sidewalk. Belief had been suspended—I had no inkling that the soldier was serious. The sun was shining, the birds were singing, and a small group had gathered around us. Someone put out a hand to grab the canister off the ground. Astonishing. It was my own hand that threw it hard and long, all the way across the street and onto some grass. Tear gas for walking on 3rd Street, I thought to myself. To my surprise, my husband was talking calmly and logically to the soldier in charge. All of a sudden, I didn't know him very well—could not imagine why he was engaging a soldier in polite conversation. What happened to the guy who'd always had incurable problems with authority? OK, I thought, now I'm scared, but I'm not going to back down. Trying to be calm, and looking the soldier straight in the eye through the cloudy plastic of the mask, I said, "This is a real baby with a real tear-gas canister right in front of a real stroller. If it goes off, I'll give you a real reason to arrest me. If that happens, he goes with me. He's breast-fed, and he'll be hungry in around forty minutes."

Clearly this soldier had never heard a declaration like that. His eyes through the gas mask were wide and confused. I heard his buddy say, "Just get the hell out of here." They were younger than we were, and suddenly didn't seem so militant, even when they prodded us along with rifle butts. My husband scooped up our three-year-old and grabbed our daughter's hand. They ran and so did I, pushing the stroller as fast as I could, crying with burning eyes and sadness. After we'd gone up the street a bit, I turned and watched the Guardsmen head back toward the Mall. I was overcome with guilt as I realized my kids were coughing and choking on the cloud of gas.

Today the family laughs and says Scott is so independent and confident because he met authority head-on at a very young age. I suppose I'm proud that we stood up as a family for what was right and shouted a message our government needed to hear. But on a beautiful day in May, would I suggest such an outing today? Well, yes, I guess I would. We are a nation of individuals, even the ones who are only seventeen months old.

May 1970

North and South, Mountains and Deserts—and Blood

JOHN HUNTER GRAY

John Salter Jr. (John Hunter Gray) became an assistant professor at Tougaloo Southern Christian College, in Jackson, Mississippi, in 1961. He quickly became a leader in civil rights and community organizing activities. Following the shootings at Kent State and Jackson State, he joined the chorus for justice. One demonstration he attended was in Chicago. He recounts the story below. This piece was written in 2000.

Early on, I could tell it was going to be one hell of a big protest march, even for Chicago. My car safely parked, I walked north through and with increasing numbers of people—people of all ages and all colors—all of us heading to the edges of the downtown central business section. There, where the massive crowd was gathering, other people were streaming in from every direction.

The early afternoon sky in May 1970 was as clear as a chemically tinted Chicago cover could ever get and the sun streamed through. But the mood of the people—all of us—was dark, somber, exuding suppressed anger, bitterness, and some hope—hope that this mass action, and all the others taking place at the same time across the nation, could prevent hideous things from occurring and continuing. And maybe, too, that the once-bright springtime spirit of the 1960s—our time!—could be restored and we could go on, in a mighty wave, to build a society where a full measure of bread and butter and a full measure of liberty and peace were all permanent parts of the social/cultural geography.

In all our minds—every one of us—were the pictures shown throughout the world of the recent bloodbath in our good land: dead and injured students at Kent State, peaceful young people seeking peace but sent to funeral homes and hospitals by National Guard troopers often no older than they.

But behind those troopers and behind the hideous and sanguinary "commitment" of the United States military forces to Southeast Asia were the glowing, calculating, and sanctimonious faces of the properly dressed Old Men (and some not all that old) who start the wars that they themselves never fight.

I was hard-pressed for time that afternoon. In only a few hours, I was leaving by train—the old IC, the Illinois Central—for Jackson, Mississippi, where I was involved in a long-pending court action with civil rights dimensions that was finally coming to trial.

But this was a march I couldn't and wouldn't miss. And I'd made it.

The huge crowd was directed by an army of parade marshals who were arranging the vast number of organizations into a lineup. I learned that those of us who were not affiliated with any of these formal groups would fall in behind the others—and that could be a long, good while.

The Chicago police, somewhat on their better behavior, signaled the start, and the great march began with Grant Park, many blocks away, as the destination and designated locale for the subsequent huge rally.

Organizations and groups, each with its banners held high, moved out briskly.

One pulled up near me and stopped for a moment. Its participants were somberly and darkly dressed, and their faces were all grim, committed, and intense. I had no idea what their particular tribal flag of the Left was and I didn't care. I walked up to its leader, a tall old man in a black suit with a blood-red emblem on his lapel, and said, "Fellow worker, I don't have much time, but I want to march before I take the IC down to Mississippi for a civil rights case. Can I join you?"

He looked me over quickly and carefully. "I haven't heard that used for a long, long time," he said. There was a very faint smile with a hint of decades now far, far away. "You certainly can join us."

So I did, and we marched along.

And as we marched, I remembered.

It had been ten years since the Berkeley students had so effectively, through nonviolent demonstrations, defied the witch-hunting House Un-American Activities Committee at San Francisco, and only a few months before that since the first civil rights sit-ins had begun in the Upper South and the Student Nonviolent Coordinating Committee had formed. At that time, I was in my native Arizona, where for half a decade I'd been deeply involved in militant, radical labor campaigns and Indian rights activities—learning my organizing art and trade—even as I completed my basic academic work in sociology.

In the summer of 1961, my wife Eldri and I went down into Mississippi, where I became a professor at Tougaloo College, a private black institution near Jackson. And there I quickly became, too, the adviser to the Jackson Youth Council of the NAACP and a close colleague of the extraordinarily committed Medgar Evers, and then a primary organizer and chair of the Strategy Committee of the historic Jackson Movement of 1962–63. Along with countless others, I was beaten and arrested—many times indeed. In mid-June 1963, Medgar was killed, shot in an ambush, and we fueled the Jackson Movement to become the biggest mass upheaval in the history of that blood-dimmed state.

Our march protesting the murder of Medgar and the racist system that had manipulated his assassin and pulled the trigger took place on June 15, 1963. Six thousand of us from all over Mississippi and elsewhere participated in the first "legal" civil rights march in the history of the state—legal simply because there were too many of us to arrest.

We marched two miles in 102-degree heat, past hostile police at every point, through grimly supportive black neighborhoods, and through frightened and hostile white ones. When that march was officially over, we had a huge spontaneous demonstration that was attacked by hundreds of lawmen of all kinds with guns, dogs, tear gas. I was one of twenty-nine arrested.

Out on one of my now numerous bail bonds, I in my car and a colleague riding with me were, less than three days later and one week after Medgar's murder, seriously injured and almost killed in a wreck precipitated by the son of a prominent segregationist family. Our civil lawsuit against these people, pending for seven years and now at the very point of trial, was the reason I was heading to Mississippi this day.

As we marched along the Chicago turf, I remembered other times, other marches.

After Jackson—and we left that city deeply jarred with national and international focus on Mississippi for years to come—I became a full-time civil rights field organizer for the radical Southern Conference Educational Fund, doing grassroots organizing and anti-Klan work in some of the toughest and most isolated parts of the Deep South. Much, much later I went into militant antipoverty organizing and leadership training in the rural South and then, in 1967, Eldri and I and our growing family went to the Pacific Northwest on the organizing trail and then on and on.

Now in Chicago, where I'd been since 1969, I was the Southside director, a new position, for the Chicago Commons Association, one of the city's oldest and largest private social service organizations. My vision was a brand-new service area on the turbulent, pervasively violent South/Southwest side. With an excellent interracial and completely committed staff, we were breaking new activist ground on the Toughest City's urban frontier. Here, large numbers of white people were moving out to the suburbs and beyond, and much larger numbers of nonwhite people—black, Puerto Rican, Chicano—were moving in. The newcomers were finding that city services were now suddenly and sharply curtailed by the Richard Daley machine, they were targets of police harassment, and there were continual attacks by white racist gangs. We were beginning a long-term project, organizing multi-issue block clubs and federations of block clubs, made up mostly of these new minority people but including any whites who remained and who wanted to work with us.

Chicago—especially Richard Daley's era—was, it often seemed to us, almost pure blood in ethos. Not too long after I arrived, Black Panther leaders Fred Hampton and Mark Clark were murdered in a cold and calculated fashion—"under color of law"—by Cook County State Attorney Ed Hanrahan, an army of lawmen, and with FBI backup and assistance. On the borders of our own massive project area, in a white location called Canaryville, often known as "The Bucket of Blood," a black man from Tennessee, driving in Chicago for the first time and lost at night, was pulled from his car by a mob of three dozen white men, many with baseball bats, who murdered him.

As we were moving into a storefront field office, a horde of white Chicago riot police swarmed into the yard of a nearby elementary school, attacking black and Puerto Rican children and clubbing and arresting their parents. We got the parents out and our protest rally was big—very big! Our organizational efforts jumped ahead with great rapidity.

Long, long before all of that for sure—and maybe even long before I got to Mississippi—I had ceased to be surprised by official and vigilante murder, brutality, and frame-ups.

I was certainly not surprised by the shootings at Kent State.

And I was not at all surprised by the huge throng of people on these Chicago streets.

We arrived at Grant Park. My tribal host group and I parted amiably with mutual handshakes and, as they went off to a close-in rally vantage point, I camped under a tree on the edges. I listened for a while to the speeches, then went back to my car and went home briefly, and then I was on the Illinois Central heading to Mississippi.

There were always some positive changes there when I returned for visits. And now I could see even more of them: the hard lines of resistance to social change were weaker, even broken in parts; there was more desegregation; the old atmosphere of terror was fast waning substantially; and there was more black political activism and new unionization efforts.

But economic deprivation—poverty pure and simple—was still starkly evident in the Mississippi countryside from the train window and in Jackson when I got there. Still, in that very early May, Jackson somehow seemed far more sedate and serene than Chicago.

But I was not sanguine. Mississippi storms were often preceded by, and in the context of, hot and momentarily placid and languid afternoons.

A few hours after my arrival, I was in a chancery courtroom where our case was scheduled. The walls hung with portraits of the founders of the system and the wood-paneled walls and doors and everything else were polished to a shine, befitting the high status of Deep South court proceedings.

As it turned out, the most interesting thing about our case that day was the intriguing social scene that whirled around us before the case formally began. My colleague, white Mississippi civil rights activist Rev. Ed King, and I and our lawyers, veteran black activist R. Jess Brown and gutsy white maverick Dixon Pyles, were surrounded by a flood of spectators who seemed to be from the Bad Old Days: a former sheriff, a once outspoken racist and still practicing Criminal Court judge, various old-time white politicians, and police officials. Their faces were *very* pleasant, their voices gracious and cordial. The same swirl surrounded our formal adversaries: the young white man—now completing a professional degree at Ole Miss—who had driven the car precipitating the wreck, his obviously worried parents, and an older brother.

We were, naturally, very wary of the good fellowship and friendliness exhibited by once very hostile judges and lawmen. But one could not help wonder—was this a real change?

Compared to the old days, the court proceedings certainly were. The presiding judge was the same old man who, seven years before, had issued the most sweeping, venomous, anti–civil rights movement injunction in the history of the Southern struggle—*City of Jackson vs. John R. Salter, Jr. et al.*—which we promptly defied. But now he was scrupulously fair and even-handed. And the jury had blacks (still new but not that new) as well as women, which was very new this spring to Mississippi juries!

The court proceeding moved along routinely. Midway, the adversaries indicated a wish to settle quickly out of court and, with the proceedings temporarily adjourned, this was effected satisfactorily. The judge then reconvened, thanked the jury and everyone else, and adjourned. It was late afternoon. People were now leaving quickly. But I stood in the corner of the courtroom and looked at the other side where the young adversary stood with his parents and older brother.

I, too, was the older brother in our family. The brother's eyes and mine locked. As one, we moved toward each other and, close in, held out and shook hands. "Tell your brother," I told him, "that we wish him very well in his career."

"I will," he said, "And you have no idea how much that means to us. It means so much."

And there, for those of us in that little group, locked together for seven years by a bloody and hideous spectacle, that *was* change—significant change.

But what of the world beyond? I still wondered as the Illinois Central now carried me through the dark Mississippi night and the dim countryside back to Chicago.

After I got back, our organizing work rapidly became wildly intense. Waves of white violence were directed—month after month and beyond—against our black, Puerto Rican, and Chicano constituencies. We fought that off, found our key field office set afire, and I had to barricade my home. A key staff member was viciously framed by the police, but we got him quickly exonerated. Red-baiting was prevalent, especially against me.

But three years later, we had helped minority people organize almost three hundred block clubs and related groups; we had maintained and expanded city services; we had pushed a dozen court actions; we had played the key role in preventing what would have been one of Chicago's very worst race riots—Labor Day, 1971—by forcing poser structure concessions on the one hand and "cooling the streets" on the other. And we'd fought the Daley machine, the Republicans, and the police to the point where our new grass-roots organizations—democratically led and hard-hitting—were widely respected and quite effective and essentially permanent mountains on the South/Southwest side scenery.

But now, of course, back in time—back to Mississippi.

Just after I returned to Chicago after that early May 1970 trip to Mississippi, still wondering how much had really changed down there, came news of the Jackson State shootings: college kids—black kids, essentially peaceful demonstrators—were shot down at night by an army of white Mississippi lawmen. And so now if the question of how much change had taken place in Mississippi was at least partially answered for the time being, other questions seeking sharper and much more focused answers forced their way up and out.

What *did* all of this mean—the shooting of college kids, North and South? Had Mississippi—and the Deep South—become more like the rest of the country? Or was the rest of the country starting to do what Mississippi and the Deep South had traditionally done so very well: killing the victims?

Or were the South and North so vastly different from one another?

I decided that May 1970 was not so very different—that they were always much more like one another than many of us had wanted to concede. For no matter how you cut the pie, the pieces are always connected.

And then the really heavy question: *Can any of us break the skeleton hand of the past and build a better society?*

I said *Yes!* during May 1970. And so did many others all over our land.

We kept going and many of us still do and many more indeed will continue over the mountains and through the long, arid stretches and far, far beyond.

Always organizing. Always fighting.

The 1976 march around the Kent State campus (Source: John Rowe)

The 1977 march around the Kent State campus (Source: John Rowe)

RESPONSES NEAR AND FAR

PART VI

Hallowed Ground

The 1977 Kent State Tent City (Source: John Rowe)

Kent State

Destruction of Civil Liberties

WILLIAM G. ARTHRELL

William G. Arthrell was an undergraduate student at Kent State University in 1970 and was active in the antiwar movement on campus. He was one of the Kent 25, the students and faculty who were indicted by a grand jury on criminal charges in conjunction with the events of May 1970. Bill was also involved in the 1977 student movement to oppose the construction of the gymnasium annex on the site of the shootings on the Kent State University campus. This piece was written shortly after the 1977 Kent State Tent City.

> Kent State is the white man's Wounded Knee.
> —VERNON BELLECOURT, American Indian Movement

I had heard the other analogies: It would be like putting a bowling alley at Gettysburg, a Pizza Hut at Bunker Hill, or a K-Mart at Valley Forge. But this one fit the best: "the white man's Wounded Knee."

I was crying as I left Blanket Hill. Seven years of injustice flashed before me. Seven years of murder, court cases, appeals, insensitivity, and now the ultimate injustice of putting a building over it all. I was leaving Tent City behind me, too. It was a place where we had lived together for sixty-two days. Instead of letting them build a gym on that site, we simply occupied the land for two months with our tents and our bodies.

Now that was all behind me. The state had issued a restraining order making our encampment illegal. But instead of going obediently and meekly turning the other cheek, we were going to make a stand, with arms and legs locked in an act of defiant civil disobedience.

I was crying uncontrollably now. I sat with 193 other protestors on the edge of Tent City. In front of me sat Albert and Ann Canfora, whose son, Alan, was wounded in 1970 and Martin and Sarah Scheuer, whose daughter, Sandy, was killed. Behind me sat the May 4 Coalition—193 of the hundreds of people—some of whom had given up jobs, school, and now their legal record to preserve this site. Among them were two paraplegics in wheelchairs, Ron Kovic and Bill Schultz. In their vulnerability was manifested the fear and the courage to overcome that fear that we all shared.

I was going to jail for the right to remember—the drive to preserve my own history, the Gettysburg of the student movement, the white man's Wounded Knee. There was a note of finality as the police disentangled us to drag us off to jail. The courts had acted against us, ironically making the land we had fought so hard for illegal for us to occupy. This seemed our finest hour, the climax of our resistance. There seemed no recourse after our civil disobedience. We had fought the good fight, but were beaten by a system that wanted to literally cover up its crimes. If Nixon had covered up with lies, then Kent State was covering up with a building and we were the final victims of that cover-up.

The 194 arrests of July 12, 1977, were not the first time Kent State was a battlefield. Seven years earlier Kent State gained infamy as the place where it happened—the place where America turned its guns on its own children, the place where the war came home. This time, the war came home not as it usually did to the black, the poor, the disenfranchised, but to its own children—white, middle-class college students.

Despite the heinous results of 1970, it was a more innocent time than 1977. On July 12, 1977, we *knew* what the result would be and we were going to jail for our beliefs. In 1970 we couldn't predict the results—we didn't even know the guns were loaded.

Never to be forgotten is the mood on campus after Nixon announced his "incursion" into Cambodia. The moment when all hell would break loose hung only by a string. On May 1, 1970, the string broke. Protests swept the campus for four days. Despite the anger and destruction, there was a prevailing innocence, a lack of sophistication in gut-level rebellion. If the May 4 Coalition was an organized and disciplined protest movement, May 4, 1970, was a disorganized outpouring of human emotion. Either way, things pointed to a noon rally on the Commons on May 4.

I went to that first rally with the same innocence, or perhaps naïveté, that most students had. I was angry about the "incursion" into Cambodia, angry about the invasion of KSU by the Ohio National Guard, angry about the bayoneting of eleven students the night before. Two or three thousand other students seemed to share my anger as they assembled on the Commons.

Although it was Governor Rhodes who sent in the National Guard and approved of their live ammunition, it was the university that ordered the rally to be broken up—peacefully or otherwise. The rally was peaceful; but the Guard acted otherwise. They moved on the crowd with tear gas and fixed bayonets. We were forced over Blanket Hill onto the practice football field. The Guard followed. They huddled on the football field (where the proposed gym annex would be). When they broke the huddle, they went back up Blanket Hill and, reaching the crest, they turned in unison and poured their bullets into the crowd for thirteen seconds. When the smoke cleared, four lay dead and nine were wounded.

These painful memories had pretty well faded by July 12, 1977, and our group was overwhelmed with high spirits as the police booked 194 of us in the Portage County Jail. It was beginning to look like a moral victory; political commitment and nonviolence pitted against gross insensitivity and a lack of respect for history. Perhaps the finality I felt earlier in the day wasn't so final. The decision to stay at Tent City and force our arrest had been the right one. Our morale had never been higher. We were psychologically preparing ourselves for a struggle that might last all summer or even longer. The chants outside the jail from our supporters—"The people united will never be defeated"—were real.

The struggle did go on all summer and longer. Because of our constant political pressure, the door was open for a series of brilliant courtroom maneuvers by Tony Walsh and our team of National Lawyers Guild members. With some timely advice from William Kunstler and unlimited work and brainpower on their part, they postponed construction all summer. This was clearly our victory. Any delay, any snag slowing up or halting construction was advantageous for the Coalition, and any publicity, whether it came in the form of a demonstration or not, aided our cause. Publicity kept our issue alive. For the university, it continued to expose the very thing they were trying to hide.

But that was gone now, and deliberately so. Not only did the police confiscate our tents (and to date have not returned them), but their restraining order made any tents, temporary structures, or sleeping bags illegal anywhere on campus. They knew what they were doing. They were not only taking away our free rent, but our organizing base as well.

Now our eclectic strategy switched into second gear. The heat. It was July and we'd keep the heat on them all summer. Almost daily there were pickets, rallies, marches, or civil disobedience. On July 22, twenty-seven more were arrested for briefly reoccupying the site. On July 29, sixty-two more dramatically took the hill by night, set up tents for several hours, and were finally dragged off by police.

On July 26, 1977, the trustees met for a final debate on the gym. Since early June two of the nine trustees, Joyce Quirk and David Dix, had courageously opposed the gym. The others had clung stubbornly to their decision. (Later, one of them admitted that it was a "mistake," but it was "too late now," so we must build our mistake.") They met in a tense, closed session inside a building of the KSU Branch campus in Canton. Outside, 150 picketers reminded them how bad their mistake was.

Our argument was strong. The land was part of the legal evidence and should be preserved pending any trials. It was a beautiful site and building upon it would entail destroying two hills and cutting down thirty-five to forty-five trees. The proposed structure was excessively large: it was designed for thirty thousand students and KSU was now eighteen thousand and dropping. Because of excessive size and poor design, maintenance and heating costs would be four times the current expense of Physical Education buildings. According to polls, 70 percent of the students opposed the gym and many more Americans were revolted by the insensitivity of the KSU board of trustees.

Most importantly, Kent State is a historic site; the place where public opinion was turned around on the most divisive foreign war in history; the place where the government got away with killing peaceful protestors. The site had to remain intact as a constant reminder so that such an event could never happen again. Because of all this, the Department of Interior had been pressured to study whether or not KSU should be officially designated as a historic site.

Despite the barrage of good reasons, the trustees sat icily in their meeting with little intention of acquiescing to the demands of the protestors outside.

Finally, the trustees left their meeting and assembled at a large table in the lobby. George Janik, the chairman of the board, read their statement: "The construction of the proposed HPER facility will proceed as soon as possible." The word *gym* now had too much sting to it.

Our strategy all summer had been eclectic. Tent City had not just been a free place to live, a microcosm of a socialist alternative, but a tactic. It gave us a twenty-four-hour-a-day visibility to the people and the press. It was an open, loving, communal place that embodied the best values of the counterculture. It also served as a base of operation, a place of organizing and exchanging information.

That was the hard sell. For those who didn't buy it, there were other tactics. There were letter-writing campaigns to Congress, the state legislature, the board of trustees. There was door-to-door canvassing in Kent and petitioning, speaking troupes, appearances on radio and television, and lobbying in Washington and Columbus.

In Washington, Presidential Aide Midge Costanza invited the Coalition and parents of the slain students to the White House. At that time Democratic Senator Metzenbaum (Ohio) condemned the gym site. In Columbus we learned that the Democratic leadership of the state legislature had offered to seek the needed money to move the gym, but the trustees had refused to even request it.

Regardless, our flexible strategy was working. People were participating in tactics they were comfortable with and we were getting a response—even from the White House.

Unfortunately, our responses and sympathy seemed to come from everyone but the board of trustees. They had taken a final vote on July 26. George Janik had stated that they were going to build their mistake—a monument to repression and injustice—a mockery of the events of 1970.

We had tried everything from writing letters to breaking the law in acts of civil disobedience and we would continue to do so. Coalition members had hand-delivered individual packets of gym information to the home of each trustee. We were dealing, however, with classic examples of the power elite. George Janik was an executive with IBM, another trustee was with Pepsi Cola, another with Goodyear. Others were newspaper publishers or had lucrative law practices and lived in the plush suburbs of northeastern Ohio. Few had ever attended KSU and none lived in the city of Kent. Ironically, only one was an educator. She was Joyce Quirk and she sympathized with the Coalition all along.

Perhaps because of machismo, because of the class they represented, because they really did want to bury the memory once and for all, the trustees voted finally to build the gym.

There seemed to be nothing in the way of the bulldozers, buzz saws, and earthmovers now. We could use our bodies again, but we could not physically stop them. We could draw attention to the problem and catalyze the courts and legislature with our protests, or we could make it so politically expensive that the university would be forced to back down. But we couldn't physically stop bulldozers guarded by scores of armed cops. We had realized that all along.

All of those tactics were used. On July 29, after the sixty-two had been arrested and destruction of the site had begun, Chic Canfora, a member of the Coalition, got a phone call from New York. It was William Kunstler. He had an idea for a brief in Federal Court. Chic knew shorthand and got the brief down in a matter of minutes. It was 4:00 P.M. and Chic drove to Cleveland with Tony Walsh, a Cleveland version of Kunstler. Tony, like our brilliant defense attorney, Bill Whitaker, had worked with the Guild team on this case from the beginning—for free. Usually we weren't even able to pay their expenses. When Tony or Bill Whitaker or Alice Rickel or Chris Stanley or Chris Koneybeare or Ted Mechler did a case for us in Cleveland or Cincinnati or even in Washington, they drove their own beat-up jalopies, crashed on friends' couches, and ate in greasy spoons. By contrast, university lawyers were paid seventy to eighty dollars per hour, stayed at the plushest hotels they could find, and went into court with their twenty-five-dollar dry-look haircuts.

Now Tony and Chic were on the way to Federal Court in Cleveland and had to catch a judge before the 5:00 P.M. closing. It was Friday, so if they didn't find one who would listen, the bulldozers and buzz saws would eat away into the hill over the weekend. At five minutes before five, Tony and Chic entered Judge Thomas Lambros's courtroom. Lambros listened carefully, staying until 6:30. Then, a miracle! Lambros agreed with the plaintiffs and issued a temporary restraining order to stop construction.

I was in the Portage County Jail with the twenty-seven when I heard the news. Radical Professor Jerry Carr announced the restraining order outside with a group of supporters. Inside, the jail rocked with approval from protestors and inmates alike. We may not have stopped construction with our bodies, but it was our bodies that forced the courts to do it for us.

Appeals and resulting restraining orders worked their way through August and early September. In the meantime, we continued our "keep the pressure on" strategy with more rallies, pickets, and marches. Some were as small as five or six people picketing the trustees at home to fifteen hundred people showing up at a Joan Baez–led rally. Our tenacity surprised even ourselves. We were relearning some of the old-fashioned values of hard work, perseverance, and sacrifice.

I had given up my teaching job to work full-time on the struggle. Chic Canfora had quit her teaching job in Connecticut. Her brother, Alan, and John Rowe had fallen behind in their work toward master's degrees. Mim Jackson, a KSU graduate, had taken a leave of absence from grad school at Purdue. Rev. John Adams, a Methodist minister from Washington, came to Kent to work full-time to help mediate a settlement in favor of the Coalition. My parents, who could ill afford it, put up $1,000 to bail out of jail my lovely girlfriend, Bonny Stringer, whom they had never met.

The parents of the slain students suffered as much as anyone. They must have relived their own personal tragedies every time they returned to Kent for a press conference. I remember Mrs. Schroeder—whose son Bill died in 1970—standing at the Pagoda where the Guard stood as they fired, shaking as she read a statement against the gym to the TV cameras. And as usual, it fell on deaf ears.

At a meeting in June, the parents invited the trustees to discuss with them their concerns. The only two trustees who attended were Joyce Quirk and David Dix, who were in sympathy with the parents' wishes that the gym facility not be built on the site approved by the other trustees.

Seven years after the killings in 1970, none of the parents had ever received even a note of condolence from the university.

It was now September 24, 1977. The Commons was filling with protestors from all over the country. "Rutgers says 'Move the Gym,'" "Oberlin Remembers," U. Mass, "Long Live the Spirit at Kent and Jackson State!" Wisconsin, "Save the Site!" Over three thousand people filled the Commons in an incredible display of national support. Kunstler spoke, claiming that the courts and legislatures had "chickened out" by failing to halt construction. Rev. Charles Rawlings of Cleveland, who had been arrested along with other clergy at the site, praised the persistence of the Coalition. More speeches were made and music was heard. Then the crowd marched thunderously around campus.

At each of the buildings named for a slain student, Carter Dodge gave a somber and powerful eulogy. The names of Jeff Miller, Sandy Scheuer, Bill Schroeder, and Allison Krause were stenciled on the sides of the appropriate buildings.

Finally, the march approached the contested site. Street-wise radicals ripped the fence to shreds in a matter of minutes. The crowd surged onto the site waving flags and banners as they sat on bulldozers and piles of dirt. I held back. I had been arrested twice for protesting the gym site. Certainly, with the police churning their ever-present video cameras, I would be busted again if I participated. I ate my heart out with envy and pride. The crowd outside the fence chanted, "The people united will never be defeated."

I talked with Dorothy Fuldheim on the phone. She is a tough, crusty news commentator from Cleveland who had been one of our ardent supporters. We were both angry and sad. The week before September 24, bulldozers and buzz saws had chopped Blanket Hill and the practice football field to a virtual moonscape of rubble and dirt. The university had desecrated the site of the 1970 massacre. The destruction, the monstrous bulldozers, and ugly buzz saws were an affront to any sensitive person. Julia Cochrane, student government representative, and three other protestors could restrain

The parents of Sandy Scheuer and Alan Canfora at the Tent City arrest (Source: John Rowe)

July 12, 1977, arrest at Tent City (Source: John Rowe)

July 12, 1977, arrest of the Tent City 194; Neil Kielar being taken away (Source: John Rowe)

themselves no longer. They buried themselves in piles of dirt as the construction company tried to remove some of the trees. Supporters stood in horror as the police let the dozers continue to dig over the head of Julia. Finally, they arrested the four for disorderly conduct and Julia for resisting arrest because she fainted when the bulldozer's blade barely missed her head.

I had told Dorothy Fuldheim that Kent was virtually an armed camp. Police guarded the site in full riot gear: helmets, nightsticks, guns, and cattle prods. Some even patrolled the site on horseback. This kind of police presence was a frightful flashback to 1970. I kept thinking, "This proves how 'popular' the gym is," if they needed a small army to protect the site. Ms. Fuldheim echoed my sentiments, "They've got the bullets and they've got the bulldozers. What can we do?"

Unfortunately, putting a gym on Blanket Hill was not all they were trying to do. The trustees were trying to rewrite history. In Orwellian fashion, the university knew that "He who controls the past controls the future."

The week before, the new president of KSU, Brage Golding, had issued a so-called "peace proposal" urging that the gym be named not only for the four slain students but for the Ohio National Guard as well! He stated coldly that the Guard had suffered as much as the students and therefore deserved the same recognition.

In this nightmarish attempt to deny the truth, the trustees wanted not only to obliterate the site, they wanted to obliterate any memory of what it had seen. The year 1984 seemed less than seven years away.

I couldn't bear to go to the site unless it was to protest. But Joe McDonald begged me to take her there. She had just been released from jail and hadn't yet seen the destruction. Under cover of night, we approached the fence and saw the bulldozers and mud glistening in the rain. "They've taken away our land," I thought. "They've filled the campus with police and sent 330 of us to jail. They've lied to us, harassed us, and made our lives miserable. Now they've taken away our hill. What's left to fight for?"

Someone had answered that question before. "It wasn't the land we were fighting for; it was the idea." It was the right to remember; it was the Bill of Rights. You either have a right to protest in this country or you don't . . . period. So far at Kent State, they've said, "NO." In the age of *Roots*, people are getting in touch with their pasts. Kent State is a part of *our* past that we can't afford to forget. It is the Gettysburg of the student movement, the white man's Wounded Knee.

I thought back and remembered the confidence and hope of the 194 arrests. I thought of September 24 and other protests and acts of civil disobedience. I said to Joe, "God damnit, someday we're going to return this hill to exactly the way it was in 1970. Somehow, we're going to stop that gym."

I remembered the chanting outside the County Jail: "The people united will never be defeated." And Tony Walsh and I chanting, "The people united will never be defeated."

The people united will never be defeated . . .

Someday that hill will look exactly the way it did in 1970.

Where Were You on May 4, 1970?

JAMES HUEBNER

James Huebner began work as a student on the main campus of Kent State in 1975. Two years later, he became an active participant in the May 4 Coalition. As a member, he sought to prevent construction of a new gymnasium annex in the center of campus. In addition to being a resident of Tent City, he served as chairperson of many of the mass meetings of Coalition members that took place during the last few weeks before the arrests of July 12, 1977. This piece was written in 1980.

WHERE WERE YOU ON MAY 4, 1970? The question, when directed to contemporary May 4 "activists" or "groupies," is intended to lend legitimacy to the argument that unless you were here, you don't know what you're talking about. Oddly then, it's likewise rare when the person asking the question wasn't here either, but never mind, everyone "knows somebody" who was. Well, I wasn't, OK? But I can come off with some quasi-legitimacy. On April 3, 1970, I received the following message: "Sergeant Huebner, you have a new assignment to the Republic of Vietnam." So on May 4, 1970, while other members of my unit were on duty in Oklahoma City at the University of Oklahoma and Oklahoma State, I was packing.

Memories of that date are vague. I remember sitting in a bar that evening getting drunk and fantasizing about what I'd do to the recruiter back in Ohio who'd told me two and a half years before that I'd never go to Vietnam if I enlisted. "We'll be out of there in a year or so anyway, no sweat." A lifer at the end of the bar was saying something about students being killed in an antiwar rally at Kent State in Ohio. "Wow, that's where I'm from!" Well, almost; Massillon was my home, thirty miles from the city of Kent. But when you're in Oklahoma, a few hundred miles away, and going to Vietnam, a few thousand miles away, it's like your backyard! "Yep, and they're sending the 3rd MOB downtown to OU and OSU 'cause them draft dodgers are fixin' to riot there too." Well, that's my unit, but I won't have to go because I'm "short"—processing out. I remember the thought of two groups of young people both wishing there wasn't a war, facing off with one another and how absurd that was crossing my mind. At the time I believed we had to be there—to stop communism and all—but I sure didn't want to go. Yet, at the same time, the people who had me convinced that we had to be there had me equally convinced that people who said we shouldn't were either commies or cowards. Then thoughts returned to a woman I knew I'd never see again and vodka.

AUGUST 1970

Home on leave. "Those pictures in the *Akron Beacon Journal* made those kids look real clean-cut—they shoulda put pictures in that showed how they really looked." Mom was real proud of me now—going to Vietnam. "I hate to see you go, but I'm glad you're going too. The Boswells sure haven't got anything on us now with one son hiding behind a conscientious objector status and the other stretching out his college career until it's over." Mom was gentle and kind, but fired by the same anti-antiwar sentiment that I was. She believed college kids protested against the war because they were afraid of being drafted after graduation. All this crap about an immoral war was a front. She'd heard the neighbor, John Boswell, yelling about the National Guard being nothing but a bunch of goddamned draft dodgers. What about the students—like his son? Mom had a friend whose son was in the National Guard and in Kent, off campus, on May 4. "Ruth says Jack told her those boys up there were covered with bruises from head to foot except where their helmets and belts were from rocks." (Everybody knows someone who was there, right?) Still, Kent State didn't mean much to me at the time. I had other things on my mind and didn't especially care whether the Boswell kids were scared or not—I just knew I was. Maybe Mom was right after all. Things sure quieted down when Nixon ended the draft. But whether the immoral war issue was a front or not, it sure was legitimate.

AUGUST 1971

Coming home. Boy, am I pissed—and have been for the longest year of my life. That's a lot of anger. I'm no longer believing what I hear anymore—from anyone. Who the hell can you trust?! And who the hell are ya gonna tell what you're feeling? Mom's first question: "Did you kill anyone?" Jesus!

MAY 4, 1974

My first May 4 memorial program at Kent State. I enrolled at the Stark branch in 1973 because it was all there was to do. I wasn't black or female so the job market was closed. I saw a lot of Vietcong flags and, while I had a great deal of respect for the Vietcong and the NVA, I didn't believe the people carrying those flags understood that. And the memories of a lot of good people who died and did understand made me resentful. I left.

MAY 4, 1977

What's this gym shit?! "They'll have to bury a thousand students in the cement!" "Another attempt to COVER UP the killings!" Fiery speeches and a march back to the Plaza. Everyone begins breaking up as they always have the past two years since I came to the main campus and the May 4 rallies. Then, from atop the fountain: "The trustees are meeting right now in Rockwell Hall. Let's go tell them how we feel about their gym!" I didn't follow the march. I went to dinner with some friends and someone suggested that we go by Rockwell to see what was happening. When we arrived, they were just putting the chamber door back on its hinges and University President Glenn Olds and Board Chairman Janick were coming out to talk to us. "It's not a new gym—it's an annex to the already existing gym and it's not going to interfere with the May 4 site." BULLSHIT! "Let's stay right here until the trustees move the gym!" Few of the people there were prepared to go to jail, but no one wanted to be the first to leave either—so there we were—and until about 2:30 in the morning the rhetoric that was to become the dominant background of my environment for the next six months cranked on.

MAY 12, 1977

Tent City is born. I moved in May 15. Two weeks later I moved out—it was becoming a joke. A week after that, a friend came to my house and asked me to come back. Yeah, it was getting to be a joke. But that's because the people who needed to be there were leaving it to the clowns. "Just come to the meeting tonight, OK?" It was at that meeting that it was decided that the major focus should be on the political aspect of the site. Others argued that there were economical, architectural, and environmental concerns that should be considered as well in order to bring together a broad base of support for moving the gym. My own feelings were that there were other reasons for moving the facility that were being ignored, such as those that supported the political claim of a cover-up. To no avail, Alan Canfora et al. emerged victorious and the position paper not only stated that the political issue was *the* issue but that any other approach was an attempt to distract from that fact and would thus support the cover-up. I was disillusioned again, but that night I was also elected to the steering committee of the May 4 Coalition. I moved back to Tent City with a banner on my tent that read VIETNAM VETERANS AGAINST THE GYM.

Joan Baez with Ron Kovic at August 20, 1977, rally on the Commons (Source: John Rowe)

The 1977 nationwide march on the Kent State campus (Source: John Rowe)

Tent City's "mass meetings" were chaired on a rotating basis by members of the steering committee. Up until late June these meetings were held about twice a week. On the date that my turn came, the contracts were consummated and the fate of Tent City became imminent. Carter Dodge introduced a resolution: "Since a bust could come anytime now, I think we should hold a meeting every night and I think the same person should chair those meetings so there is less confusion and everyone knows who to bring agenda items to and I think you're doing a fine job so I nominate you." It passed, and for the next three weeks those nightly meetings became my whole life. I was fired from my job, my VA benefits were suspended, and anything that was not related to the gym issue in general and "tonight's meeting" specifically went into an indefinite hold status. A few meetings went smoothly, most were long and grueling. Attendance ranged from several dozen to several hundred and the dominant issues were the "Sparts" (Spartacus Youth League), the question of nonviolence versus violence, and the limits of the power of individuals and committees.

The May 4 Coalition became, by far, the greatest personal commitment I had ever made to an issue in my life, although there were several other issues about which I felt quite as strongly. And while it all ended with the dismantling of Tent City with a feeling of having accomplished something of significance whether they built the gym there or not, subsequent events led to deep feelings of resentment and bitterness toward those parasitic elements of campus activism that always seem to effectively prevent the successful achievement of the goals they espouse. Tent City was, for me, the greatest classroom of my academic career at Kent State. Many of the lessons came hard and some had to be repeated over and over until they sank in. Perhaps I know something of how Tom Hayden must have felt when the Progressive Workers Movement sucked the life from SDS. The image I hold now is not the gym or the meetings or Tent City or William Kunstler. It's the gentle anguish in Martin Scheuer's eyes.

MAY 4, 1980

The kids with the flags are back again. They're not Vietcong flags now, although many of the symbols of that time have been revived, borrowed, or, in a sense, stolen. Now they're just red or say things about Iran or Mobile or the draft or pot or nukes or a hundred other things. And I think they still don't really understand—or maybe I don't. But who the hell can they trust? Who the hell can they talk to about what they're feeling? How many are really feeling anything beyond the hype of the theater? Are they just another bunch of draft dodgers? Is this whole May 4 thing just another clown act? Not in Martin Scheuer's eyes. But I don't think many look there—and because they don't, I think the last May 4 hasn't happened yet.

PART VII

Legal Maneuvering and the Courts

The Ruse of the Kent 25 Indictments

ROSEANN "CHIC" CANFORA

Roseann "Chic" Canfora was an eyewitness to the May 4, 1970, shootings at Kent State University. Her brother Alan was one of the nine wounded students. This piece was written in 2001.

MAY 4, 1970: THE AFTERMATH

In the aftermath of the Kent State shootings, a haunting sense of shock was felt throughout Ohio and much of the nation. Even as campuses across the country erupted in massive protests over the shootings at Kent and Jackson State, parents of the Woodstock generation demanded a national pause. Dissent in our country had reached astonishing proportions in May of that year, and America, under Nixon's misdirection, was stunned by the backlash that resulted from his expansion of the war into Cambodia.

Campus protests mounted at the news of the shootings at Kent State. They now numbered a hundred a day, and civil unrest in America reached historic heights. Henry Kissinger, in a memoir of his White House years, described Washington as "a besieged city" following the Kent State shootings. Police had surrounded the White House and buses were used as a shield on the grounds of the president's home. Congress, too, had been deeply affected by a tidal wave of criticism launched by the student movement and the news media. "The very fabric of government was falling apart," Kissinger reflected. Nixon reached a point of exhaustion that caused deep concern among his advisers. H. R. Haldeman, in his own memoirs, called May 4, 1970, the turning point of Nixon's downhill spiral toward Watergate.

Those of us who witnessed and survived the shootings at Kent State were not surprised at this backlash. After all, we had been very much a part of it in the months preceding and in the days following the senseless invasion of Cambodia. Many of us had fought together in the streets of Kent, Cleveland, and Washington, demanding an end to the war. We had seen in Chicago, and now at Kent and Jackson State, the depths the Nixon administration would go to stifle righteous protests against the war. With the blood of our fallen friends still fresh in our memory, our hope for justice now turned to the courts. Surely, the Grand Jury in Ohio would find what all of us knew in our hearts—the blame for the Kent State shootings rested first with the triggermen, who unloaded their military weapons for thirteen seconds as students crouched in horror. Also, blame surely rested with the leaders of the Ohio National Guard, Ohio governor James Rhodes, Vice President Spiro Agnew, and President Richard Nixon, all of whom instigated the bloody deed.

Our hope for justice mounted in the two months following the shootings, when key portions of a secret Justice Department memorandum were published in the *Akron Beacon Journal*, declaring the shootings "unnecessary" and calling on prosecutors in Portage County to seek criminal charges against six Guardsmen. This declaration was whitewashed immediately by Attorney General John Mitchell, who issued a statement one week later charging that both students and Guardsmen likely violated federal laws, and suggesting that if Ohio did not act on such charges, the federal government surely would.

It was then that Gov. James Rhodes ordered a special state Grand Jury to oversee the criminal investigation of the shootings in Ohio. When the jury convened, we were hopeful they, too, would view the compelling evidence that prompted the FBI, the Justice Department, and the President's Commission on Campus Unrest before them to conclude that students had done nothing to warrant such an excessive use of military force.

On September 26, 1970, the president's own commission concluded that the shootings were "unnecessary, unwarranted, and inexcusable." To the surprise of many, the special state Grand Jury ignored key evidence and totally exonerated the Ohio National Guard of any wrongdoing for the shooting deaths. The Portage County Grand Jury released their findings on October 16, 1970. Led by Special Prosecutor Seabury Ford, who openly told newsmen the Guardsmen should have killed four hundred rather than four students, the Grand Jury chose to indict twenty-five individuals, mostly students, with thirty-one indictments covering forty-three offenses committed prior to the shootings.

In an inflammatory report that shocked the nation, the Grand Jury condemned the students, the faculty, the administration, and the police department at Kent State for their actions, while hailing the killers for their bravery. The Special Grand Jury exposed its prejudice against students by openly referring to them as "intellectual and social misfits," criticizing the use of four-letter words in antiwar chants, and admonishing the university administration for granting permission to the YIPPIES and the Jefferson Airplane to perform in the campus auditorium five months after the shootings.

The Special Grand Jury, faced with mounds of evidence to the contrary, concluded that the Guardsmen "fired in the honest and sincere belief . . . that they would suffer serious bodily harm had they not done so." In so doing, the jurors completely ignored prior testimony of several of the Guardsmen that their lives were never in danger that day. Even more, the jury discounted the conclusions of the Scranton Commission and Justice Department's summary of the FBI findings that claims by the National Guard that their lives were in danger were most likely "fabricated subsequent to the event."

THE KENT 25 INDICTMENTS

I was working at my desk at Harvard University when my mother phoned me with news of the Kent 25 indictments.

"It's awful," she said. "Just awful. They didn't indict a single Guardsman, not the leaders, not Governor Rhodes, not anybody but students and one professor."

"Oh, God," I said. "Who in the world did they blame? The kids that were shot? Who in the world would they choose to blame for this?"

"Alan, for one," my mother said.

My brother had been vocal and visible on May 4. He had been pictured in the center spread of *Life* magazine, waving his black flag as he approached the Guard that fateful day. Even knowing that, I was still surprised to hear his name among those indicted.

"Alan? Oh God, who else?"

"Jimmy, Aquinas, Jeff . . ." she went on.

I was numb as she read the list, which included not only my brother, but several of our friends. Jimmy Riggs, whom I credit with pulling me behind a car, which saved my life that day, had himself carried a black flag to the rally. Was it that he, too, was highly visible? I couldn't remember a thing either Alan or Jimmy did that day that would warrant a criminal indictment. Tom

Miller, whom we all called "Aquinas," had been the most peaceful of all of us during this and other protests that spring. He, too, had been indicted by the Grand Jury. Perhaps it was because after the shootings, Aquinas had found Alan's black flag lying on the ground near where Alan and his roommate, Tom Grace, fell wounded during the bloody fray. In Aquinas's anger and confusion over the shootings, he lost control and began waving Alan's flag in the air, screaming at the top of his lungs: "Take this blood home! Remember what you've seen here today!" He screamed as he jumped in the pool of blood left on the pavement where Jeff Miller had fallen. "The blood is on all of us! The blood is on all of us!" he screamed.

Aquinas had been jumping up and down in Jeff's blood in a sort of death dance, dipping Alan's flag into the pool and flinging it on all of us within reach. He was screaming and crying at the Guardsmen as they left the hill, screaming at students and at everyone after the shooting stopped. We were watching Aquinas in disbelief when Jeff Hartzler came up behind us and said softly, "Alan got hit. Tom Grace too."

Now, months later, Alan, Jimmy, Jeff, and Aquinas had all been indicted for riot by the Ohio Grand Jury.

"For what?" I asked my mother. "They didn't do anything wrong!"

"There's more," my mother said. "The Grand Jury also indicted you."

My mind raced over the events of the day. There had been no riotous condition that I could recall. In fact, when a member of the Ohio National Guard had driven up in a jeep to read the Ohio Riot Act over a bullhorn to the students gathering at noon, his actions were met with taunts and laughter. Most of the day, we had simply chanted antiwar slogans and ran from their tear gas. Where, in fact, would they find evidence that we had rioted?

Perhaps it was after the shootings, I rationalized. When I came out from behind the car that shielded me, I ran immediately to Bill Schroeder, who was lying dead several feet behind me. Later, as I raced to find my brother, I came upon Sandy and Jeff on the spots where they had fallen with mortal wounds. Eventually, after learning that Alan and Tom, too, had been hit with bullets, I ran frantically into a large lecture class in Bowman Hall, screaming at everyone that my brother had been shot, that students had been killed by the National Guard. It was there that I had first vented my anger after the shootings. Perhaps that constituted riot in the eyes of the Grand Jury, I thought.

Or perhaps my riot charge stemmed from my actions when I returned to Blanket Hill that day. After leaving Robinson Memorial Hospital, I learned that Alan and Tom had survived their wounds. I returned to the campus with my parents to pack my bags. Students had been ordered to move immediately out of the dorms. As we left Lake Hall, my father asked me to show him where it all happened. As we approached the crest of the hill, just beyond the backyard of my dorm, I noticed what appeared to be hundreds of spent shells on the slope near the Pagoda. Reaching down, I grabbed a handful of shells. Looking down the hill, I could see the remaining Guardsmen lined up on the Commons where it all had begun.

"Murderers! Murderers!" I screamed. "You murderers!" I shouted over and over, while my father held me tightly in an attempt to restrain me. It was the first time I cried that day. Perhaps *that* constituted second-degree riot on May 4 in the eyes of the Grand Jury.

I hated being away from home when I heard of the charges against us. I had no idea what "second-degree riot" or any of the indictments meant. As news of the Kent 25 indictments spread throughout the nation, more protests over the injustice mounted on college campuses. My phone at Harvard began ringing with calls from the news media, from political groups in the Boston area, and from professors at Harvard and Radcliffe volunteering to hold fundraisers for my legal defense. I was in a whirlwind and all I wanted was to go home.

"You'll have to wait until Monday," my mother cautioned. It was Friday, and if I returned to Ohio immediately, I would have had to spend the weekend in jail awaiting a bail hearing. "It's best to wait until we can take you directly from the airport to turn yourself in and we can have a bondsman waiting," she told me.

It was then that I began to worry about the prospect of going to jail for our actions on May 4. It was then that it hit me what the Grand Jury had done.

"This is where it ends? We exercise our First Amendment rights and get shot at? The Guardsmen fire indiscriminately into an unarmed crowd and *we* take the blame?"

THE REACTION

I did return to Ohio to face the charge against me. In fact, I curled my hair and wore a black velvet dress, with a cameo pin positioned just beneath the white-lace Victorian collar, as I turned myself in at the County Courthouse in Ravenna, Ohio. I wanted to be sure that if my mugshot were ever to be placed in a post office for my "criminal" conduct on May 4, I would be the portrait of the All-American girl.

Once I left Ohio and returned to Cambridge, there were fundraisers already in progress on the Harvard campus in preparation for my defense. A law student, who lived across the hall from me in our Central Square apartment house, had arranged a meeting for me at Harvard with noted attorneys Leonard Boudin and Alan Dershowitz. Within a week of that meeting, attorney Mark Lane, of *Rush to Justice* fame, came into Cambridge with Jane Fonda and the Winter Soldiers' Investigation and over dinner at an Indian restaurant in Cambridge, he, too, asked to take my case.

Back at home in Ohio, New York lawyer William Kunstler, who had defended the Chicago 8, was already on the scene organizing an aggressive defense of the Kent 25. The jury had indicted most of us on riot charges, including inciting to riot, second-degree riot, or first-degree riot, with maximum penalties of three years in prison.

While I had been treated almost like a celebrity on the East Coast, reactions toward the Kent 25 were noticeably different in Ohio. My family and the family members of the other victims and defendants endured hate mail, vicious phone calls, and even bomb threats from hateful citizens in the months following May 4. This came as no surprise to us in Ohio, considering the fact that the groundwork for this brand of hatred had long festered.

In the days leading up to May 4, the president of the United States had called campus protesters "bums." Vice President Spiro Agnew likened student protesters to Nazis and Klansmen and called on law enforcement officials to imagine student protesters were "wearing brown shirts or white sheets" and to "act accordingly." Two weeks before the Kent State shootings, California governor Ronald Reagan announced, "If these students want a blood-bath, let's get it over with." Finally, in the most inflammatory rhetoric of all, Ohio governor James Rhodes had painted an even more inciteful portrait of student activists: "We are up against the strongest, well-trained, militant revolutionary group that has ever assembled in America," he said. "They're worse than the Brown-shirts and the Communist element and the night riders and the vigilantes . . . They're the worst type of people that we harbor in America."

Following his statement the night before the shootings, Governor Rhodes made it clear to the press that protests against the war would no longer be tolerated in the city of Kent. "We are going to do something about it and with them," he warned. His prophetic words were echoed by Kent Police Chief Roy Thompson, who added, "I'll be right behind with the National Guard to give our full support—Ohio law says, use any force that is necessary, even to the point of shooting."

Many of us who attended the peaceful antiwar rally at noon on Monday, May 4, 1970, were either too young or too naive to realize the danger of their inflammatory words. Beginning with President Nixon, the groundwork for the shootings had been laid, and with Rhodes's final threat, armed gunmen had been sent onto our campus, conditioned to view us eighteen- and nineteen-year-old college students as military enemies. Within twenty minutes after our peaceful rally began, we realized the danger our government leaders had put all of us in. In a thirteen-second barrage of gunfire, thirteen Kent State students lay bleeding and dying.

Now, months after the National Guard killed four and wounded nine of us without warning and without provocation, we saw the depths to which the citizens of Ohio would go to justify their bloody deed. A jury of middle-class Americans in Ravenna, Ohio, could not fathom that American soldiers would turn their guns on American citizens without a reason. It was their job to find that reason, and they did, with their indictments of the Kent 25.

After numerous petitions, the prejudicial findings of the Special Grand Jury were studied by the US Department of Justice and were ordered by US District Judge William Thomas to be physically destroyed and expunged from the record. While we relished the burning of the Grand Jury report in a wastebasket outside the Portage County Courthouse in November 1971, Judge Thomas allowed our indictments to stand. In spite of the jury's prejudice, the Kent 25 were left to blame for the shooting of students during a peaceful protest at Kent State on May 4, 1970.

THE TRIALS

I am bitter to this day that the Special Grand Jury chose to indict not merely those they deemed "responsible," but what appears to have been a "cross-section" of the campus on which to place the blame for the shootings. Among us, there were protesters and nonprotesters, hippies and straights, students and nonstudents, and one member of the faculty. The president of the student body was charged, as were four women and two of the wounded students. All but two of us turned ourselves in to face the charges, but those of us who did knew the trials would present our first opportunity to expose the truth of what had happened that day. A gag order had been placed on everyone associated with the shootings once the Grand Jury convened, and the trials would, at last, bring the Guardsmen to the stand to answer publicly for their actions.

Eventually, David Scribner, from the Center for Constitutional Rights in New York, moved into Kent to head the legal defense of the Kent 25. While a number of other attorneys assisted or held the reins in several individual legal battles on behalf of defendants, it was David who lived and breathed the

Chic Canfora speaking at the May 4, 1976, commemoration (Source: John Rowe)

trials of the Kent 25 in the year that followed. During that time, he resided in a tiny motel room at the Kent Motor Inn, where a box of saltine crackers and a jar of peanut butter, kept in the bottom drawer of his file cabinet, provided sustenance for the twelve- and fourteen-hour days he put in without a break. As the only defendant with shorthand and typing skills, I had the privilege of serving as David's legal secretary that year. I marveled at the manner in which he would dictate legal briefs word for word off the top of his head, always pacing as he spoke, in passionate treatises that required little or no editing once they were transferred to paper.

David was brilliant in his strategy and in his leadership of a team of countless volunteers who worked for more than a year to prepare for the trials. None of us who worked seven days a week in preparation for the trials expected that after the first five appearances, the cases against the remaining twenty defendants would be abruptly dismissed. The first five courtroom appearances of the Kent 25 centered on actions leading up to May 4, and had resulted in only one conviction on a misdemeanor charge and with two plea-bargained guilty pleas. Each of the cases centered around actions that occurred during the burning of the ROTC building two days before the shootings. It was now time to focus the courtroom action on the events of May 4, 1970.

The courtroom was packed when the trials of the remaining twenty-five began, most of which stemmed from actions that occurred during the fateful protest on Monday, May 4. As we assembled and waited to hear the opening arguments, the state prosecutors shocked everyone when they stepped before the court and announced they were dropping the charges against the remaining Kent 25.

Their action was prompted by Ohio Attorney General William Brown's conclusion that there was insufficient evidence to convict any more of the remaining twenty defendants. In reality, the state had simply succeeded in buying time. Attention, for more than a year, had been taken off Governor Rhodes and the triggermen in the Ohio National Guard and was placed squarely on the victims. The state alone was free during that time to distort the truth and place the blame squarely on student protestors for the tragedy at Kent State.

When the prosecutor made the announcement that he was dropping the Kent 25 indictments, students, defendants, and members of the legal defense team erupted in joyous celebration in the courtroom. Everyone was jumping over the benches, leaping into each other's arms, cheering and embracing everyone within reach. In the midst of the excitement, I saw David Scribner, alone in the back of the courtroom, pacing silently, with his hand on his chin. Even as the jubilation continued around me, in that one moment, I understood why David had not joined in our celebration. He knew then what all of us would realize in the days to come: We had just lost our chance to tell the world what happened on May 4.

May 4, 1988, Speech

WILLIAM MOSES KUNSTLER

William Moses Kunstler first came to Kent in 1970, when he was invited to speak at a memorial rally at which time he also offered his legal assistance to anyone at Kent State who might be charged with crimes involving the events of May 4, 1970. When a grand jury indicted twenty-four KSU students and one professor on various riot charges, Bill helped to organize a team of defense attorneys. In 1976 when the university announced plans to build a gym annex on the May 4 site, Bill once again came to the aid of the May 4 families by helping to file a federal lawsuit to declare the site a national landmark. This piece was written in 1988.

Thank you very much. I have come here many times before—five or six, I think—in rain and in sunshine, in gymnasiums and out of gymnasiums. Tom [William Kunstler is referring to Tom Grace, who had just introduced him and who had been shot by the National Guard at Kent State on May 4, 1970] spoke only of me, but there were many lawyers and the latest ones tried desperately to stop the building of that gymnasium on Blanket Hill and to have Blanket Hill turned into a national monument, as it should be. We went to Federal Court in Cleveland. We had a sympathetic federal judge, but he could not bend the law to force the government to make this a national monument.

And so we lost and when I left the Federal Courthouse in Cleveland, the judge said to me, "If I had it in my power," he said, "I would grant the relief you wanted, but I don't." But he said Blanket Hill should be a national monument, so we came out of his chambers feeling that although while we had lost to the powers of darkness, we had at least shown one federal judge what the right path would have been.

Now a gymnasium covers part of that hill and it is a shame. There should be a monument there. It was a place where American patriots lived and died on May 4, 1970. It was a place where young blood was shed by people no older than themselves. It was a place of tragedy, and yet out of it sprang a revulsion around this country that caused the closing of most of the institutions of higher education, which really brought an end to that ghastly war, if you can call it a war, in Southeast Asia.

The four who died here, the nine who were wounded here, the many who faced a Portage County Grand Jury and Petit Jury, they did more for their country than all the Nixons and the Agnews and the Reagans could possibly do. And they did it without consulting astrology or any other science.

They did what they did because they believed in what they were doing. They learned the hard way what was happening to their brothers and sisters abroad, to themselves here and to their society. May 4 is a particularly memorable day in American history because eighty-four years to the day before May 4, 1970, there was another demonstration at the Haymarket Square in Chicago. And so similar to what happened here because on May 3, 1886, strikers at the McCormick Harvester Plant outside of Chicago had demonstrated. The mayor had called out the police. The police broke up the demonstration outside the Harvester Works, killing one striker and wounding many others. And so, just as here, a demonstration was planned for the next day, the next evening, at the Haymarket Square in Chicago.

And at that demonstration a provocateur exploded a bomb. The bomb killed seven police officers and two members of the audience and wounded many others. And, as many of you know, the state of Illinois and the city of Chicago retaliated by trying eight of the demonstrators who were present at that rally, convicting them of murder and executing four of them by hanging at Joliet Prison. The remaining four were commuted by a true American, although he wasn't born here—John Peter Altgeld, who had the courage to jeopardize and eventually ruin his own career by commuting the death sentences of four of the eight. And as Clarence Darrow said at his funeral, "He freed the captives. He freed the captives." So May 4 in the labor movement has always been an important date. And interestingly enough, the city of Chicago erected, on the site of the Haymarket explosion, a statue of a police officer with a commemorative sign in bronze and I was happy to be present after May 4, 1970, to see students from the University of Chicago and elsewhere topple that sign as a sign of solidarity with another May 4 in their own lifetime.

William Kunstler speaking at a 1977 rally (Source: John Rowe)

Some of you here will remember that in 1977, we came back on May 4 and it was a bad day as far as the weather was concerned. It rained heavily, so we moved inside to the Memorial Gymnasium and on the platform sat two men, each in a wheelchair. There was Ron Kovic, a Vietnam veteran who was paralyzed from the waist down stemming from rifle fire that first struck his right foot, and from a paralyzing round that entered his shoulder and severed his spinal column in Vietnam. And there was Dean Kahler, a student of this university, who was paralyzed for life by a National Guardsman's bullet. Toward the end of the services, Ron Kovic wheeled his wheelchair over to Dean Kahler and these two men embraced each other with tears rolling down their cheeks. Ron Kovic said—and I will never forget the words, and there are people here who will remember them too—"Today, at last, Kent State and Vietnam are united as one." It was a moment that I have never forgotten and each year I hope that I am invited back because I relive it in my own mind. It is the stuff of which human emotions are made. Dean Kahler is not here today and Ron Kovic is not here today, but close your eyes and think of two paralyzed young men in wheelchairs, one with his legs destroyed by a mine in that useless, senseless, immoral conflict in Southeast Asia, and another having the same thing happen to him so many miles away on what should have been a peaceful American campus. Just visualize those two wheelchairs rolling toward each other and those two paralyzed human beings, paralyzed by the same war, the same conflict, embracing each other and saying, as it is true, Vietnam and Kent State are and were as one.

I would conclude with a sonnet that I wrote after Alan Canfora invited me to come here. I was sitting in a courtroom in New York going through the endless process of jury selection where I write all my sonnets. It saves your own sanity sometimes. You turn to other means of expression other than objection or overruled or what have you. The sonnet came out almost as if it had been written already in my brain, and I wanted to end by reading it to you.

A sonnet is a political form of expression that has been used since the early seventeenth century by writers in English, Italian, German, and many other languages. I decided to write sonnets after reading one by Edna St. Vincent Millay about the murders of Sacco and Vanzetti by the Massachusetts judicial system in 1927. This is called "Kent State Revisited."

Can it be true that it's been eighteen years
Since Blanket Hill soaked up the youthful blood
Of those whose only crimes were earnest tears
For each who had died in Southeast Asia mud?

They are united now who fell upon this hill
With all those who dropped ten thousand miles away
Destroyed by those they came so far to kill.
They never lived beyond the fourth of May.

Today they perish still around the world.
The guns have not forgotten how to speak
The flags of lunacy remain unfurled.
And earth yet does not comprehend the meek.

So now as then, impatiently we yearn
To know at last when will they ever learn.

Thank you.

The Big Chill

The Stifling Effect of the Official Response to the Kent State Killings

WILLIAM WHITAKER

William Whitaker is a trial lawyer in Akron, involved in both civil and criminal litigation. He began his career by coordinating the defense of the Kent 25 and has continued to represent those charged with crimes because of their political activity. This piece was written in 1990. It was slightly updated in 2019.

> Against perception so solidly in place it is all but useless
> to assert anything so subversive as fact.
> —Lewis Lapham

The official version of the events of May 4, 1970, was contained in the report of the Special Grand Jury issued on October 16, 1970, on behalf of the State of Ohio. The report also indicted twenty-five people, including students and one faculty member, and completely exonerated the state and the National Guard for the consequences of their actions. The report, which played to public perceptions, was orchestrated to further solidify those perceptions and was completely unencumbered by fact. The most startling example of the state's refusal to deal with the truth is that the Grand Jury, despite making seventy findings, did not find, acknowledge, or even mention that four students had been shot and killed and that nine others had been wounded.

The manipulation of public perceptions was not new then and has since, of course, been raised to an art form. What made the successful manipulation of perceptions in 1970 most insidious, however, was the fact that it in effect condoned the killing of those engaged in dissent, condoned the criminal prosecution of the survivors, and created an immediate chilling effect on the exercise of fundamental constitutional rights, which continues to this day.

Although two credible investigative bodies produced reports more consistent with the facts—that the shootings were unjustified, unwarranted, and inexcusable criminal acts—their effect on public perceptions was carefully minimized. The first report prepared by the FBI was sealed from the public and never published except for a short summary, which was leaked to the press. The second report, prepared by the President's Commission on Campus Unrest, chaired by William Scranton and hereinafter referred to as the Scranton Commission, was released to the media and thus the public in two carefully thought-out stages. The main body of the report, which contained general, nice-sounding findings about student dissent without conclusions or accusations, was initially released at a press conference amid great fanfare. The findings about Jackson State and Kent State were released in two separate reports at later dates after Mr. Scranton and other commission members had left town and were unavailable to the press. At the time, one commentator, I. F. Stone, made a remarkably accurate prediction. Commenting on the fact that the Scranton Commission Report honestly and thoroughly showed that the killings were unjustified and unnecessary, he went on to say, "And yet there is not the slightest chance that anything will be done about it. The Chairman of the Commission William Scranton will turn up at the White House one of these days to be photographed with the President, an innocuous statement will issue from the White House, and that will be the end of the finding."[1]

As it turns out, there were photographs with the president, an innocuous statement was issued, and fifty years later, *absolutely nothing has been done about it.*

It was against this background that the official story emerged from the Special Grand Jury in Portage County, Ohio. The extent of the distortions and the viciousness with which the Grand Jury reported them is as startling today as it was fifty years ago. A review of the official story and its effect is in order.

The main purpose of the report appears to have been the complete exoneration of the National Guard, thus clearing Gov. James Rhodes and other state officials responsible for permitting the troops to kill. The report's central conclusion:

> We find however that those members of the National Guard who were present on the hill adjacent to Taylor Hall on May 4 fired their weapons in the honest and sincere belief and under circumstances that would have logically

caused them to believe that they would suffer serious bodily injury had they not done so.

This most complete exoneration was in direct contradiction to the Scranton Commission's Report, the FBI Report, and all available evidence. The Scranton Commission found unequivocally that "the indiscriminate firing of rifles into a crowd of students and the deaths that followed were unnecessary, unwarranted, and inexcusable." The FBI found that "six Guardsmen, including two sergeants and Captain Srp of Troop G stated pointedly that the lives of the Guardsmen were not in danger and that it was not a shooting situation." The FBI Report, which was available to the prosecuting officials running the Grand Jury, also noted: "We have some reason to believe that the claims by the National Guard, that their lives were endangered by the students, was fabricated subsequent to the event."[2]

The Grand Jury went on to support its conclusion with "facts": that "58 Guardsmen were injured by rocks and other subjects"; that the Guardsmen were "surrounded by several hundred hostile rioters"; and that two hundred bricks taken from a nearby construction site were used. After interviewing every Guardsman and checking all the medical records, the FBI found that only one Guardsman—Lawrence Shaffer—was injured on May 4, 1970, seriously enough to require any kind of medical treatment. That injury occurred ten to fifteen minutes before the shooting (and apparently did not hinder the said Mr. Shaffer when he shot Joe Lewis shortly thereafter because, according to Mr. Shaffer, Mr. Lewis, who had nothing in his hands, gave him the finger). Photographs, the Scranton Report, the FBI Report, and every other study of the May 4 shooting established that the Guardsmen were not surrounded at any time.[3] No bricks were ever found on the Commons or on the hill that day.

That the Grand Jury so flagrantly distorted facts and exonerated the Guard should not have been surprising. Governor Rhodes called for the Grand Jury and he appointed his good friend and political associate, Attorney General Paul Brown, to direct and supervise the Grand Jury. Paul Brown then hired as special assistant prosecutors for the Grand Jury the chairman of the Portage County Republican Party, Seabury Ford, and another close friend, Robert Balyeat. The local Republican judge, Edwin Jones, presided and gave the grand jurors their instructions. Although most jurors were selected randomly, Judge Jones and prosecutor Balyeat handpicked the Grand Jury foreman, a Mr. Robert Hastings, who was a former client of both men. The tenor and tone of the direction the Grand Jury received was revealed in an interview given by Seabury Ford to William Schmidt, a reporter for the *Detroit Free Press*. The interview was published in both the *Free Press* and the *Akron Beacon Journal*. Mr. Ford stated, "they should have shot all the troublemakers," and he asked, "why didn't the Guard shoot more of them?" He went on to justify it all with what he perceived to be brilliant logic: "The point about the shooting is, it stopped the riot—you can't argue with that. It just stopped it flat."

Many of the falsehoods contained in the Grand Jury Report are obviously deliberate, beginning with the preface, which was designed to influence public perceptions about the fairness of the report. The Grand Jury claimed that it had available the FBI Investigative Report and that the report was examined in detail. The truth, as one of the prosecutors later testified to under oath, was that the prosecutors did not show the FBI Report to the Grand Jury. The Grand Jury also claimed that the witnesses called had "fairly represented every aspect, attitude, and point of view concerning the events," and further claimed that this "clearly indicated an effort at complete impartiality with a full and complete disclosure of all available evidence." In fact, the Grand Jury failed to call the commander of one of the units that fired the fatal shots. That commander was one of those who had told the FBI pointedly that the lives of the members of the National Guard were not in danger and that it was not a shooting situation. There were also many other witnesses in a position to provide objective information about the shootings who were not called.

The Grand Jury found it somehow probative to write that "It is obvious that if the order to disperse had been heeded, there would not have been the consequences of that fatal day." It did not explore the fundamental question: By whom and by what authority was the prohibition against the exercise of constitutional right issued? It appears from all reports that the prohibition and the subsequent order to disperse was issued by the National Guard even though there was no declaration of martial law. By what authority is another question. The state attempted, after the fact, to give the Guard such authority by claiming that a proclamation issued April 29, 1970, empowered the Guard to act against a Teamsters strike. That proclamation, however, did not mention Portage County, Kent, or the university. It read:

> Whereas, in Northeastern Ohio particularly in the Counties of Cuyahoga, Mahoning, Summit and Lorain, and in other parts of Ohio in particular Richland, Butler, and Hamilton Counties, there exists unlawful assemblies and roving bodies of men acting with intent to commit felonies and do violence to persons or property in disregard of the laws of the State of Ohio and of the United States of America.

. . . The Commanding Officer of any organization of such militia, is authorized and ordered to take action necessary for the restoration of order throughout the State of Ohio.

That order was amended on May 5, 1970, to include Kent and Kent State University.

Obviously, there was no authority permitting the military to prohibit the exercise of constitutional rights. The significance of this issue is that constitutional law and fundamental Democratic principal clearly forbid the military from usurping civilian authority. On May 4, there had been an absolute abdication of civilian authority and Kent State became "a model of exactly the kind of military suppression of civil disorders that the historical principal of due process forbids."[4]

Notwithstanding the clear violation of due process under color of state law, and notwithstanding the clear violation of state and federal law, all of which resulted in the direct deprivation of the most sacred of all constitutional rights—the right to life—the perpetrators remain today untouched by the criminal justice system. The Grand Jury Report exonerating the Guard carried the day and the Justice Department, following the state's lead, declined to present any violations of federal law to a federal Grand Jury.

The state Grand Jury was not content to merely exonerate the Guard in its deliverance of the official story. It felt the need to lay the blame and further chill the exercise of First Amendment freedom. The manner in which the blame was cast, as well as the fact that most of the observations were not supported by fact, says much about the mindset of those directing the process. The report found many to blame:

- "Those who were present as cheerleaders and onlookers, while not liable for criminal acts, must morally assume a part of the responsibility for what occurred."
- "Protestors . . . engaged in their usual obscenities, rock throwing, and other disorderly conduct."
- Those who, when ordered to disperse on May 4, "quickly degenerated into a riotous mob."
- a group of "intellectual and social" misfits called the Yippies.

The Grand Jury was clearly affected by matters of lifestyle. In noting that epithets came from male and female rioters alike, the grand jurors found it "hard to accept the fact that the language of the gutter has become the common vernacular of many persons posing as students in search of higher education."

In an attempt to profoundly and adversely effect change in the manner in which a university is run, the Grand Jury cast much of the blame on the administration and the faculty. In attacking the administration, the report stated: "The administration at Kent State University has fostered an attitude of laxity, over-indulgence, and permissiveness with its students and faculty to the extent that it can no longer regulate the activities of either and is particularly vulnerable to any pressure applied from radical elements within the student body or faculty."

The Grand Jury made this finding despite the fact that in April 1969, the university banned SDS from campus; expelled most of its members; and initiated prosecutions that resulted in four of its leaders spending six months in the Portage County Jail and one of its leaders being sentenced to prison. As the FBI Report noted, the university had experienced no problems with student unrest since that time. What the Grand Jury was suggesting to the university remains unclear (assuming Seabury Ford was not positing their solution in his interview, in which he also suggested that, "this country won't simmer down until the police have orders to shoot to kill") but the threat of draconian penalties was obviously implied. The attack on unspecified members of the faculty was particularly chilling: "The faculty members to whom we refer teach nothing but the negative side of our institutions of government and refuse to acknowledge that any positive good has resulted during the growth of our nation." The Grand Jury also accused the faculty of attempting to inflame their students in the hopes of inciting unrest. As one of the twenty-five indicted was a faculty member, and as the charge against him was inciting to riot, the message was clear: such behavior on the part of the faculty would not be tolerated.

The immediate power of the Grand Jury was the threat to send twenty-five people to prison. For nearly a year the lives of a group of people called the Kent 25 were disrupted by this very real threat (given the atmosphere at the Portage County Courthouse, the judges, who must be elected, were not about to consider probation). The uncertainty of the future, the difficult and all-consuming task of preparing the defense, and the disgrace and ridicule many felt created an enormous and often psychologically damaging burden. It was later revealed, after the infliction of this punishment, that as with the rest of the Grand Jury Report, the indictments were not based upon fact.

By the time the trials began, a new prosecution team had been installed. The Republican administration had been defeated in the fall of 1970 and the new governor and attorney general appointed three new special prosecutors. In order for the new prosecutors to prepare for trial, they needed to read the transcript of the Grand Jury's proceedings, including the testimony of the witnesses. Upon completion of that reading, the new prosecutors realized that there was not a shred of factual evidence to support the charges. That fact, however, did not dissuade these folks from attempting to obtain convictions.

The prosecution team devised a strategy by which they would begin the trials with their strongest cases involving the most serious charges. They had hoped these early cases would result in such severe sentences that the remaining defendants would, out of fear, negotiate pleas for lesser sentences. The plan did not work. Under the expert guidance of attorneys Benjamin Sheerer of Cleveland and David Scribner from the Center for Constitutional Rights in New York, a thorough and effective defense was prepared.

The prosecutors chose the case of Jerry Rupe to begin the trials. They chose Mr. Rupe, a former student, because he was charged with arson in the burning of the ROTC building on May 2, 1970, a crime sure to incite the passions of the jury and, more importantly, because Mr. Rupe had been convicted of selling marijuana, a fact that they were sure would cause the jury to convict regardless of the evidence. Their strongest case, however, did not result in the necessary conviction; the jury was hung, the felony charges dismissed. The second case, also an arson charge, had to be dismissed when the only prosecution witness testified that he was not sure the defendant was the man he had seen at the ROTC building on May 2. This witness later explained that he had been attempting to tell the prosecutors since the time of his testimony before the Grand Jury that he could not identify the defendant, but no one would listen. The third and what would be the final trial was so weak that the court had to direct a verdict of acquittal. With defense lawyers Jim Hogle and George Martin (who had also tried the Rupe case) still seated at the counsel table, the chief prosecutor rose and stated that he wanted a short recess because he had an announcement to make. A short while later he told the court that there was no evidence to support the charges against the remaining defendants, and he requested that they all be dismissed. The motion was granted.

The Grand Jury Report itself ultimately went down in flames—literally. A lawsuit was filed in the United States District Court in Cleveland on behalf of the Kent 25, various faculty members, and others who might suffer from the chilling effect of the report. In *Hammond v. Brown*,[5] Judge William K. Thomas ordered that the report be expunged from the county files and publicly burned, although he recognized that the report had already begun to take its intended effect.

Judge Thomas ordered the report expunged and destroyed for several reasons. First, he found that it was illegal under state law and that the Grand Jury had no authority whatsoever to issue a report. Second, he found that the report's continued existence "irreparably injure[d] the right of each of the accused indicted to fair trial, protected by the Due Process clause." Finally, he found that "A report of the Special Grand Jury, an official accusatory body of the community, that criticizes faculty members for 'over-emphasis on dissent,' thus seeking to impose norms of 'behavior and expression,' restricts and interferes with the faculty members' exercise of protected expression."[6]

Indeed, after many days of testimony the court found that the interference and restriction was already happening, and that it was happening because of the report.

Because of the report, instructors have altered or dropped course materials for fear of classroom controversy. For example, an assistant professor of English, after reading the report, "scratched three poems" from her outline in her Introduction to Poetry course. The poems are "Politics" by William Butler Yeats, "Prometheus" by Lord Byron, and "Dover Beach" by Matthew Arnold.

In "Politics," Yeats writes: "And maybe what they say is true / of war and war's alarms."

A university professor may add or subtract course content for different reasons. But when a university professor is fearful that "war's alarm," a poet's concern, may produce "inflammatory discussion" in a poetry class, it is evident that the report's riptide is washing away protected expression on the Kent State campus.

Other evidence cumulatively shows that this teacher's reaction was not isolated. The report is dulling classroom discussion and is upsetting the teaching atmosphere. This effect was described by other faculty witnesses. When thought is controlled, when pedagogues and pupils shrink from free inquiry at a state university because of a report of a resident Grand Jury, then academic freedom of expression is impermissibly impaired.[7]

The combination of the exoneration of those who were responsible for the shooting and killing of students, the charging of innocent students and faculty with criminal acts, and the thinly veiled threats against the university community by the only official body with the power to take action and which published a report on the May 4 tragedy clearly had an enormously chilling effect on a variety of freedoms protected by the First Amendment. There is much evidence that the effect of the "washing away of protected expression" continues to exist today. The "dulling of classroom discussion" and the upsetting of the university atmosphere was, as the court noted, irreparable.

In commenting on the years of unrest immediately preceding the tragedies at Kent State and Jackson State, the Scranton Commission noted that "It is not so much the unrest of the past half-dozen years that is exceptional as it is the quiet of the twenty years which preceded them." Equally exceptional but not as surprising in light of the official response is the twenty years of quiet that followed.

NOTES

This piece originally appeared in *Kent & Jackson State 1970–1990*, edited by Susie Erenrich.

1. I. F. Stone, *The Killings at Kent State: How Murder Went Unpunished* (New York: Vintage Books, 1971), 15; emphasis in the original.

2. Peter Davies, *The Truth about Kent State: A Challenge to the American Conscience* (New York: Farrar Strauss Giroux, 1973).

3. An excellent analysis of the evidence is provided in Davies, *The Truth about Kent State*.

4. David E. Engdall, "The Legal Background and Aftermath of the Kent State Tragedy," 22 *Cleveland Law Review* 3 (1973), 24.

5. Hammond v. Brown, 323 F. Supp. 326 (1971).

6. Hammond v. Brown, 323 F. Supp. 326 (1971), at 349.

7. Hammond v. Brown, 323 F. Supp. 326 (1971), at 350.

Eulogy for Galen Keller Lewis

REV. BARBARA CHILD

Rev. Barbara Child began her professional life teaching English at Kent State University, where she barely escaped the National Guard's gunfire on May 4, 1970. She became an attorney, first practicing poverty law and then teaching as a plain-legal-language advocate in law schools and among state legislative drafting bureaus. This piece was written in 1992.

> She changed everything she touched.
> Everything she touched was changed.

Galen Keller began devoting her life to the families of the Kent State dead and wounded from the earliest time that I knew her, from the very early 1970s. We shared our labors of love together in the American Civil Liberties Union, and I remember her in those early days in her house on Crain Avenue with her infant son Barney. In those days in this place, the ACLU was devoted to students' rights and the rights of the Vietnam Veterans Against the War. The ACLU in those days was inclined to say that women's organizations ought to look out for women's concerns. Galen Keller would have none of that. She started an ACLU Women's Rights Project.

But then came the litigation on behalf of the Kent State families. You need to understand that this litigation took place before the age of computers—computers that can manage the documents and information for massive litigation so that you can get what you want to know in a couple of keystrokes.

Not then. I remember Galen in the little ACLU office on the second floor on North Water Street, going through file drawers full of newspaper clippings about individual Guardsmen, figuring out the patterns, the contradictions, the lies.

Today people—lots of people—go to school to learn to be paralegals and legal assistants. Nobody taught Galen. Nobody could have taught her to be the genius she was. Managing the information involved in that litigation became her labor of love. She gave her life to it. She moved out of the house on Crain Avenue, and moved from the little ACLU office on North Water Street to the state ACLU office in Columbus as part of what some people called the litigation team representing the families of the dead and wounded.

All of us who had our lives newly forged in the crucible of the Kent killings began to think not of the Kent State "families" in the plural, but the Kent State Family in the singular, so coming back to Kent on May 4—or any other time—is coming for a family reunion.

Galen had transformed her thinking, her life, to be part of this family. She had been a housewife in Hudson, Ohio, with a husband and two sons. But she had decided to study political science, and when I first met her, she was a graduate student here. When the Kent State Family's civil litigation against the Guard reached the discovery stage—the stage of seeking documents and then discovering what they say and, more than that, what they mean—then Galen and her toddler son Barney moved to Columbus, where the file drawers of newspaper clippings multiplied into a roomful of documents to be pored over and order brought to their chaos.

Eventually the litigation team, including Galen, moved to Cleveland for the civil trial in Federal Court. Galen the genius—the one with the photographic memory, who could sit by the side of the lawyer who happened to be questioning a given Guardsman, any Guardsman, and she could say to the lawyer, "Ask him what he said about X to Y on Z occasion." And when the Guardsman had answered, she would whisper to the lawyer, "Now ask him what he said on that same subject to this other person on this other date." And she would have her documents ready to serve as evidence. Galen was the keeper of the documents and most of the information in them, information that was also in her head.

What a grueling, ghastly long period that trial was. What a toll it took on the families. But there was a glory in it too. For during that time, a love grew between Galen and Joseph Lewis. You have seen the pictures of Joseph, lying on the walk to Taylor Hall, gravely wounded, with wounds over time no longer visible, such as Dean Kahler's paralysis, but grave and lasting. So when Galen and Joseph had had all they could take of Ohio, they and Barney, Galen's youngest son, moved to Oregon. And I remember her exuberant phone call when she told me that there was new life that the Guards' worst doing had not been able to prevent. And she sent me pictures of this new son, Christopher, her fourth.

Galen continued to fill her life with loving work. She taught children with special problems, and if the loving care of a certain child at school was not enough, she brought that child home. And she still worked for women needing shelter.

At one point, Peter Davies, the author of *The Truth about Kent State*, asked Galen to collaborate with him on a new book about KSU to bring forth all those horrid truths that lay stored in her brain, truths that the rules of evidence had prevented the world from knowing. She called me and we talked about it. She agonized about it. But she and Joseph had chosen Oregon, and working for women and children. They needed her energies now. The book did not happen.

It has been a long time since Galen and I lived in the same place, but I will always treasure my memories of two reunions with her. The first was in Tacoma, six years ago, where she and Joseph drove to visit me when I was there on business. We sat at an outdoor restaurant on Puget Sound and caught up on our lives. We laughed a lot. She made light of her long sleeves and hat in the summer sun. There had been a melanoma, nothing to worry about, but she would just have to be careful in the sun.

The second reunion was two years ago, here at Kent State. She and Joseph weren't going to come. It was so far. I begged. Everybody would be here for this family reunion. It was the twentieth anniversary, and I cannot tell you how glad I am that I did not give up. They came. And we stood in that historic parking lot in the rain, and Galen's youngest son rode on his father's shoulders. When that sweet boy climbed on the memorial stones, and people told him to get down, she told them that boy could climb anywhere he liked.

And she slid down the hill through the daffodils. I remember the smell of her wet sweater and the grass stain on her skirt when we hugged and said good-bye.

Joseph called the next winter to tell me of the brain tumor. After that, all I had was the sound of her voice on the telephone, that wonderful lilting voice, miraculously at first still laughing, joking about her bald head and the target tattooed for radiation.

Later the laughter left. I sent her Starhawk's books to read. And when she could no longer read, I sent her the beautiful chants of Libana to listen to.

She lasted until the summer. She lasted for a visit to her school class where they put on a special program for her. She lasted for Barney's graduation from high school. She lasted to listen to one more birdsong outside her window. Joseph called me in the summer to tell me when she was gone.

Galen Keller Lewis was a civil libertarian of the finest sensibilities. She was a feminist before it was fashionable. Mother of four sons, and wife of her beloved Joseph, she proved that feminism is about a better life, a loving life, for men as well as women. There is a chant of Libana's that I like to think Galen listened to often and that I hope sustained her, for it is about her. It goes this way: "She changes everything she touches, and everything she touches, changes. She changes everything she touches, and everything she touches, changes." Galen brought out the best in everyone. She changed us all.

The Kent State Shootings after Nearly 50 Years

One Lawyer's Remembrance

SANFORD JAY ROSEN

Sanford Jay Rosen was the lead attorney for the dead and wounded students of the May 4, 1970, shootings at Kent State. Rosen came to the case in 1977 as lead counsel for the appeal following the victims' loss of their cases in federal district court in Ohio. After he won the appeal, the cases were sent back to the district court for retrial. Rosen continues to practice law in San Francisco and is a founding partner at the San Francisco law firm Rosen, Bien, Galvan & Grunfeld, LLP. This piece was written in 2019.

To understand my involvement in the Kent State cases, we begin with my father's mother long before I was born in December 1937. Aida Grudsky was born in the late 1860s in Kiev, Ukraine. In 1905, she fled to America with her husband and two sons from Czarist Russia's latest oppression of Jews. Neither son survived the journey. Her eldest, born in the United States, also died as a child. Perhaps because of her unspeakable suffering, Aida had an innate sense of injustice, which she passed on to me.

My late wife Catherine was born in January 1940, just three weeks after she was smuggled into the United States in her mother's belly. Pregnant Jewish women were not allowed into the United States on visitors' visas during World War II. The Nazis murdered Cathy's maternal grandmother and that branch of Cathy's family, except my mother-in-law. Cathy, her siblings, and their children and grandchildren are all who remain. Cathy and I were together from when we were teenagers until she died nine years ago. Her story is also of mine, and has informed my passion to confront injustice.

By May 4, 1970, Cathy and I were raising our family in the sure and certain knowledge that, with all of its many faults, America was the best place in the world for us to live. I knew this even though we had suffered the assassinations of John F. Kennedy, Robert Kennedy, Martin Luther King Jr., Malcolm X, and others. I knew this even though I had paid my dues in advancing civil rights, including by representing curfew violators around the clock during the riots in Baltimore, Maryland, following Dr. King's murder in 1968. The courtrooms were guarded by National Guardsmen armed with bayonets affixed to their rifles, and troops were bivouacked less than a mile from my house.

On May 4, 1970, I learned of the shootings at Kent State. My confidence was shaken. What happened there was unique. Soldiers had shot and killed civilians before in America. But this was the first time it had happened on a college campus where white, middle-American citizen-soldiers had shot similarly white, middle-American students. My closest African American friends were as shaken as I was. They feared that since American soldiers were killing white students on college campuses, all hope was lost for them. Horribly, ten days later, on May 14–15, 1970, two black students were killed, and many more blacks were wounded by police during demonstrations at predominantly black Jackson State College. All of the victims were students at Kent State University:

- Jeff Miller was killed. He was 20 years old and a junior. He was shot down approximately 200–220 feet from the line of fire.
- Allison Kraus was killed. She was 19 years old and a sophomore. She was shot down approximately 325 feet from the line of fire.
- Bill Schroeder was killed. He was 19 years old and a sophomore and member of the ROTC. He was shot down approximately 330 feet from the line of fire as he was walking to class.
- Sandy Scheuer was killed. She was 20 years old and a junior. She was shot down approximately 350 feet from the line of fire.
- Joe Lewis was wounded. He was 18 years old and a freshman. He was at least 60 feet from the line of fire. He was shot twice, in the abdomen and in the leg. He later worked in Oregon as a manager in a water plant.
- John Cleary was wounded. He was 19 years old and a freshman. He was at least 60–75 feet from the line of fire. He was shot in the chest. He later became an architect.
- Tom Grace was wounded. He was 20 years old and a sophomore. He was at least 150 feet from the line of fire. He was shot in the left foot. The

bullet took away a large portion of his foot. He later worked for a state government.
- Jim Russell was wounded. He was 23 years old and a postgraduate student. He was at least 160 feet from the line of fire. He was shot in the right thigh and right forehead. He became a city planner.
- Alan Canfora was wounded. He was 21 years old and a junior. He was approximately 175 feet from the line of fire. He was shot in the right wrist. He later became a law librarian.
- Dean Kahler was wounded. He was 20 years old and a freshman. He was approximately 205 feet from the line of fire. He was paralyzed from the waist down and rendered a paraplegic. He later became an elected county government official.
- Doug Wrentmore was wounded. He was 20 years old and a sophomore. He was at least 340 feet from the line of fire. He was wounded in the left knee and leg. He later became an investor.
- Robby Stamps was wounded. He was 19 years old and a sophomore. He was at least 500 feet from the line of fire. He was hit in the right buttock. He later became a social worker.
- Donald MacKenzie was wounded. He was 21 years old and a junior. He was approximately 500 feet from the line of fire. He was hit in the back of the neck. The bullet exited through his cheek, shattering his jaw. He later became a professor.

It was bizarre that three of the four students who were killed and one of the nine wounded were Jews. Horribly, like my in-laws, Sandy Scheuer's father Martin had fled the Nazi Holocaust to find a safe home in the middle of America.

America in the 1970s was not Hitler's Germany. Despite the Vietnam War and the terrible rift in our country at that time, our legal system had not been co-opted by the government. I knew that I could be involved in responding to the shootings. I had a really good cockpit because I was about to spend the spring and summer of 1970 as special counsel in the American Civil Liberties Union's national office. My boss, Mel Wulf, sent me to Ohio to investigate possible lawsuits to respond to the shootings.

Upon my return to New York, I proposed several lawsuits, including damages suits, on behalf of the victims. I did not expect to be involved in prosecuting them because at the end of the summer, I returned to my regular job as a law professor. Yet, at one stage or another, I became involved in several of the lawsuits.

I assisted in the defense of Craig Morgan, Kent State student body president, against charges of inciting to riot. I tried the lawsuit that contested illegal searches of the Kent State students' dorm rooms in the week that followed the shootings. And I argued the appeal to the US Court of Appeals of the suit to get court orders to reform National Guard weaponry, orders, and training for control of civil disorders.

We won Craig Morgan's case and the illegal search case. We lost the suit to reform the National Guard in the Supreme Court, but likely were instrumental in reforming it.

The thirteen damages cases were tried together for fifteen weeks in US District Court in Cleveland during the summer of 1975. I was not involved in it. The trial ended in a nine-to-three jury verdict against the plaintiffs and in favor of the defendants: Ohio governor James Rhodes, the president of Kent State University, the Ohio National Guard adjutant general, the assistant adjutant general, and the National Guard officers and enlisted men who were responsible for the shootings.

Well before the 1975 damages trial, the families of the thirteen victims formed the Kent State Family as a political force that strived for justice. Rev. John Adams, of the United Methodist Church, was largely responsible for bringing them together. The Kent State Family included other close friends and supporters. The Family insisted on appealing the damages cases after losing at trial.

In the fall of 1975, I was about to make a transition from my job as MALDEF's legal director into private practice. I planned to take several months off to write two books that were sponsored by the ACLU. I never wrote them.

Aryeh Neier, the executive director of the ACLU, asked me to take on the Kent State victims' appeal. He told me that I could not expect to win. He said that "it is hopeless, but for the sake of history, the appeal must be taken. It must not be written that the victims did not appeal, therefore they acquiesced." I agreed to take on the appeal, but decided that we could win.

Michael Geltner, then a law professor at Ohio State University and the lead attorney in much of the Kent State litigation, agreed. He added that if I won the appeal, I had to be prepared to be lead counsel at any retrial. I took his advice to heart, having heard of conflicts among counsel for the victims that played out poorly in the first trial.

I assembled a team of lawyers and paralegals to work with me on the appeal. We worked out of my house. My children and friends remember the disruptions.

Preparing the briefs took more than six months. Our opening brief was 159 pages long and included several pertinent photographs and maps of the Kent State campus. A separate appendix, including a larger number of pertinent photographs, was also provided to the Appellate Court. The defendants responded with briefs totaling more than 159 pages and included several additional photographs and a map.

The victims were in the courtroom at the oral argument in Cincinnati. Dean Kahler sat up front in his wheelchair. Their presence was acknowledged by the three judges.

In 1977, the Court of Appeals unanimously reversed the trial court and sent the case back for retrial. The court's clerk, who was almost as excited as I was, called to tell me the news. Defendants moved unsuccessfully for reconsideration in the Court of Appeals, and equally unsuccessfully petitioned the Supreme Court to review the case.

Now, the clients collectively had to decide which lawyers were going to represent them at the retry. A member of the original trial team attempted to take the case back. However, I was designated as lead counsel.

I assembled a trial team. The late Rees Davis of Mansfield, Ohio, and David Engdahl then of Boulder, Colorado, were my principal trial cocounsel. Our back-up lawyers were Ellen Sue Goldblatt of Berkeley, California, and Robert Baker of Beckley, West Virginia. Our paralegal was Steven Keller, who later became a lawyer. Engdahl and Keller had worked on the first trial, and provided us with some continuity.

We submitted more than twenty pretrial motions designed to improve the chances of winning the case. We also began to prepare another motion, this one to disqualify Judge Don J. Young, who had presided over the first trial. We believed he was prejudiced against the victims. He withdrew before we filed that motion, but he could not resist taking a parting shot at the victims and their legal team. In a press interview when he withdrew, he declared that the victims were foolishly refusing to settle the case and that they could not win regardless of the number of times the case was tried.

William K. Thomas was assigned as the new trial judge. He had presided over and favorably decided the Kent State illegal search case. He also had ordered expunged an unauthorized and illegally unsealed and published Portage County, Ohio, Grand Jury report that excoriated the Kent State students.

We believed Judge Thomas was a no-nonsense and fair judge. He proved us right. During opening statements at the retrial in 1978, for example, he ordered one of the defendants' lawyers to use the real words, rather than substituting the nonsense phrase, "da-da-da-da," when that lawyer repeated the protest chant: "One, two, three, four. We don't want your fucking war." In that instant, Judge Thomas demystified the chant and much of the events leading up to the May 4 shootings.

We were disappointed that Judge Thomas limited our pretrial discovery. However, he granted all but one of our pretrial motions, including one to exclude bricks and rocks from the courtroom. At the first trial the defendants' lawyers brought sacks full of bricks and rocks into the courtroom, where they remained in plain view as a reminder that similar items were thrown at the Guardsmen before the May 4 shootings.

Lt. Gen. Walter Giles Johnson (US Air Force, retired), the former adjutant general of the Mississippi National Guard, was in charge of the Mississippi National Guard troops when blacks were killed and wounded at Jackson State College. None of General Johnson's troops had fired a weapon.

General Johnson agreed to testify as an expert witness. Before his deposition, the defendants' paralegal told Judge Thomas that General Johnson did not want to testify, and that I had been harassing him. The judge got the general, who was at his golf club in Mississippi, on his speakerphone. General Johnson said I had not harassed him and that he was willing to testify. As we left the judge's chambers, I said heatedly, "Your Honor, we should question the defendants' paralegal under oath now." Judge Thomas responded, as if speaking to an unruly nephew, "Sandy, why don't you take a run around the block and cool down."

At General Johnson's deposition, one of the defendants' lawyers made an anti-Semitic comment featuring my mother. "Sandy," the lawyer said, "I have this image of your Mama as a little old Jewish lady making chicken soup and leaning out of her window in Brooklyn." He must not have known that General Johnson had defied his father to get into World War II, had been shot down, and spent more than a year as a German prisoner of war. As tempers flared, General Johnson said, "Mr. Rosen, is it true that Jewish people believe that chicken soup is like penicillin?" "Yes, General," I said, "some do." To which the general responded, "I love chicken soup." The deposition went on and his answers just got better.

Our jury consultants from the National Jury Project told us that most people's initial reactions to an historic or traumatic event usually remain their final reactions. They also told us that the majority of potential jurors in northern Ohio were hostile to the Kent State victims, and many would try to hide their biases so that they could be on the jury to decide against the victims.

We asked for and got a rigorous selection process. After filling out extensive questionnaires, each potential juror was taken into the judge's chambers and questioned at length by the judge and the lawyers.

Several potential jurors tried to get off, but were not excused. We wanted one of them, a paratrooper in the Korean War, on the jury because we believed that he knew that well-trained and soldiers under good officers would not have opened fire at Kent State.

Many jurors were disqualified for cause. One was a young black mother who was on welfare. Judge Thomas refused to believe her assurances that she had sufficient family help to take care of her child during the trial. I reacted furiously in front of the judge. When we returned to our "war room" in the courthouse, I threw my briefcase across the room. The next day, Judge Thomas apologized for his decision.

Several potential jurors, whom we believed were biased against the victims, tried hard to stay on the jury. We had to strike (excuse) several peremptorily, but could not get rid of all the potentially biased jurors. The defendants struck the brighter and freethinking jurors, including a young woman who had identified herself as a Druid.

We did the best we could in selecting jurors, but we were not happy with some on the panel. This weighed heavily on me.

Early in the pretrial proceedings, Judge Thomas said that he wanted to explore settlement. All parties and their attorneys agreed that he could act as a settlement judge. He interviewed the victims, and examined some of the deformities and scars (both visible and invisible) caused by the shootings. He fully evaluated the case. He proposed a settlement figure of $675,000, limiting attorneys' fees and expenses to $75,000 of that amount, plus an additional sum for court-awarded costs. Rees Davis, my experienced Ohio co-counsel, agreed that this was a reasonable recovery based on his knowledge of damages recoveries in Ohio. He was not happy to settle. He wanted to try the case to judgment and hold the defendants' feet to the fire.

John Adams met privately with the parents of the students who had been killed. I have wept only three times in public since I have been an adult. One of those occasions was when the parents came out of their private meeting. With tears and pain they had made the difficult decision to accept the settlement and end that part of their fight for justice and accountability.

My clients agreed to settle on the condition that the defendants, and only the defendants, each sign an acknowledgment that the victims had been wronged. The words of the defendants' statement were hard-fought. Years later, Rees Davis told me he understood the value of getting the statement. Here is what each defendant, including Ohio's governor, signed:

> In retrospect, the tragedy of May 4, 1970 should not have occurred. The students may have believed that they were right in continuing their mass protest in response to the Cambodian invasion, even though this protest followed the posting and reading by the University of an order to ban rallies

and an order to disperse. These orders have since been determined by the Sixth Circuit Court of Appeals to have been lawful.

Some of the Guardsmen on Blanket Hill, fearful and anxious from prior events, may have believed in their own minds that their lives were in danger. Hindsight suggests that another method would have resolved the confrontation. Better ways must be found to deal with such confrontations.

We devoutly wish that a means had been found to avoid the May 4 events culminating in the Guard shootings and the irreversible deaths and injuries. We deeply regret those events and are profoundly saddened by the deaths of four students and wounding of nine others, which resulted. We hope that the agreement to end this litigation will help to assuage the tragic memories regarding that sad day.

The settlement had to be funded by the State of Ohio. Before the state officials agreed to the settlement, the politicians floated it to legislators and in the public press. Time passed and we started the trial on December 19, 1978, my forty-first birthday.

We worked on our opening statement for weeks, and it took less than an hour for me to deliver. It had a Psalm-like cadence and structure, featuring repetition of form and transitional sentences and phrases. Several jurors brushed tears from their eyes, while others sat stone-faced.

We called our first four witnesses, each of whom testified well. Then, suddenly, it was over. The State of Ohio agreed to the settlement.

The next day, I visited with Judge Thomas and told him how much my clients appreciated his fairness. He responded, "Fairness satisfies the appearance of fairness."

More work had to be done. Some of the victims' previous lawyers attempted to collect full contingent fees from the settlement fund. They were spurned by Judge Thomas and then by the Court of Appeals. As one of the appellate judges in Cincinnati, Pierce Lively, said during oral argument, "What do you want us to do? Send these people back to retry the case a third time?"

The Kent State Family has not yet gotten to the bottom of why the shootings occurred. It is still doing that, and the Family's determination in the damages cases itself has had a powerful impact on America. For instance, I believe the Family became the model for future victims' families, such as the relatives and friends of the victims of the Pan Am Flight 103 bombing over Lockerbie, Scotland.

Moreover, the Kent State damages case was the first in US history in which damages were paid to the victims of shootings by soldiers and in which state government officials acknowledged in writing that a wrong had been done to the victims.

I understand that the Kent State shootings and litigation caused reform of National Guard weaponry, orders, and training to control assemblages and civil disorders. The shootings are taught in National Guard training classes as an example of what not to do in controlling civilian disorders. National Guard troops no longer patrol with their weapons "locked and loaded." They lock and load their weapons only when ordered by an officer. They also are provided with and trained on the use of nonlethal weapons.

Since the Kent State and Jackson State shootings, I do not believe there has been a single civilian fatality in the United States caused by National Guard troops in the control of an assembly or civil disorder circumstances, possibly excluding siege situations.

I wish I could say that ending the case gave the victims some peace of mind. Certainly, the money helped Dean Kahler to lead a better life, and it assisted the other victims. But did it bring peace of mind? No. No resolution could.

Reentering my real life in January 1979 was difficult. It took a lot of time. My absence and preoccupation had been difficult on my wife and children, and on me. Even now, nearly fifty years after the shootings and more than forty years after the settlement, I become a bit moody as each May 4 approaches. Sometimes I have buyer's remorse about settling, rather than trying the case to a judgment. Then again, after the settlement, Judge Thomas told me he was concerned that we could have lost the case.

The wailing from the parents of the slain students I heard in our war room in the Federal Court still haunts me. I continue to mourn for the lost lives so full of promise: Allison, Jeff, Sandy, and Bill. I mourn for the wounded students' disrupted lives and the disrupted lives of their family members, friends, and witnesses. (During jury selection, one potential juror, a man who had been at Kent State on May 4, burst into tears as he remembered arriving on the Commons just after the shootings.)

I mourn for the other victims who have since died—Robbie Stamps, who died in 2007, and Jim Russell, who died in 2008—and for other members of the Kent State Family who have died, such as parents of the victims and for John Adam and Rees Davis.

I think it is likely that the Kent State tragedy would not have happened if Gov. James Rhodes, Vice President Spiro Agnew, and President Richard Nixon had not used incendiary rhetoric to demonize the antiwar demonstrators at Kent State and many other colleges around the country. It

Sanford Jay Rosen at the settlement news conference in Cleveland, Ohio (Source: John Rowe)

is beyond concerning that elected officials and other public persons in the United States are doing that kind of thing again with a vengeance, enabling the haters among us, as evidenced by the senseless killings by white nationalists, racists, and anti-Semites over the past several years.

I have heard many shocked or disbelieving reactions to the Kent State shootings from around the world from people living in countries long used to the slaughter of civilians by soldiers and police. It does not matter that measured on any world scale, few were killed or wounded at Kent State. It should not have happened in America.

One weekend some years ago, in a chance encounter in a store, I talked with a retired Marine. He had mustered out as a gunnery sergeant and was the second most senior noncommissioned Marine officer at the time of his retirement. He had served two full tours in Vietnam, the last one ending with the evacuation of Saigon in 1975. When I told him that I had represented the victims of the shootings at Kent State, he looked mournful and then angry. "They were murdered," he said.

PART VIII

Testimonials by Some of the Wounded Students

My Life Was Forever Changed

DEAN KAHLER

Dean Kahler was shot in the back on May 4, 1970. He knew almost instantly that he would never walk again. He sailed through rehabilitation and returned to Kent State after missing just one quarter. This piece was written around 2005.

Sunday, May 3, 1970, the weekend news stories of trouble on and off campus led to a discussion with my parents of my returning to Kent State University to resume classes. I lived in Wright Hall, located in the Tri-Towers complex of dormitories on campus. My parents were torn. It appeared to be a dangerous situation. The proclamation by Ohio governor James A. Rhodes stating that he was going to keep Kent State open and protect the property and people of the city of Kent was only mildly reassuring. Kent State is surrounded by Akron, Canton, Cleveland, and Youngstown and was not known as a hotbed of political dissent. The academic nature of Kent State and the blue-collar students enrolled there would not lend itself to danger once classes resumed on Monday, May 4. This was my rationale for deciding to go back to KSU on that day. Little did we know that the events of the next twenty-four hours would alter our lives and the lives of everyone who attended the university during the spring of 1970.

The forty-five-minute drive to Kent State was tense as my parents and I talked about returning to campus. Governor Rhodes's speech was interpreted as more political than substantive. When we reached the city limits of Kent, we encountered National Guardsmen stationed at a checkpoint. All traffic was stymied and questions about our destination reminded my father of the US occupation of Korea following World War II. Prior to my parents' departure, they asked me if I really wanted to stay. I reasoned that I would not get into trouble if I stayed out of the way of the National Guard. I assured them that I would be safe. I know my parents were worried and apprehensive about my safety. Our good-bye was difficult and eerie. I saw the fear on their faces as they drove off.

The rest of that afternoon, I wandered around campus looking for a neighbor from back home and discovered he would not be in KSU until Monday. Early that evening, I found myself by the Student Union, where a group had gathered to protest the Guard's presence. A suggestion was made to visit the various dormitories, recruit additional students, and march to the university president's house. As we approached President White's home, we were teargassed and chased away. I immediately went to my dorm, cleaned my face, and calmed myself. I heard students were assembling on the front campus, so several of my dorm mates and I went to face the music once again. We were greeted by National Guard troops and local police officers. Students sitting on the curb, the street, and the campus lawn were singing and chanting antiwar slogans. An announcement was made alerting students that the mayor and university president would speak at 8:30 P.M. The troops increased and helicopters flew overhead. Shortly thereafter, rounds of tear gas were fired and that familiar smell filled my throat. I headed back to my dorm, trying to dodge the troops. The dormitory door was jammed with students, residents, and nonresidents. They were trying to get away from the mayhem. I had to struggle to get inside. Students on the outside were rounded up and arrested. The National Guard continued their maneuvers and helicopters circled the dorms. It was a frightening night.

Monday, May 4, I called my professors and skipped my morning classes. I still wasn't sure about our rights and responsibilities. I tried to sort through rumors and stayed indoors. Later, a few of us walked to the Commons. There was a demonstration planned for noon. I had never been to a mass rally and was curious. It wasn't as I imagined. There were people with bullhorns talking about the *-isms*. What this had to do with the National Guard leaving campus and life getting back to normal was beyond me.

A campus policeman and a National Guardsman drove onto the Commons and proclaimed that we were assembled illegally and read the Riot Act. We were ordered to disperse. Boos, chanting, and a bit of stone-throwing ensued. Troops hurled tear-gas canisters into the crowd. I ran to the other side of Taylor Hall to escape. The troops appeared to be chasing students past Taylor Hall and onto the practice field. I ran through Prentice Parking Lot, across a street, and onto a gravel construction pit. My eyes burned from tear gas. I wiped my face with a wet handkerchief. Frustrated, I grabbed a handful of gravel and heaved it toward the kneeling Guardsmen. The stones fell on unsuspecting students in front of me. The troops were more than one hundred yards away, so there was no possibility of hitting them.

The Guard formed a line and started marching back up Blanket Hill toward Taylor Hall. There weren't many students close by. Nobody wanted to be near them. The students on the Taylor Hall slope moved away from the advancing troops. I followed at what seemed a safe distance, about one hundred yards. When the troops reached the hilltop, beside Taylor Hall, they turned around, lowered their weapons, and fired. I was stunned. I was in the line of fire. "Oh my God, they're shooting at me!" I jumped to the ground, covered my head, and prayed that I would not be shot. Terror overcame me as the ammo hit the ground around me. Then I felt the sting of a bullet. After experiencing a violent uncontrollable contraction, I knew I was seriously injured. I had no sensation in my lower body.

The barrage of gunfire lasted what seemed like forever. When it was over, I reached down, touched my thighs, and felt nothing. I was terrorized. I frantically wondered how badly I was wounded. A student who came to my aid asked if he could contact my folks. I gave him the phone number. By this time, a crowd had gathered around me. I saw horror in their faces. I wondered how many other students were shot. Were any killed? A couple of students knelt beside me and tried to comfort me. They assured me that the ambulance was on its way. It seemed like an eternity. When the emergency vehicle finally arrived, I told the medics I had sustained a back injury, so they should be careful putting me on a backboard. During the loading, I saw a familiar student giving me the peace sign and I gave him the thumbs-up sign as the transporter took off.

The hospital was in total chaos when I arrived. Someone shouted, "Get blood types on all of these people." I handed my blood donor and insurance cards to the technician. I think it saved my life.

Luckily, my parents were reached before the telephones were cut off on campus. Mom called a minister friend of the family. He was able to get to the critical-care facility. I was very surprised to see him. We talked and prayed before I was rushed to emergency surgery.

On Thursday morning, I slowly came out of an induced coma, full of questions and in tremendous pain. I didn't have much information regarding the incident. All I knew was that several students were shot and some were killed. I wanted to know more. I wanted to know everything. I wanted to see my parents. I wanted to see my doctor! There were tubes in my throat, nose, sides, and intravenous needles in my hands, elbows, and feet. I couldn't move.

Above: Dean Kahler and Alan Canfora on May 4, 1976 (Source: John Rowe)

Left: Dean Kahler during the 1979 settlement news conference (Source: John Rowe)

Three ribs were broken so the doctors could examine my chest cavity, search for bullet fragments, check internal organs, stop the bleeding, and inspect the damaged vertebrae. I survived and was in rehabilitation until late October. I returned to the Kent State campus in January 1971 for the winter quarter.

Now when I reflect on the events of May 4, 1970, certain images still come to mind: the fear on my parents' faces and the terror-stricken students staring down at me as I lay in a pool of my own blood.

Over the years, I have listened to the stories of the other victims, eyewitnesses, and families. All of us were traumatized by the episode. We lost our basic rights on that fateful day—our right to speak out against abusive power. And some of us lost our lives. Questioning our elected representatives and holding them accountable for their actions is what makes up a democracy.

I continue to attend the annual commemoration and to discuss May 4, 1970, events with the current generation of students. I encourage them to study their history and learn their rights.

Speech on May 4, 1984

TOM GRACE

Tom Grace was one of the wounded students on May 4, 1970, at Kent State University. He is a scholar and instructor of American history. He specializes in dissent and the protest movements in the 1960s and is the author of Kent State: Death and Dissent in the Long Sixties, *published by the University of Massachusetts Press. This piece was written in 1984.*

Fourteen years ago today, our surroundings were disturbed by the din of agitated protest, by clouds of tear gas, and finally by the horrifying sound of gunfire. Impassioned voices were stilled, some forever, by thirteen seconds of terror—sixty-seven shots in all—from M1 rifles, shotguns, and .45 caliber automatics.

By the time National Guard officers finally regained control over their gunmen and ordered them to cease firing, thirteen Kent students lay dead, wounded, or dying. Hundreds more were stunned as if they had been hit. None who saw defenseless people shot down—save the Guardsmen responsible for the shooting—will ever be the same. Our lives were permanently changed.

How far away that day must seem for many of you as we gather inside on an overcast afternoon, on a day unlike the pleasant one of fourteen years ago. How profound the contrast between those seconds and minutes of terror and the misty serenity of this day.

For those assembled here who are too young to remember, for those who were guilty of the wanton killings, and for the legions of Americans who cried out for peace in 1970, we are here today to tell all who will listen that our dead classmates will not be forgotten.

Every year for the past fourteen springs, hundreds—and sometimes thousands—have come to pay respects to the memory of Allison Krause and Sandy Scheuer and Jeff Miller and Bill Schroeder. Some of us who still bear scars from wounds suffered on May 4 have come from distant parts of the country to recall our classmates' sacrifices.

With the recent birth of my second child, I have been more aware than ever of the magnitude of the sacrifice made by Sandy and Jeff, and of what was stolen from Bill and Allison. They will never know the joys and trials of parenting. Their families will never see their children grow into adulthood. Why? Because a group of armed men robbed four people of their futures by gunning them down just as they entered the threshold of their adult lives.

I will not attempt to retrace the events that led up to the burst of fire. The outcome has become part of our heritage, even if the facts and meaning of the killings remain in dispute.

Rather, we will address ourselves to the legacy of Kent State and of what we are memorializing.

The deaths of four students here and of two more at Jackson State occurred because some had the audacity to protest, in sometimes militant fashion, the invasion of Cambodia by US ground forces. The then governor of California surely spoke for many in the establishment when he intimated a bloodbath for those who opposed the country's policy. It was left to the governor of Ohio, James Rhodes, to make good his western counterpart's admonitions.

Yet if the killings were supposed to silence antiwar critics, then the tactic failed, for the shootings only served to intensify the movement. Never before or since were so many campuses racked by protests. Even today, when I meet a college-educated person of my age, they are able to recall their involvement in protests against the killings and the invasion of Cambodia.

The demonstrators accomplished what electoral activity alone could not—to force the issue of Vietnam and Cambodia into the body politic in such a way that it could no longer be ignored. Over Richard Nixon's strong objections, two US senators, Sherman Cooper and the late Frank Church, cosponsored an amendment restricting future operations in Cambodia. Its terms required the executive to withdraw the US forces two months after the original April 30, 1970, invasion.

The politics of protest grew to such magnitude that the system was compelled to respond or face further measures. Cooper-Church passed in final form as the War Powers Act, marked the first time during the Vietnam experience that Congress acted to restrict a president's ability to wage undeclared war.

I have been told by combat veterans who were a part of the Cambodian invasion that they felt their lives had been saved by the protests. If true, then the lives lost here have greater meaning.

Most recently, the War Powers Act served as the basis for the Lebanon debate. Had Congress exercised their power instead of showing only their timidity, some three hundred Marines would undoubtedly now be alive. Missing in the fall of 1983, however, was the vibrant mass movement of the late 1960s and early 1970s. The apparent lesson is that mass pressure is required to prevent the introduction of US soldiers into unpopular foreign conflicts.

While a mass movement opposing imperial penetration of Third World countries such as Lebanon or El Salvador does not exist on the scale it once did, there remains a widespread skepticism about American foreign policy objectives.

This is a legacy of Kent State and of Cambodia, which has become known as the Vietnam Syndrome. There are millions of Americans who agreed with George McGovern when he said it was wrong for our country to support every two-bit dictator in the world. And part of the appeal of Gary Hart and Jesse Jackson is their often-stated opposition to the commitment of US forces in conflicts in the underdeveloped world. In Jackson's case, he has questioned the very motives and aims of corporation and government policies.

We have today an entire generation of Americans who came to a newfound political understanding during the Vietnam War. Our political outlook was shaped and fashioned by the utter ruthlessness of American policy in Indochina, as well as on the home front in Kent, Ohio, and Jackson, Mississippi. Commentators speaking of a largely white, university-educated group have dubbed us the "Big Chill" generation. While the consciousness of many of the college-schooled 1960s generation reflects primarily middle-class aspirations and, hence, is often found wanting on issues concerning working Americans, the poor, and disenfranchised minorities, it nevertheless forms a basis of opposition to reckless foreign adventures. This, too, is a legacy of Kent State and Vietnam.

On the domestic front, the Kent State and Jackson State killings awoke millions of our countrymen to the ugly realities of which minorities and the urban poor have long been aware—that the police and National Guard are the ultimate instruments of rule. At KSU and Jackson State, deadly force was used to contain what, in retrospect, was resistance not to government rule but only to its war policies.

"Kent State," in the words of former presidential aide and convicted felon H. R. Haldeman, "marked a turning point for Nixon—a beginning of his long downhill slide towards Watergate."

Some apparently are anxious to rehabilitate Nixon. I will always remember him for the siege mentality he developed during the years of protest that engulfed his administration. Illegal countermeasures first used against Black Panthers were next employed versus the antiwar movement. Reactionary steps were then taken toward the press and were finally directed at the opposition party headquartered in 1972 at the Watergate Apartments in Washington.

During the unraveling of Nixon's administration between 1973 and 1974, three attorney generals, two of whom were convicted for criminal wrongdoing, occupied the office directing the Justice Department. The first two, John Mitchell and Richard Kleindienst, blocked federal action on Kent State. Hence, four years passed before the Justice Department, badly shaken by Watergate, succumbed to pressure from fifty thousand people who in their petitions demanded action against the Ohio National Guard. A large measure of credit is due to author Peter Davies and churchman John Adams, who pleaded and prayed for justice from a department whose stated mission is to uphold the law.

When indictments were returned against eight Ohio Guardsmen for their roles in the shooting deaths, they were charged only with conspiring to violate our civil rights. Rather than indict the Guardsmen for charges easily proven, the Department of Justice, as they recently did in the case of the shooting deaths of five anti-Klan demonstrators in Greensboro, North Carolina, chose to prosecute the killers under hard-to-prove sections of the US Criminal Code. This "let's indict the killers for charges we can't prove" mentality led to predictable results.

In 1974, a federal judge dismissed the cases against the Guardsmen before sending them to a jury. The charade was played out again three weeks ago when an all-white jury exonerated nine Nazi party and Ku Klux Klansmen in the execution-style killings of five protestors.

The lesson of Kent State? Simply that Mississippi justice prevails in Ohio and North Carolina if the victimized are protestors calling for peace or racial justice. Jesse Jackson's statement that the Greensboro travesty "threatens everyone in a free society" rings true for Kent State as well.

These are unpleasant realities for some, but important lessons for all. For those of us present on May 4, 1970, the foregoing constitutes a lasting legacy. Yet, lessons seldom outlast the living and legacies survive, in part, because of permanent memorials.

Following years of disputes and no small amount of callousness, the new Kent State administration is giving serious consideration to the erection of a fitting memorial to the dead.

Even an unrepentant antiwar activist like myself can feel a welcome sense of openness from Dr. Schwartz. His administration has a chance, as all new administrations do, to right many wrongs and to help heal our wounds.

Here at Kent State we already have a grossly placed monument to insensitivity, for the construction of the gym on the other side of the Commons stands out as the single most unfeeling act ever committed by a post-1970 Kent State administration. If the building of the gym represented callous disregard, other memorial ventures, such as were proposed by former KSU President Brage Golding, were simply ridiculous.

The most serious—and in my mind appropriate—tribute to date was created by the renowned sculptor George Segal. His memorial was rejected by Kent State as being too violent. Imagine that. A university administration that cooperated with police in employing all manner of repressive tactics and public humiliation against its students, its alumni, and—on one occasion—even the parents of slain student Sandy Scheuer, rejected a thought-provoking sculpture of Abraham slaying his son. One can only assume that the thoughts the sculpture provoked would be ones that past administrations could not bear.

The current efforts by the May 4 Committee to choose a suitable permanent memorial will serve as a litmus test of the new administration's sincerity. The committee, which I understand has an appointed chairman, cannot escape the sad fact that violence was done to defenseless civilians. While shape and design are not unimportant, what is inscribed or not inscribed will be of lasting significance.

I submit that an inscription that tells in unadorned fashion what happened here is essential. We do not need more gymnasiums to conceal what occurred at Kent State. Rather, we need a committee ready to act with moral fortitude so future generations can stand near the Pagoda and read of how thirteen Americans were killed and wounded by the Ohio National Guard in a protest over the invasion of Cambodia.

"Why should it say that?" some will ask. I answer, "Because that is what happened."

While a student at Kent State I majored in history with a particular focus on the Civil War. The battlefields of that war—America's bloodiest and most-remembered conflict—dot the landscape from southern Pennsylvania to western Missouri. Decades after the war, veterans returned to the sites to dedicate monuments to their fallen friends and to commemorate their sac-

Doug Wrentmore, Tom Grace, and Scott MacKenzie during a commemoration (Source: Brad McKelvey)

rifices, deeds, and actions. Today, long after the last veterans have died, we can still visit the fields of conflict. We can read the inscriptions on the granite monuments and understand what happened on the banks of Antietam Creek or on the hills surrounding Gettysburg.

It may be inevitable that the committee's charge of memorializing the controversial killings will itself generate controversy. Yet we must remember who it is that comes back to remember and pay homage. Certainly not James Rhodes or General Canterbury or General Del Corso. No, it is those of us who were wronged and our supporters, both old and new. Our feelings—the views of the four families—must not be dismissed again.

None of us are anxious to refight past battles, but all of us, like Civil War veterans who fought either for or against freedom and the Union, will someday be dead. This memorial can ensure that future generations will know and understand the bloody day of fourteen years past. We owe that to the memory of those who died on the other side of this campus.

If Kent State truly wants to make peace with the past, they must make peace with the living. We will not rest until we are certain that our classmates are never forgotten.

This piece originally appeared in *Kent & Jackson State 1970–1990,* edited by Susie Erenrich.

May 4 Recollections

JOHN CLEARY

John Cleary was an undergraduate student studying architecture in 1970, observing and taking photographs on May 4 when he was shot in the chest by the National Guard. John returned to finish his degree at Kent State, eventually becoming an architect in Pittsburgh, Pennsylvania. This piece was written in 2019.

I came to attend Kent State in the fall of 1969. I'm from a family with strong conservative values, and while growing up in rural upstate New York, my parents always stressed the need for a good education. They were the first generation of college graduates in their families and they wanted us to have better lives than theirs. They felt education was the key. Two of my best friends were in the military, and my brother-in-law was a veteran, working in the LAPD in California. Kent State was new territory for me with a diversity of people and values. The reason I was at KSU was to get a degree in architecture and I focused on my classes and my grades. I tended to make friends in my major and we soon formed study groups, working well into the evening to keep up with our workload. Politics were rarely discussed and antiwar rallies held on the Commons were merely background noise filtering up through the windows of our design studio overlooking the Commons from Taylor Hall.

To earn spending money for the weekends, I worked part-time in the student cafeteria washing dishes, squeezing time between classes and homework.

On one of the first warm spring days, Friday evening, May 1, I was in my dorm studying when rumors began from students coming back from downtown that rioting was going on and that property was being damaged. I remember a feeling of unease coming over the dorm.

On Saturday, May 2, rumors were circulating that the ROTC building would be burned that evening. Around 8:00 in the evening, a group of students gathered around the ROTC building chanting antiwar slogans. From my dorm room in Stopher Hall, I had a front-row seat. Attempts were made to ignite the building. At first the building did not catch fire, but later in the evening it was fully engulfed in flames. I walked out to the sidewalk to watch firefighters attempting to put it out. It was my first real exposure to the antiwar movement and students with a strong political agenda. I walked with a group of friends toward Main Street to watch a convoy of National Guard troops traveling down Main Street in armored vehicles and jeeps. It felt like the campus was being taken over by the military.

On Sunday, May 3, the weather was beautiful, but tensions were apparent, and the military presence on campus put everyone on edge. With disruptions on Friday night and Saturday night, my goal was to catch up with some work that evening that was due on Monday. That evening after dusk, several groups of students were teargassed on or near the Commons. The tear gas drifted into Stopher Hall and when we began to have difficulty breathing, we fled the building. Guardsmen deployed outside ordered us back into our dorm. We tried to explain our plight, but they threatened to arrest us if we didn't comply. We hunkered down in study lounges that were clear of gas. Helicopters with spotlights and bullhorns ordered any students outside that they were in violation of curfew. It was a frightening experience and none of us got much sleep that evening.

On Monday, May 4, classes were in session and I went to my morning classes. Each building entrance was guarded by soldiers. It was an eerie sight and many students were angry at the strong military presence on campus. Almost everyone knew that there would be a noon rally at the Commons and I wanted to be there, more out of curiosity than any political bent. I borrowed my roommate's camera as I thought I might find some good photo opportunities. I watched the rally as it gathered in size; many of the students in attendance were on their way to their next class or were curious like I was to see what would happen. The Guard at one point began to advance on the crowd after warning them with a bullhorn to disperse. I took several pictures of the Guard as they passed by me over the crest of the hill near the Pagoda. After marching to a practice field and regrouping, they reversed course and headed back over the hill. I positioned myself near the entry to Taylor Hall, taking several more pictures as they passed by. At that point I was going to head into Taylor Hall for my next class, but lingered to take one more picture before they disappeared over the crest of the hill. As the Guard reached the crest of the hill, they suddenly turned and fired in my direction. I remember it felt like I was hit in the chest with a sledgehammer. That was my last memory after being shot until I came to in the hospital.

I was in a room in Ravenna Hospital with Joe Lewis, who was the closest to the Guard when he was shot. He was in a lot of pain and they had to change his dressings often, which put him in agony. I remember having difficulties breathing with all the tubes attached to my body. I was in critical condition for the first few days and then upgraded to stable after the threat of infection subsided. My parents and Joe Lewis's parents were in our room whenever possible. I remember my parents being thrilled when the nurses surprised them by moving me from the bed to an upright chair, a real sign of progress. After two weeks, I was discharged and quietly made my way to the airport for a flight home.

When I arrived home, I was surprised to find news trucks camped out across from our house looking for any sign that I was home. We lived in a very small community where everyone knew you and this attention was not welcome. The FBI questioned my high school teachers and my neighbors in an effort to determine how "radicalized" I may have been before and after my first year at Kent State. My neighbors were very supportive of me, but strangers often sent me hate mail, which my parents screened for me. I spent the summer recuperating. My professors mailed me homework and projects to do over the summer, enabling me to complete my work and obtain grades for the spring semester, which had been cut short. People asked me if I was transferring to another college, but the thought never occurred to me. I had made good friends that year and after how my professors worked with me long distance, I was going back to complete my education at Kent State.

Over the next four years I worked hard on my studies, staying clear of any antiwar protests. I did attend the May 4 commemoration observances, but always kept a low profile near the back of the crowd. At the first annual observance, I was introduced to Kathy, a girl I immediately took a liking to, and when I graduated, Kathy and I were married in Kent, and had our reception in the Student Union.

When I came back to campus, reporters often asked me if it was traumatic to see the spot where I was shot. It was at the entrance to Taylor Hall, which I passed every day for the next four years while going to classes. If anything, it spurred me on not to waste the opportunity I was given—to accomplish as much as possible with my new lease on life.

When Kathy and I moved to Pittsburgh after graduating, the economy was not doing well and it was a struggle to find work. When the civil trials began, I had to travel to Cleveland to testify. I was strongly encouraged to spend time attending the trial to show my support for the plaintiffs, but as I was responsible for supporting my family and starting a career, I could not take that amount of time off and keep my job.

I immersed myself in work, and my goal was to take the tests to become a registered architect as soon as I was ready.

Meanwhile, several trials were occurring over the years in Cleveland. I attended only when required to testify, which I believe created friction between myself, the parents of the slain students, and others at what they perceived as my apathy toward the proceedings. It was not apathy on my part, but fear of jeopardizing my career and alienating friends we had made in Pittsburgh. It was convenient to live far enough away from Ohio, where I could keep a low profile and the tragedy of Kent State was rarely discussed.

On the tenth anniversary, I was in New Mexico attending my mom's second marriage. I was the only wounded student who did not attend. One year later, my first child was born on May 4, perhaps a message that May 4 could not be conveniently tucked away and would always be an important part of my life.

On the twentieth anniversary, I did attend, after granting *Life* magazine the opportunity to do an article on where I was twenty years later after appearing on the cover after the shootings. *Life* magazine arranged a meeting with Joe Cullum, who was on campus that May 4. Joe is shown on the cover kneeling over me, helping to tend my wounds. He was instrumental in saving my life. It was an opportunity to meet Joe and thank him for his lifesaving efforts. As a result of always being portrayed as a victim, I wanted to be the person kneeling over people helping them with their injuries. It started me on a path toward becoming a first responder with the National Ski Patrol. I volunteer at the Hidden Valley Ski Resort and find it a richly rewarding experience. I have served with a great bunch of people for over twenty-five years.

On the twenty-fifth anniversary, I took my son and a friend of his to the May 4 observances. It was a chance to teach him what had happened there and what my involvement was. I listened to the people who knew the four slain students speak about their loss; they described each student's life before the shootings and I felt a profound loss, especially with my son at my side, knowing just how lucky I was to have survived.

Work and family kept me extremely busy in the late 1990s; there was an economic downturn and I went through several job changes, which was stressful and demanding. We were also renovating older homes and had several triplexes, which we rented out. After working all day, I spent the evenings and weekends working on our properties.

By the thirtieth anniversary, work had turned around and I had become a shareholder in our firm and was finally enjoying a successful career. I was more comfortable attending the May 4 commemorations and beginning to know the other wounded students and those actively involved in the May 4 Task Force.

Another change that brought us back to Ohio was our son's decision to attend Kent State. We began to visit him more regularly and reconnect with our Kent State friends. Andy, while living on campus, understood the importance of May 4 and one year volunteered to stand vigil in the parking lot for his allotted hour.

In 2007, I saw Jim Russell standing during the speeches near the Liberty Bell and had a very nice conversation with him. He was warm and engaging with me, making me feel welcomed. I was shocked to learn that less than two months later, he died of a heart attack. Jim was the first of the wounded students to pass on and I felt his loss after just beginning to know him.

In 2008 I was invited by the May 4 Task Force to speak on behalf of Jeff Miller, one of the slain students. When I was researching Jeff's life, I felt that I understood him better. He was a sensitive student who liked to write poems and expressed compassion toward both sides of the conflict in his poems, describing his antiwar sentiments. Perhaps he was targeted that day because of his appearance, with his long hair and the way he dressed. Certainly his actions did not warrant the way his life ended.

In the ensuing years, Kathy and I attended more regularly. We brought our daughter Lizzy, along with our golden retriever Rocky, to one of the observances. To see my family sitting on Blanket Hill listening to speeches reminded me of how lucky I was to have survived and how I was able to prosper and live a rich life, while other people's lives were cut short and they never had that opportunity.

I have met people who have made it their passion and purpose in life to keep the memories of May 4 alive. Carole Barbato, who was a communications professor and active in the creation of the May 4 Visitors Center, always had a big hug for me when I returned and she went out of her way to make me feel welcome. Her passing several years ago was a big loss, which I felt deeply. The May 4 Task Force, in conjunction with the university, hosts a breakfast the morning of May 4 prior to the observances and it has become an opportunity to visit with other wounded students and other people actively involved in keeping the memory of May 4 alive. These friendships have expanded and we have spent time together outside of the confines of the May 4 observances.

I have come to respect and admire those who are passionate about their political beliefs and work toward making the system work. I have never been political in nature. I keep my beliefs closely guarded, and when people pry, I tell them that's why they put curtains on voting booths. It takes courage to openly express your beliefs and defend them from those who disagree with you. I have never been comfortable with doing that. I take comfort in swinging a hammer and painting a wall.

As we approach the fiftieth anniversary of the May 4 shootings, social media has become another avenue for those of us who were there on May 4 to reconnect and share common experiences. The current president of Kent State has embraced and participated in recent commemorations, showing the university's growing acceptance and acknowledgment that what happened at KSU is historic and needs to be properly observed and not swept away to be forgotten by future generations. Dr. Beverly Warren recently gave a speech at Chautauqua Institute in which she outlined how she envisions the university plans on commemorating the fiftieth anniversary of May 4 by "remembering, reflecting and renewing."

Last year, the nephew of Bill Schroeder gave a speech on behalf of his family. His mother, Bill's sister, introduced her son. She said that on the anniversary of each May 4, her mother always wanted to know "Are people still coming?" I reflected on that afterwards and came to understand why I need to attend. It's not just for me; it's to respect and remember the other wounded students, those who were witnesses of that day and those whose lives were cut short. It's for us who were there to keep the memory of May 4 alive and, hopefully, teach a new generation of students never to forget the historical import of what occurred that day.

Russell and Me

Surviving Kent State

JOSEPH LEWIS

Joseph Lewis was sixty feet away from the guns when he was shot twice by the Ohio National Guard on May 4, 1970, at Kent State University. This piece was written in 2018.

YOU DIDN'T HAVE TO BE SHOT AT KENT STATE TO BE WOUNDED

It's no accomplishment on my part to have been wounded at Kent State on May 4, 1970, but it is my responsibility to speak up for those who lost their voices that day. I used to see Allison Krause, one of the four students who were murdered, all the time because her boyfriend was my dorm room mailbox partner. She was an activist; she would have spoken up for me if I had been killed and she had survived. For a long time I was quiet; I didn't share with people my experiences. I now look at Parkland survivors Emma González, David Hogg, and the others. They're so ballsy and savvy, and they spoke out immediately. I was quiet for years. But then in 1995, twenty-five years after the shooting, a reporter for the *Oregonian* newspaper, Steve Duin, came out here to Columbia County, and interviewed me and Jim Russell. After his article came out, Russell and I began to be contacted by high school teachers and college professors to speak in their classrooms. We were hesitant to do it at first, but found it cathartic to share with students what we had witnessed and experienced.

I have all the Blood Brothers—that is, the nine students who were wounded and survived—in mind as I write, but this essay is mostly about Russell and me. Jim Russell and I probably never would have been friends if it weren't for what happened that day. We were very different people. I knew him by sight from all the alternative movies he was putting on every weekend in one of the halls at Kent State. Russell was a twenty-two-year-old frat boy senior, while I was an eighteen-year-old pseudo-hippie freshman. He was the oldest and I was the youngest student shot that day. As for me, I was the first person in my family to go to college. I was paying my way; I'd saved enough to attend the first year. I would drop out not long after the shooting, while Russell would stay on and finish his degree. He used to say that he spent "five good years and one bad day" at Kent State. After the shooting I knew him by name, but it wasn't until our civil trial in 1975 that I really got to know Russell.

There are so many things I've been made aware of because of Kent State. The story doesn't end with the shootings; the story and the pain and the message go on. You didn't have to be shot at Kent State to be wounded.

NOT UNLESS YOU HIT ME ON THE OTHER KNEE

We were so sheltered and idealistic then. The twenty-four-hour news cycle didn't exist. When we heard news from Vietnam, it was on videotape that had been transported across the ocean a couple of days before. But when "Uncle Walter," Walter Cronkite on *CBS News*, showed these tapes, they included scenes of war. I'll never forget seeing a young soldier who had been shot in the lungs, had a gaping chest wound, and was dying in front of the camera. Americans would see the carnage with their families at dinnertime. There was no way you couldn't react to it. People formed strong opinions, were prowar or antiwar. Nixon played to that division. One of the biggest lies he told, and that politicians continue to tell, was that he wanted to "unite" the country. He did everything he could to divide the country. His backers, the so-called "silent majority," blamed the antiwar movement on communist infiltrators. We weren't, of course; we were people who were aware of what was going on and objected to it. And many were smart asses, like Russell and me.

On April 30, 1970, Nixon announced that he had authorized bombings and troops to go into Cambodia to cut off supply lines to the Vietcong. People like me who were opposed to the war saw this as an escalation. On Thursday night there was a demonstration on campus. On Friday there was a disruption downtown that caught the mayor's and the governor's attention. On Saturday, there was a rumor on campus that the ROTC building would be burned down. And it was. The building burned to the ground as I watched from my friend Tommy Thompson's dorm room. I know it seems unbelievable, but at one point the radio was playing Buffalo Springfield's "For What It's Worth" ("Something's happening here / What it is ain't exactly clear"). It was very spooky. There were three helicopters circling overhead with searchlights. My parents called to tell me to stay out of trouble, and I told them I would.

On Sunday, Governor Rhodes made an inflammatory speech: "They're worse than the brown shirts and the communist element and also the night riders and the vigilantes. This is the worst element of people we harbor in America," he said, pounding the table and setting the tone, I think, for the Guardsmen's response the next day. That night the campus was occupied by the Ohio National Guard, enforcing an 11:00 curfew at bayonet point, deploying tear gas, and chasing students into the dormitories. A girl carrying books and trying to get into the library was bayoneted in the upper leg. Russell was outside; Guardsmen came up to him and said, "There's a curfew. You'd better keep moving." And Russell said, "This is my fraternity house here. I pay taxes on this area, and I'm not going anywhere." So one of them took out his billy club and smashed Russell on the knee, knocking him to the ground. As Russell stumbled back up to his feet, the National Guardsman said, "I guess you'll be moving now." And Russell said, "Nope. Not unless you hit me on the other knee, and then I'm just going down."

WELL, EVERYONE ELSE WAS SHOOTING HIM

The next day, Monday, May 4, there were classes as usual, with nine hundred National Guardsmen bivouacked on the campus with half-tracks, jeeps, trucks, fixed bayonets, steel helmets, and tear gas, in full battle dress. I went to a couple of classes. There seemed to be two messages coming from the professors. One was: *Stay the hell out of sight, you could lose your life.* The other was: *This is a participatory democracy and you need to have your voice heard.* The Victory Bell was rung at noon and that was the signal for people to assemble on the Commons. At this point, it was not so much an antiwar demonstration as an antioccupation demonstration. I was determined to join it.

A jeep came out, and over the bullhorn a patrolman read the Riot Act three times (I assume that's a requirement of the law): "Students of Kent State, go back to your dorms. This is an illegal assembly." After the third time, students shouted, "Get out of here—you're the ones who are out of place!" When the students didn't disperse, the Guardsmen formed up and moved forward. Six or eight of them deployed tear gas across the Commons, firing it into the group of students. Some students put wet rags on their faces and hurled the canisters back at them. It was like a bizarre tennis match. Russell was dressed for the occasion—he wore a jean jacket and a headband—the one bad fashion choice he made was a T-shirt with a bull's-eye on it. The Guardsmen went down to the practice football field. They knelt and directed their guns at the most vocal part of the crowd, including Alan Canfora with his black flag, alongside a parking lot.

It all went down near the Taylor Hall School of Architecture and Journalism and my dormitory, Johnson Hall. When the Guardsmen left the Commons, they had gone between these two buildings, forcing students ahead of them. When they knelt and aimed at the students in the parking lot and didn't fire, students thought that it was over and went back to their places. Then the Guardsmen marched back up the hill. They were coming directly at me, so I moved to one side. They were so close to me that I could hear their equipment jostling. They kept looking back toward the parking lot; I think they were picking targets. They marched past me. They reached the top of the hill and came to a railing at the front of Taylor Hall. Either by previous agreement or by command, the first three guys turned in unison and aimed their rifles at me (a sound recording suggests that there was an order to fire). So there I was, eighteen years old, naive and foolish. I gave them the finger. The previous night, I had considered but ruled out the notion that they would bring live ammunition onto a campus. Now I heard these sounds. The ground was churned up in front of me. Two bullets hit me, one in the abdomen. (I learned later at the civil trial that when I went down, a second soldier shot me. And that bullet went through my lower leg right above the ankle. Asked why he did it, he said, "Well, everyone else was shooting him.") The shooting went on for thirteen seconds. Bodies were lying on the ground. There was a pause. And then students started screaming, just going crazy. A guy approached me. I tried to get up, but couldn't. I asked him, "How bad is it?" He said, "I think it's just a flesh wound." I was calmed by that, although it wasn't true. I still couldn't get up. A young woman named Ellen Mann held my hand. There were medics around, but they didn't offer us any help; they walked away. It may have been thirty minutes before the ambulance arrived. Years later, Ellen Mann commented online about a photograph of herself holding my hand that had been posted: "I'll never forget the look of terror and fear in Joseph's eyes." (Ellen and I met up years later at Longfellow's Inn in Scappoose, Oregon, and talked afterwards at my home. That meant the world to me.)

The ambulance came. We were loaded two to an ambulance; John Cleary and I rode together. He was wounded through the lungs, so our ambulance ride was nightmarish. With every bump and corner, he was screaming bloody agony; he was in so much pain that it freaked me out. And I thought I was dying. When you're eighteen, you're not very profound about death, so what I thought was "This could be it." I had been raised in the Catholic tradition, so I made the act of contrition for my sins, just in case that would apply.

In intensive care, Dean Kahler was six foot four, I was six foot three, and John Cleary was six foot five. There we lay, injured in a shared room. We were all too big for our beds; our feet were sticking out from them in a row.

And these are all my Blood Brothers: Dean Kahler had some familiarity with firearms; when he heard the gunshots, he knew they were live rounds and dropped to the ground. He was paralyzed for life when his spinal cord was severed. Dean is an amazing person. Whenever I call him up and ask how he is he says, "I'm doing great, Joe, how're you?" He's from the Church of the Brethren. Dean was forgiving right away because that's his tradition. He's my best friend; he's the person I think of when I think that I've got it tough. Tom Grace's left foot was practically shot off. Tom is maybe the smartest among us. He's an historian from Buffalo, New York. Tommy wrote a book called *The Long Sixties* about the Students for a Democratic Society. He and his wife send a Christmas card to all of us every year. When Tommy Grace's Christmas card comes out, I say, "Tommy, Tommy, Tommy. I love that boy." And Russell used to say the same thing: "Tommy, Tommy, Tommy." John Cleary recovered from his chest wound and became an architect. Robby Stamps was shot in the behind; he died years later of Lyme disease. Alan Canfora was hit in the right wrist. Doug Wrentmore was shot in the leg; Doug doesn't participate in the gatherings. Scott (Donald) MacKenzie was shot from seven hundred yards and sustained a neck wound. Russell was hit with buckshot at the temple and knee. Luckily, the Guardsmen had missed the bull's-eye on his T-shirt.

RUSSELL WAS A TALKER

Afterwards, I didn't continue on at school for long. In retrospect, that's not surprising. Initially I was under indictment. I was recovering from my injuries. I felt anger against the citizens of Ohio for blaming the students for the shootings. I was self-medicating grandly.

My friend Jerry Higgins and I came to visit his brother Kevin in Scappoose, Oregon, in the summer of 1972. We stayed at first with the Kozlowskys. They were amazing people, an older couple from the Bay Area originally. Albert had been a card-carrying communist during the McCarthy era. He was a leftist—so far left that the hippies sometimes had to reel him in because he thought that Russian communism was the way to go. While I was here that summer, I found a job and a place to live. The beauty of Oregon was breathtaking to me, the wide-open spaces, the forests, the ocean and mountains. It was healing, and I've lived here ever since.

But I had to go back to Ohio for the civil trial in 1975. I was freaked out, coming from the rural hills of Scappoose to a trial in downtown Cleveland. It was Jim Russell who got me through it. He was a fascinating, hyper guy. Russell was a talker, a meticulous genius with all kinds of interests. He talked me past reporters and microphones that would follow us through the streets of Cleveland during the civil trial. He was so chatty and I was so nervous and out of my element that he calmed me and took me through it and *almost* kept me sane.

ASSAULTED, HELL—THEY SHOT ME!

Ten days after the Kent State shooting, two students were killed at Jackson State in Mississippi, in a huge fusillade that has marked the building even to this day, so many rounds went into the side of that stairwell. I'm sure Nixon intended to whitewash his administration's policies. He assembled the Scranton Commission on Campus Violence to study so-called "campus unrest." There was an FBI investigation. And there was the Portage County Grand Jury. All the Guardsmen and other people involved in the Kent State shootings testified at each one of these venues. Eventually, we got a federal Grand Jury to investigate. Galen Keller, a paralegal for ACLU, had a photographic memory and was able to compare the various testimonies and demonstrate where the Guardsmen had impeached themselves.

We tried to get the federal Grand Jury to indict the Guardsmen. I was suspicious that the government was involved. Remember, this was the time of the COINTELPRO (Counter Intelligence Program), which infiltrated dissident groups. Members of the Justice Department were our attorneys in a federal case against eight Ohio National Guardsmen who were charged with conspiring to deprive us of our civil rights, but the trial was before a judge with whom I think the governor had a political connection. The case was presented. Our lawyers gave their initial arguments. The state moved to dismiss the charges on the ground of insufficient evidence. Our lawyers were saving their best evidence for rebuttal. The judge's order went through. And there was no rebuttal.

These eight guys, we figured, had fired into the crowd, so we tried to sue them in civil court for damages. The Ohio Supreme Court denied the case, arguing that you could not sue the state or the agents of the state. So we went to the United States Supreme Court and our thirty-five-year-old attorney won the case to proceed. We could now go ahead with a lawsuit against the governor, the president of the university, the officers of the Ohio National Guard, and the Guardsmen. We broke precedent in being able to take it to court.

So we went through this trial. Federal District Court Judge Don Young was ludicrously biased. For example, he wouldn't let the jurors see the photographs of the students who had been killed and wounded because they might prejudice the decision. The Cleveland, Ohio, courtroom in summer was humid and hot, unbearable. I had cut off my ponytail. Alan Canfora didn't get his hair cut; he had a short-hair wig; every day in court we sat behind him and could see a big long strand of hair dangling down from it. The Guardsmen were on one side of the aisle laughing and flirting with the reporters, as if they already knew they were going to be acquitted. We were on the other side with the parents of the students who had been killed.

Our lead attorney was Joe Kelner, a former president of the American Trial Lawyers Association. And so the State of Ohio, its deputy attorney general, was always saying shit like, "Mr. Kelner, I don't know how you do things in New York City, but 'round here . . ." Joe Kelner was a Jewish dude; they were slamming him in all kinds of ways.

Governor Rhodes came in to testify. I held (and hold) him and Nixon ultimately to blame for what had happened. I can still see him; he had this blue hair. Rhodes lied his ass off in court. And then the Guardsmen came up and talked about how afraid they were of us, how close we were, etc.

Russell got on the stand and was questioned by Charlie Brown, assistant attorney general for the State of Ohio. Charlie Brown was a big guy and wore a brown suit. He'd always come back from lunch red as a beet, three sheets to the wind, and had just drunk his lunch. He'd pull out his pocket handkerchief and cough up a gob and put it back in his pocket. He would fuck with us on the stand, and he tried to fuck with Russell. Russell says something about First Amendment rights, and Charlie Brown asks, "So Mr. Russell, you're not a constitutional lawyer, are you?" And Russell goes, "No." "So how much do you know about the Constitution?" So Russell started with the Preamble, went through the whole Preamble, and launched into the Bill of Rights. And Charlie Brown says, "OK, OK, enough . . ." Russell was a genius.

So Alan Canfora's on the stand. He was a little bit older and more self-assured. I was a freshman; I had a little survivor's guilt. Alan didn't. He was older and more radical, positive he had played a part in ending the war in Vietnam. So here's Alan in his short fuckin' wig. And they're trying to imply that he hadn't been threatened by the National Guard. "So Mr. Canfora, you weren't assaulted by the National Guard, were you?" And Alan goes, "Assaulted, hell—they shot me!"

The jury sided with the governor, the university, and the Guardsmen.

I think of the parents of the students who were murdered. Elaine Holstein was Jeff Miller's mom and feisty as hell—New York City feisty. Her husband blamed her for filling their son's head with all those liberal ideas. They divorced, of course. Her new husband Artie Holstein and she had a wonderful life together. She was the last of the parents to die. Sandy Scheuer's parents were Martin and Sarah—Martin was a Holocaust survivor. The university wanted to build a gym over part of the shooting site. And the Scheuers, then in their seventies or eighties, got arrested trying to stop it. Lou and Florence Schroeder were Bill's parents. Lou was a factory worker guy, a little rough around the edges, and Florence was this sweet, sweet homemaker lady. Lou and I had Reubens and beer in a Cleveland bar. He was a Scout leader; Bill had been a Scout. But the man who taught me how to be a man was Arthur Krause. His daughter had been killed. And he was fucking outraged. And he had a booming voice. He spoke in public for us. Oh, man, the heartbreak. Arthur and Doris; Doris just passed away a couple of years ago. Allison's sister Laurel Krause is my friend, my sister. We had an in-house chaplain, Rev. John Adams. He was from DC, from the United Methodist Church. I don't know how he came on the scene, but he counseled us all. Later he came to our farm up here in Oregon with a box of oranges. Russell asked, "Do you think we're gonna get scurvy?" A great man. My son Christopher John Adams Lewis is named for him. I was really worried when I first met these parents, especially Lou and Florence, because they were pretty straitlaced, hard workers. But they were just as sweet as could be; they understood the TV was lying. My own parents weren't so sure at first.

We lost the trial. The jury did not find the National Guardsmen culpable. Twenty-eight people fired sixty-seven live rounds at students at Kent State and not one of them has ever been held accountable for killing four people and wounding nine. Twenty-four of us students and one professor had been baselessly indicted and the people who fired at us got away with it. There was no counseling and no sympathy for us. The Guardsmen had claimed that they had "feared for their lives"—fully armed against a rowdy and outraged but essentially unthreatening assemblage. And this relates to the truth of what goes on in our inner cities today. I often think of Michael Brown.

SMOKE SOME HASHISH?

The appeal went to the Sixth Circuit Court of Appeals. Our attorneys challenged the ruling of the jury, and said there'd been a mistrial. And they won the appeal, so there would be a second civil trial and they wanted to depose us. Russell and I used to take the midnight plane out of Portland. You'd get to Chicago at about 5:00 A.M. We were walking between gates at O'Hare. Nothing's going on. The people from our plane are there, nobody else. So we walk past this guy and he's got a turban on. That stood out, pretty much, at O'Hare. And as I walk past him, he says, "Smoke some hashish?" I said, "Excuse me?" And he says, "Smoke some hashish?" And I say, "Well, yeah! Russell, come here!" So Russell and I go down to Gate 15 and there's nobody there. So this guy with a turban sits in the middle and I'm on one side of him and Russell on the other, and we smoke hashish at O'Hare Airport during our layover in Chicago. And we get on our plane and go to Cleveland. And then Russell gives me that look like, "We're in for it now." Yeah. He gave me that look.

The second civil trial was short-lived, lasting maybe one or two days. A different set of lawyers, a different approach. And an ACLU lawyer, a great man, Sandy Rosen. Going through the first trial had been almost as bad as being shot. Negotiations began, and we accepted an out-of-court settlement. They divided the amount of money set aside for the cost of the trial between the survivors. The person most in need was Dean Kahler. My settlement was $42,000. The parents of the students who were killed were offered $15,000. I'm not certain how all of the parents dealt with the money, but I do know that some donated the funds. And we got a framed letter of regret. Not apology. Signed by the governor and all the Guardsmen. A lot of days I regret taking the settlement. My comment at the time was that in the state of Ohio, that was the best possible outcome. Another consideration is that I used the money as a down payment for my seven acres on Apple Valley Road, which provided me with the healing I needed to come through it. Sometimes I do regret settling, but not when I'm sitting in my backyard with my sweet wife Lisa.

YOU KNOW, JOE, WE'VE REALLY GONE OVER THE EDGE THIS TIME

In 1975, after the trial was over and we had lost, we were pretty much heartbroken. I invited Russell to move to Oregon. At this point we had a kind of communal living place on a hill seven miles above Scappoose, renting a few buildings on a farm owned by a man named Burt Smith for the cost of his property taxes—twenty-five dollars a month. Lots of my friends would come out to visit during the summer and a number of them ultimately stayed. We were known to the locals as "the hippies on the hill." They thought it was a wild orgy every night. At least two dozen people came here from Ohio after Kent State and settled down. Confounding expectations, most of us found employment serving our local communities—as a midwife, a city planner, an engineer, public works employees, and teachers. We serve on school boards, take up other elected positions, volunteer.

During the course of our first civil trial, Russell became acquainted with the paralegal assistant I mentioned earlier, Galen Keller, this beautiful, brilliant blonde; all the guys were interested in her. During the trial I was focused on the proceedings and shied away from anything else, but Jim encouraged me to ask her out after the trial was over. And so I did and eventually Galen and I got married and had a child. Sadly, Galen died of cancer in 1991. Chris is thirty-five now. And I also had someone for Russell to meet, my good friend, Nelda Pelosi, and I said to her, "I think you'd like this guy." So I got Nelda and Jim together, and they eventually got married and had a kid—her name is Becca. After such a sad, tragic event, two children are in this world who would not have existed had it not happened.

Russell lived in the communal space for a while, but he annoyed everyone and moved up to Deer Island. Russell bought land up there that was inexpensive because the Trojan Nuclear Plant was within sight. He was going to build a house. He was so finicky that he wanted every joint and fitting to be just so. It took about two or three years for him to finish designing and redesigning this house. Nelda is a saint. For two or three years they lived in a tent with a woodstove through the winters. Of course, it turned out to be a wonderful house, which Nelda still lives in. Russell worked for the City of St. Helens in its design department. Later, he worked for the City of Beaverton, where he got to design what he loved—curves and radiuses, sidewalks, where roads intersected, and the like. He was so detail-oriented; that's how he approached things.

Every now and then on a Friday night, he'd bring over a six-pack of beer to my house. We'd sit there and talk and laugh and remember old days. He had this way about him. It would happen later in the evening when we both had had sufficient quantities of beer and whatever. He'd have a sort of shit-eating grin on his face and get a little look in his eye and he'd say, "You know, Joe, we've really gone over the edge this time . . . Oh yeah, we've done it now."

Like so many people, the things that drew Russell and me together also annoyed the shit out of me. He just talked on and on, but he was brilliant. He knew what he was saying. Everything that Russell did he did wholeheartedly. Our mutual friend Bill Eagle persuaded us to join the Kiwanis Club, and Russell became the president of the St. Helens Kiwanis Club. Russell joined the Sherlock Holmes Society. And pretty soon he was the president of the Sherlock Holmes Society. Like me, he was fascinated by railroads. He joined the Oregon Model Railroad Association and, sure enough, he became the president of the Oregon Model Railroad Association. One year the national conference was going to be held in Oregon and he was the one who made it all happen. So when he became convinced that he had a duty to talk about Kent State, he jumped into it with both feet.

DO YOU EVEN KNOW WHAT THE SHOOTINGS AT KENT STATE INVOLVED?

Our classroom presentations were very effective because our perspectives and experiences had been different. We gave this presentation dozens of times. We were good friends; one of us would be speaking and the other would jump in and there was no overlap and no interruption. It was a free-flowing narrative from two differing points of view. We were reluctant activists at first, but we felt compelled to tell the truth about how the Kent State shootings happened. We used to go in and say, "How old were you when Kent State happened?" and then it was "How old were your parents when Kent State happened?" and now it's "Do you even know what the shootings at Kent State involved?" It didn't take much planning; we'd have a few basic notes on a small piece of paper. It was never the same, and it always affected the students profoundly. And us, too; we'd usually stop and have a few beers afterwards and decompress a bit.

We became a formidable team when it came to telling the story and relating it to people. We did a "Teach-in for Peace" at Humboldt State University about fifteen years ago or so. We were with some wonderful and talented Vietnam Vets for Peace, including Charlie Liteky, congressional Medal of Honor winner, who threw his medal at the White House during Iran Contra; Brian Wilson, who protested the armament trains in California railyards during Nicaragua and had both of his legs cut off; Michael Hastie, who was a Vietnam-era medic; Marvin Simmons, Special Forces. And Camillo Mejia and Tim Goodrich, who were Iraq Veterans Against the War. When Russell and I put it together, it was seamless. The vets acknowledged our teamwork and tried to copy it, but no one else could pull it off as we did.

JUST AS HE WOULD HAVE CHOREOGRAPHED IT

Yeah, Russell was so fuckin' annoying, he was such a detailed person—and that's not me, I'm on the opposite end of that spectrum. I just treasured him so much, but I didn't realize how much I would miss him until he was gone. In 2007 Jim Russell, my dear friend, had a heart attack and died in his wife's arms, just as he would have choreographed it.

PART IX

Troubadours of Conscience

The Kent State Massacre

BARBARA DANE

Barbara Dane is a blues and jazz singer who has lent her voice to the cause of racial and economic justice since 1945. She became a significant part of the 1960s political folk scene. A guest at May 4 commemorations, her essay and unflinching lyrics underscore the weightiness of racial and economic justice to the overall struggle for social change. This piece was written in 1970.

This is a powerful ballad, written mostly by Jack Warshaw in England, sent to me soon after the events on the Kent State campus by mutual friend Peggy Seeger. I sang it many times during the years I traveled from one army base to another across our country; to Japan, where we have several naval bases; to the air force base at Mountain Home, Idaho; and wherever I was called by the groups of GIs organizing to resist the war in Vietnam. I sang it at campus rallies everywhere, at the huge peace demonstrations in Washington, and, most memorably for me, at the Kent State rallies commemorating the awful day of the killings and the students who died. I recorded it during that time, and these are the notes that appeared with the album.

The capitalist system, since its earliest days when little children were employed in the mills and sweatshops, has destroyed its young. In recent times it has demonstrated that it will not tolerate the most modest challenge to its power by murdering students during peaceful demonstrations on campuses.

There is a direct line of continuity from the murders at Orangeburg, South Carolina, of Sam Hammond, eighteen; Delano Middleton, seventeen; and

Henry Smith, eighteen, to the murders at Jackson State in Mississippi of Phillip Gibbs, nineteen, and James Green, seventeen, to the murders at Kent State, Ohio. The line continues to the needless victimization of hundreds of thousands of their generation who were sent away to fight and die or come home maimed in body or spirit, or to become addicted to drugs in Southeast Asia or Watts and Harlem, Scarsdale and Des Moines.

I have been to Cuba and China, and seen how enthusiastic and wholesome young people can be, even in 1973, when they are allowed a place in the building of a society rather than converted into a by-product of the death of a system. It is possible to get an idea of what it will be like someday when we have pushed our own society up onto the next stage of human development, but we won't have the satisfaction of seeing how it will work out in the full flowering genius of our own peoples until we get there. One thing is for sure and certain: the young people will stop being victims and become the hope and joy of everyone in those new times to come.

Jim Garland, miner and organizer in the notorious and bloody Harlan County mine strikes of the 1930s, wrote the song "Murder of Harry Simms" about an incident that shook him deeply. This story is something of a parallel to the original in that Harry, too, was full of idealism and he, too, was murdered in the first flight of his young hopes. In the words of Aunt Molly Jackson, Garland's sister and herself a legendary singing organizer in the struggle to organize the National Mineworker's Union, "Harry Simms was a young Jewish organizer who was murdered on Brush Creek, Knot County, Kentucky. He was walking along the railroad track with another fellow—they were going down to meet some writers who came to study the conditions of the miners—when the company gun thugs shot him." He was a young communist who volunteered to leave his home in New York and go to work with the miners during the bloody organizing drive, only to lose his life to ruling-class violence at the age of nineteen. The last line of his song is the same as the last line of this one because it is the only way we will see an end to that kind of violence.

The Kent State Massacre
Words: Jack Warshaw and Barbara Dane © 1970
Music: "The Murder of Harry Simms" by Jim Garland

Brothers, listen to my story,
Sisters, listen to my song.
Gonna sing of four young people
Who are now dead and gone.

Two of them were twenty,
And two were just nineteen,
Just stepping out to meet the world
Like so many you have seen.

It was in Kent State, Ohio
On a Monday afternoon.
The air was full of springtime,
The flowers were in bloom.
It was a scene of terror
That none will soon forget.
Young students stood with empty hands
To face the bayonets.

Alli Krause and Sandy Scheuer
Marched and sang a peaceful song.
Like Bill Schroeder and Jeff Miller,
They did not think it wrong.
They laughed and joked with troopers,
And some to them did say:
We march to bring the GIs home,
And we are not afraid.

No warning were they given,
No mercy and no chance.
The air was filled with teargas,
The troopers did advance.
Suddenly they knelt and fired,
The students turned and fled.
Thirteen fell at that moment,
And four of them were dead.

On the campus they were murdered,
In the springtime of their lives.
As angry sorrow swept the land,
Their friends and parents cried.
They'd hardly learned to struggle,
But witness they will be.
They died for those in Vietnam,
Also for you and me.

But while we march and mourn today,
There's much more we must do.
We must teach ourselves to organize,
And see the struggle through.
Blood flowed upon the 4th of May,
And we'll know its color well
'Til we sink this murdering system
In the darkest pits of hell.

As recorded by Barbara Dane on her album *I Hate the Capitalist System,* Paredon Records P-1014, available from Smithsonian/Folkways, Victor Bldg., 750 9th Street, NW, Suite 4100, Washington, DC 20001-4505 or from DNMusic@webtv.net.

Twenty Years Later

HOLLY NEAR

Holly Near has been a strong voice for integrity, justice, and peace for five decades. Influenced by social change movements around the globe, she writes and sings songs that look at the world through the lens of feminism, antiracism, and peace. She has performed during several May 4 commemorations. This song was composed in 1974. The introductory paragraph was written in 1990.

When the students at Kent State were killed, followed by the violence and killings later the next week at Jackson State, I was doing *Hair* on Broadway in New York City. *Hair* was an antiwar musical reflecting the discontent and confusion in society as a result of violence and racism. We protested the Kent State killings on the evening of May 4 by refusing to sing the finale, "Let the Sun Shine In," and instead invited the audience to participate in a silent vigil. A few years later, I was invited to write and sing a song for a Kent State memorial at which I joined Ron Kovic, Jane Fonda, Dan Ellsberg, Judy Collins, and many other longtime activists who gathered there. The song has grown over the years, new verses being added as violence continues to interrupt human potential.

Students in our country, at Kent and Jackson State
Shot down by nameless fire one early day in May
People cried out angry,
"You should have shot more of them down!"
But you can't bury youth my friend
We grow the whole world round

And it could have been me
But instead it was you
So I'll keep doing the work you were doing as if I were two
I'll be a student of life, a singer of song
A farmer of food and the righter of wrong
It could have been me but instead it was you
And it may be me dear sisters and brothers before we are through
But if you can die for freedom
Freedom, freedom, freedom
If you can die for freedom I can too

The junta broke the fingers of Victor Jara's hands
Said to the gentle poet play your guitar now if you can
Victor started singing until they brought his body down
You can kill that man but not his song
Because it's sung the whole world round

And it could have been me
But instead it was you
So I'll keep doing the work you were doing as if I were two
I'll be a student of life, a singer of song
A farmer of food and the righter of wrong
It could have been me but instead it was you
And it may be me dear sisters and brothers before we are through
But if you can sing for freedom
Freedom, freedom, freedom
If you can sing for freedom I can too

Woman in the jungle so many miles away
Studies late into the night, defends a village in the day
Although her skin is golden like mine will never be
Her song is heard and I know the words
And I'll sing them till she is free

And it could have been me
But instead it was you
So I'll keep doing the work you were doing as if I were two
I'll be a student of life, a singer of song
A farmer of food and the righter of wrong
It could have been me but instead it was you

And it may be me dear sisters and brothers before we are through
But if you can live for freedom
Freedom, freedom, freedom
If you can live for freedom I can too

One night in Oklahoma, Karen Silkwood died
Because she had some secrets that big companies wanted to hide
There is talk of nuclear safety and talk of national pride
But we all know it is a death machine and that's why Karen died

And it could have been me
But instead it was you
So I'll keep doing the work you were doing as if I were two
I'll be a student of life, a singer of song
A farmer of food and the righter of wrong
It could have been me but instead it was you
And it may be me dear sisters and brothers before we are through
But if you can die for freedom
Freedom, freedom, freedom
If you can die for freedom I can too

Women shot in Montreal by a man so full of rage
Makes me think of ancient time, back in the Middle Ages
This was not a single incident, this was not a one time tragedy
People all around the world must fight misogyny

And it could have been me
But instead it was you
So I'll keep doing the work you were doing as if I were two
I'll be a student of life, a singer of song
A farmer of food and the righter of wrong
It could have been me but instead it was you
And it may be me dear sisters and brothers before we are through
But if you can fight for freedom
Freedom, freedom, freedom
If you can fight for freedom I can too

The songs of Nicaragua and El Salvador
Will long outlast the singers who face the guns at war
They sing at the line of fire

And they sing from a fire within
All across the land the poets stand
El pueblo unido jamas sera vencido

And it could have been me
But instead it was you
So I'll keep doing the work you were doing as if I were two
I'll be a student of life, a singer of song
A farmer of food and the righter of wrong
It could have been me but instead it was you
And it may be me dear sisters and brothers before we are through
But if you can die for freedom
Freedom, freedom, freedom
If you can die for freedom I can too

This piece originally appeared in *Kent & Jackson State 1970–1990,* edited by Susie Erenrich.

Kent

GREG ARTZNER AND TERRY LEONINO (MAGPIE)

Terry Leonino is a Kent State shooting survivor, and Greg Artzner was a Kent resident on May 4, 1970. They joined forces in September 1973, becoming the musical duo known as Magpie. They wrote and performed the following song for the twenty-fifth anniversary of the shootings.

In my dream
I remember a walk with you in spring
The trees are full of blossoms
    And the air is full of song
You show me (Below that grassy knoll)
That place where just a few short years before (I heard that bell toll)
Four lives were cut short by execution (Calling us to freely speak and listen)
And others were changed for all time (With voices raised in anger)
While the killers walked away

In my dream
I see you there standing on that hill
The air is full of anger
    In the brilliant springtime sun
You're watching (We are standing)
As the soldiers in their uniforms conspire (Our innocence gone)
And together fashion this blind sacrifice (Unwitting in that moment)

And then, ascending the altar (We faced the blinding fire)
They turn and cut us down

In my dream
I see you in that moment of despair
The air full of confusion
    And hearts all full of rage
You're running
Along the bank of the river of their blood
Searching for reason where there could be none
Wondering who was next to fall before the gun
A daughter or a son

And then we knew
Those bullets were the answers to our questioning
The bell tolled for another day of reckoning
But what they couldn't kill are voices ringing still

In my dream
Twenty years had gone and we are there
Hearts are full of sorrow
    And the air is full of rain
You and I
Standing with our faces to the sky
The rage remains in our memory
Twenty years of tears
Can't wash it away

And from that time
The life that we are living full of questioning,
Our voices all the louder without cowering,
So that the voices gone will surely carry on.

In my dream
I see you on that hillside in the month of May
The trees are full of blossoms
    And the air is full of song
You and I
Standing with our faces to the wind
In a world where justice isn't just a word

Where freedom's voice above the guns can still be heard
And all our cries for peace have been answered
Bill and Sandy, Jeff and Allison
In our memory live on
They live on.

May 1995

An Eyewitness Recollection Thirty Years after the Shootings

TERRY LEONINO

Terry Leonino was on the Kent State University Commons on May 4, 1970, and an eyewitness to the shootings. This piece was written in 2000.

Like so many other times in our history, those of us who were witnesses could never imagine that we would ever be a part of what is so ugly, so wrong, one more moment of madness in the chapters of the book we call the story of America. But here I sit, just one person among many, who heard the shots that will ring forever, like the Victory Bell on the Commons that day, ring forever in the hearts and minds of those of us who lived through that time. In that one moment all we'd been taught about God and our country came into question, and we felt suspended in the deep pain of the reality that our thoughts and our words could so threaten our nation as to bring it to the place that it kills anything in its path, even its own children.

I was a commuter to campus, and came to school after days of not-so-peaceful demonstrations to attempt to gain some knowledge, only to find the doors of the Education building blocked by soldiers armed with machine guns, warning me to go in at my own risk. So, like many others, I went to the Student Union and tried to make sense of what militaristic madness had come over this campus. It was Vietnam and Cambodia permeating all the conversations. It was the voices of students and teachers and the music of James Taylor and Jimi Hendrix all loudly mixing together in a high-pitched, emotional dialogue over the questions that were bursting like the apple blossoms and the humming of the new spring, all coming to one big conclusion:

let's go outside to the Commons and talk, gather ourselves in one place and speak our minds about all we had been through and where we were all going. Many of us could not imagine what was about to happen. Many of us were just going to class as usual, but there was nothing usual about today or any of the days leading up to this day. There were tanks and there were guns and there were words and there were warnings. There were shots and there were screams, and they were herding us like cattle with their tear-gas masks and their triggers marked on targets. But I ask you, what kind of country kills its own? No, this was nothing new. It was just that no one expected it here on a "party" campus; white students, middle-class America. I have Dr. Frank to thank for he talked us all into sitting down after we were gunned down so more of us wouldn't fall. And then there were the reporters asking questions. Dorothy Fuldheim, someone I was used to seeing on TV, was now holding her microphone in the stunned faces of those who had barely gotten up off the ground, ground soaked with the blood of those who came to listen, speak, and those who just happened to be walking through the Prentice Hall parking lot, that was now the grave for four who looked like me, who could have been me, or my sister, whom I was frantically trying to find among this sea of faces.

Who was I to survive this? Why wasn't I dead? No time for such questions now; I've got to find my sister. Is she among the dead or dying? Why can't I cry? Why are they still herding us and talking to us like we were the enemy? Didn't they have the guns? "Disperse, go home, leave immediately!!"—Dr. Frank's words ringing in our ears—"It'll be a bloodbath! Only more of you will die if you don't leave now!" And so we did. I don't remember how I got home. But arriving the same time as I did was my sister. We hugged in the front yard and both of us began to cry, the first time for me. And I have been crying ever since. We were all branded troublemakers then—anyone who looked like me or called himself or herself a Kent State student. God help me to always be a troublemaker because I believe now that's why I was allowed to live: to continue to help stir things up, to use that freedom of speech they tried to shoot down that day! But they didn't shoot all of us ... they will never be able to shoot all of us! They tried again not long after KSU—at Jackson State. I am ashamed to say that my country barely took note of that or of Orangeburg, two years before, or any number of other cases of unjustified killings by authorities, summary executions that have gone unpunished. But then we in our country don't like to talk about these things anymore than we like to admit the genocide of Native Americans, slavery, racism, or many other injustices. But as long as there are those of us still here to tell our stories and people like Susie who care enough to ask us to tell them, I feel lucky enough to be alive to share mine. Thirty years and here I sit again remembering, learning, reflecting . . . isn't that what the so-called "memorial" at Kent State says to those parents who lost their children, and to the country that shot us down, to those of us who were there, and to students of today? Inquiring? We will never stop questioning "authority" . . . we're still here and your bullets can never silence us!

You Carried Us

For Professor Glenn W. Frank (1928–93)

GREG ARTZNER AND TERRY LEONINO (MAGPIE)

Greg Artzner and Terry Leonino are the musical duo known as Magpie.

With an M1 guardin' every door you said 'let's not study these books no more'
So side by side out into the sun to join the voices shoutin' down the gun
But that's when peaceful anger met the searing gas, the bayonet
Before pointed and insistent threat we marched over that hill
You carried us over that river
You carried us over that river
You carried us over that river
Where we wait still, for peace to come,
For peace to come
But over on the other side there really was no place to hide
As on the crest they wheeled 'round, a terrifying, crackling sound
The bullets flew through steel and wood where rightfully the innocent stood
You defended us, did what you could against those bound to kill

When the shooting was all done and the scarlet river deep did run
We could not see through anger blind, through chaos, raging state of mind
Until your desperate, crying plea, reminding us of what might be
The slaughter we had yet to see if we don't walk away
    To resist another day

© 2014 Greg Artzner and Terry Leonino, April 25, 2014

Rolly Brown and Magpie performing during the forty-fifth commemoration (Source: Brad McKelvey)

PART X

Annual Rituals and Historic Markers

The Candlelight Walk and Vigil

JERRY M. LEWIS

Jerry M. Lewis is professor emeritus of sociology at Kent State University. An eyewitness to the shootings on May 4, 1970, he has since been involved in researching, memorializing, and lecturing about this tragic event. He also has generously shared his experiences with countless numbers of students and visitors through presentations, interviews, and tours of the site. This piece was written in 2000.

INTRODUCTION

This year on the thirtieth anniversary, Kent State, as it has done in the past, held the annual candlelight walk and vigil to remember its fallen students. This essay describes and interprets the annual vigil held each May 4 on the campus of Kent State University. It has three parts. The first portrays events of May 4 and my involvement with them. The second part describes the origins and structure of the annual candlelight walk and vigil. It explores the meaning of the events in relation to the themes on the memorial of inquire, learn, and reflect. The third part examines the ethics of remembering.

MAY 4, 1970

In late April 1970, the United States Army and Marines invaded Cambodia and broadened the war. This sparked protest throughout the United States—

mostly on college campuses as Nixon had indicated the United States would not expand the war.

Two days after the Cambodian invasion, on a Saturday evening, the Ohio National Guard came on campus because the ROTC building had been attacked and burned to the ground. Protests continued through Sunday.

In 1970, I was an assistant professor of sociology at Kent State University, having come to KSU in 1966. Shortly before noon on Monday, May 4, I went to the Commons area to attend a rally as a faculty marshal. I thought a rally might be held to protest the presence of the Ohio National Guard on campus. Once I reached the grassy, open Commons, I passed students who had been gathering around the Victory Bell for the past hour. I watched the crowd for about fifteen minutes when the National Guard moved against the students, driving them off the Commons with a tear-gas attack. Students responded very angrily to the attack, which did little more than provoke them.

The Guardsmen continued to advance on students and drove them toward a practice football field. I had been taking care of a student near the parking lot who had been teargassed by the Guard. I looked up and saw the Guard retracing their steps from the parking lot over the hill to the Commons. As they got to the top of the hill, Guardsmen fired their rifles. We later learned that at least twenty-eight of the over seventy Guardsmen had discharged their weapons. Many Guardsmen fired into the air or the ground. However, a small number fired into the crowd, killing four Kent State students and wounding nine others. I had been standing twenty yards from Sandy Scheuer, who was killed, but took cover when the firing began.[1]

The Kent State shootings caused the first national college student strike in United States history. The pain of Kent State was reinforced ten days later by the killing of two students and the wounding of several other students at Jackson State College (now Jackson State University) in Mississippi.

Three hours after the shootings, Kent State closed and was not to open for six weeks as a viable university. When it resumed classes in the summer of 1970, it was charged with three new responsibilities. The residues of this early activity remain today.

First, we as a university had to bring aid and comfort to our own. This began early on with faculty trying to finish the quarter with a reasonable amount of academic integrity. Second, along with finishing the quarter, there was a call for the development of alternative forms of protest and conflict resolution to help prevent tragedies such as the May 4 shootings and the killings at Jackson State. The university responded to this challenge with the Center for Peaceful Change, the faculty marshals and observers, and other conflict-resolution programs. These efforts continue today with diversity programs, residence hall community-building programs, attempts at reducing conflict on campus, and the annual conference on violence.

Third, and soon after the shootings, many people began to talk about some form of remembrance and memorial for the students.

May 4, 2000, marked the thirtieth anniversary of the shootings. An extensive program, including a conference and artistic programs, carried the anniversary. An important aspect of the anniversary activities was the annual candlelight walk and vigil, begun in 1971, that has become a cornerstone of the annual commemoration. In carrying out these commemorations, Kent State refused, after the tragedy of May 4, to be frozen in the role of victim apologizing for "letting" the National Guard kill students. We as a community resisted this definition and worked hard to be more than thirteen seconds and a victim. One major way the university accomplished this was through the annual candlelight walk and vigil.

THE ANNUAL CANDLELIGHT WALK AND VIGIL

The annual vigil started, as most things do, with a brief conversation. In late fall of 1970, I was talking with Michelle Klein, who was a student of mine and was on campus in May. We were exploring issues related to an appropriate commemoration and decided the best thing would be a vigil where students, faculty, and whoever wanted to attend would stand at the spots where the four slain students had fallen in the Prentice-Taylor parking lot.

We made our ideas known to university officials. The initial response of the university administration was negative. We were told that President Robert White wanted only between four and eight people on the entire hill and parking lot at any time during the vigil. I told one of his representatives that I thought there would probably be about two thousand people on the hill, and there's not much they could do about it.

The estimate of two thousand was too high, but the numbers were clearly in the hundreds for the first vigil. Almost immediately when people heard about the vigil, we started getting calls of encouragement for our efforts.

Independently of us, another student, Jeff Auld, proposed that there be a march around campus. Under the encouragement of university officials, we got together, and the march was combined with the vigil. In the remainder of the essay, I will refer to the vigil only. However, it should be seen as two distinct events—the candlelight walk and the vigil in the parking lot.

What happens at the vigil? It has evolved over the years, but basically the candlelight walk begins at midnight on May 3. There is a procession around campus, which usually takes about forty-five minutes. There is no significance to the route followed; it's really just for convenience. There are a couple of points where you can look back to see the row of candles behind you. The walk starts from the Victory Bell on the Commons and ends at the Taylor Hall parking lot. People who are associated closely with the shootings stand during the first vigils: the wounded students; the parents of the slain or wounded students; and leaders of the May 4th Task Force.

At the conclusion of the candlelight walk, the actual vigil begins. All the vigils are half-hour segments through the night until the beginning of the commemorative program the next day on the Commons. What has evolved recently is that the people standing during the last four shifts walk to the Commons about 12:15 P.M. on May 4 to mark the transition to the other commemoration activities. The vigil concludes with the ringing of the Victory Bell at 12:24 P.M. on May 4.

Initially I was in charge of the vigil, handling the many details of planning the route, putting out sign-up sheets, and making the usual types of plans that any event requires. A number of agencies had to be dealt with, including the university police, parking services, staff and faculty in Taylor Hall, the press, and special guests who might attend the vigil. Soon the vigil graduated to being sponsored by the Center for Peaceful Change (now the Center for Applied Conflict Management). In the early 1990s, the management of the vigil shifted to the May 4th Task Force, and they have handled its administration ever since in a very commendable manner.

The significance to participants has been captured in a master's thesis by one of my students, Scott Reid, who did a dramaturgical study using participant observation of the 1990 and 1991 vigils drawing on the ideas of sociologist Erving Goffman. Reid concluded that the candlelight vigil represented a theatrical performance based on the predictability of the ritual aspects such as the same walk route, location of the vigil places, and the half-hour vigils.[2] All these aspects are very important to the participants.

One of the unique aspects about the vigil has been the effort to keep it a personal experience for the people who attend: students, faculty, Kent City people, staff, and family and friends of the slain and wounded. Over the years I have had to really, and sometimes nastily, resist people who wanted to play music, read poetry, or give speeches. Some people on the far political left have tried to have their own perspective put forward at the vigil, particularly during the walk. But these displays have been resisted by vigil organizers. However, since the early 1980s, Kaddish, the Jewish prayer of mourning, has been said. This is certainly appropriate since three of the four slain students, Jeffrey Miller, Allison Krause, and Sandy Scheuer, came from the Jewish tradition.

The vigil itself means several things. First and foremost, it allows people to work through the pain of the killings. It provides an opportunity for closure.

Second, it is a historical enactment of the event. People are placed where the students fell. When freshmen, in particular, attend, they are amazed at the distances involved. It's a teaching device. People learn about the dimensions of the protest that went on during that day in 1970.

Third, the vigil also serves a humanitarian purpose, broadly speaking, of allowing people to say that an injustice has happened and it should not happen again—ever.

Fourth, it has also become an important campus ritual, indeed, perhaps the most important one, even though some students and faculty never attend the vigil. It is a way of participating on a campus that doesn't have much tradition to it. To some, it may be a ritual to be attended because it's there.

Rituals are important for organizations. They give people a sense of meaning, tradition, and continuity. One way the military sustains itself is through rituals. I think if we're trying to reduce militarism in our society, we should provide alternative rituals to those that exist in the military. The May 4 rituals can serve this purpose.

Lastly, it facilitates the process on the memorial expressed in the words "Inquire, Learn and Reflect."[3]

THE MARKERS

The facilitation of inquire, learn, and reflect, as well as the commitment to the candlelight vigil, has been enhanced with the building of the parking lot markers. They are lighted fixtures surrounding the locations where the four students fell when they were shot. Each has six posts with light that come on at night. For me, the markers represent a permanent candlelight vigil, as well as the university's statement that it will not forget the events of May 4.

On September 8, 1999, Kent State dedicated the markers that show where Jeffrey, Allison, Bill, and Sandy fell on May 4. The markers—in the spirit of inquiry, learning, and reflection—can help us understand our own personal agendas about May 4. It is difficult to do this for people whom we did not know personally, but we can understand the meaning of the markers by contemplating the actions of the parents of the slain students.

Beginning with the marker closest to the Pagoda from where members of the National Guard fired, we stand at Jeffrey Miller's spot. I recall Jeffrey Miller's mother, Elaine Holstein, connecting with Mary Ann Vecchio (the subject of a powerful photograph) as they walked in the vigil march in 1995. Two women, linked in tragedy, reached out to each other. The next site, marking where Allison Krause was shot, leads me to think of her father, Arthur, with his powerful frame and booming voice saying, "Jerry, never let what happened here be forgotten."

We come up on Bill Schroeder's spot, the third marker in distance from the pagoda. I remember his mother, Florence, moving me to tears with her simple declaration that although there was criticism and controversy, like me, she felt that "we think the memorial is just fine."

Lastly, to Sandy Scheuer, who was on her way to class to avoid the tear gas in May 1970. Her parents, Martin and Sarah, often came to the annual vigils. I remember one cold May 3 in 1979, when they learned that I was to be promoted to full professor in the fall, they gave me a resounding "Mazeltov," forgetting their pain and wishing me success. Each of us brings an agenda to the markers. But perhaps the most important one is the reminder of what the families of the slain and wounded students have suffered. Perhaps the markers can help us imagine it and encourage us to make the world better in honor of the four families.

THE ETHICS OF REMEMBERING

In this concluding part I want to explore some issues related to the ethics of remembering.

When one talks about the ethics of remembering, what immediately comes to mind is the ethical issue of forgetting those who should be remem-

Michael Pacifico lighting candles prior to the annual candlelight march in 2015 (Source: Brad McKelvey)

Annual candlelight walk in 1995 (Source: Michael Pacifico)

bered. While that is certainly an important point, it is not one that I have set for myself in this concluding part. Rather, I want to talk about ethical issues related to active remembering.

Two core assumptions must be addressed before we examine these ethical questions. First, it should be noted that remembering is always contextual. In the case of the May 4 tragedy, the context is the university community with its culture and roles of faculty, staff, and students. Further, adding to the context at Kent State was the fact of the Vietnam War. Therefore, ethical concerns revolve around the norms and conventions of university culture.

Second, we need to explore issues around why we remember. Three come to mind. One, we remember to honor the fallen. Two, we remember in the hope that the events remembered, often very tragic, might never occur again. That is, as George Santayana said, "Those who cannot remember the past are condemned to repeat it."[4] Three, the larger society demands that we remember. The first two seem obvious, but let me develop the third. I often said that Kent State does not belong to the university but to the larger society. Many people were deeply affected by the event of May 4 and its aftermath. The larger community expects that Kent State will do something each year to memorialize the four students. In other words, the demands for remembering are extrinsic to the university culture.

Given these assumptions, I want to turn to the ethical issues associated with remembering, which I address in "Emotional Pain for Those Who Remember" and "Truth-Seeking and Remembering." Let's explore each in turn.

Candlelight vigil in 2015 (Source: Brad McKelvey)

EMOTIONAL PAIN FOR THOSE WHO REMEMBER

In order to truly remember the fallen and wounded students, one has to experience what happened in May 1970. In social psychologist Charles Cooley's powerful terminology, we must practice sympathetic introspection to truly capture the events of May 4. We must put ourselves in the situation of being students, faculty, staff members, or National Guardsmen. This can be quite emotionally difficult. So I ask this question: *Do those who encourage remembering have the right to inflict emotional pain on other people to remember?*

TRUTH-SEEKING AND REMEMBERING

A core value of a college or university is the uncompromising search for truth whatever the consequences. A college or university professor commits his or her perspectives—theoretical, methodological, and empirical to this pursuit. Yet often the process of remembering creates abstractions that move the remembered event or person away from empirical reality. For example, Abraham Lincoln is not nineteen feet tall.[5]

In Kent State's May 4 case, the May 4 Memorial is clearly not representational. Also, it is not on the site of the shootings, but near where students were killed and wounded. This question is raised: *Does the process of remembering, which is often based on an abstraction, harm the values of truth-seeking?*

SOME TENTATIVE ANSWERS TO THE ETHICAL QUERIES

The first query is the causing of emotional pain while remembering. Frankly, I do not know how this can be avoided. Every time I take people to the shooting site and they stand at the markers and look where the Guardsmen were when they fired, a look of shock or pain comes across their faces. This is particularly true of Sandy Scheuer's spot, which is over 130 yards from the Pagoda—the site from where the National Guard shot. Each of the markers help us understand the distances that the slain students were from the National Guard.[6] Perhaps the best way to cushion this pain is simply to prepare visitors for it before they come to the memorial.

The second question related to remembering is the tension between ethical issues and the values of inquiry in colleges and universities. How do we resolve this tension? One obvious answer is to try not to distort, in the *process* of remembering, the empirical truths of the event(s) being remembered. But when one looks at the May 4 Memorial, that may happen. It is clearly an abstraction.

The recently placed markers in the parking lot for Taylor Hall and Prentice Hall answer the ethical query that I raised earlier. The markers clearly show where the students fell. However, empirically there are still problems. First, there are no physical markers to indicate where the National Guardsmen were when they fired. That is a problem that must be addressed in the

The vigil's end (Source: John Rowe)

future. Second, there are no actual indicators in or near the parking lot where the nine wounded students were when they were hit by the Guardsmen's bullets. Since a memorial is a continuing process, these problems will likely be resolved in the future.

NOTES

This essay is dedicated to Sarah and Martin Scheuer in honor of their daughter Sandy.

Some aspects of this essay were drawn from a previously published article: Jerry M. Lewis, "Social Remembering and Kent State," in *Democratic Narrative, History and Memory,* ed. C. A. Barbato and L. L. Davis (Kent, OH: Kent State Univ. Press, 2012), 176–93.

1. Thomas R. Hensley and Jerry M. Lewis, *Kent State and May 4th: A Social Science Perspective,* 2nd ed. (Dubuque, IA: Kendall/Hunt Publishing Co., 2000), passim.

2. Scott Reid, "Developing a Methodology for Dramaturgical Analysis: The Results of Dramaturgical Analysis of Two Annual Candlelight Marches Commemorating May 4, 1970" (MA thesis, Kent State Univ., 1991), 51.

3. The words *inquire, learn,* and *reflect* came about in the following way. In the committee work that led to the call for a memorial, there was considerable discussion about what the memorial should accomplish. At one point in the discussion I proposed that people who came to the site were trying to find out what had happened. This process was in three stages of finding out, learning, and thinking about it. During the discussion, someone said that people should reflect on the shootings and that the site should be a reflective one. Later I was assigned to write the first draft of the call for a memorial. In that draft I framed the memorial process as inquiring, learning, and reflecting. The committee changed the wording to inquire, learn, and reflect. While the memorial was being built, I suggested to KSU President Michael Schwartz that the words be placed on the memorial. Schwartz agreed and asked the memorial designer, Bruno Ast, to do it, which he did.

4. George Santayana, quoted in *The Oxford Dictionary of Quotations,* 4th ed., ed. Angela Partington (Oxford: Oxford Univ. Press, 1992), 555.

5. *The Lincoln Memorial,* http://library.thinkquest.org/17188/lincoln.html.

6. The distances of the slain students from the National Guard were Jeffrey Miller, 270 feet; Allison Krause, 330 feet; William Schroeder, 390 feet; and Sandra Scheuer, 390 feet.

Parking Lot Dedication Remarks

CAROLE A. BARBATO

Carole A. Barbato was a Kent State University student on May 4, 1970. Her friend Sandy Scheuer was killed on that fateful day. She helped create the May 4 audio walking tour, which led to the opening of the May 4 Visitors Center, and finally National Landmark Designation for the site. Dr. Barbato, a communication studies professor at Kent State, was coauthor of This We Know: A Chronology of the Shootings at Kent State, May 1970. *She passed away on April 30, 2014. This piece was written in 1999.*

Thank you, President Cartwright. As Dr. Cartwright mentioned, I am a Kent State faculty member. In 1970, I was a Kent State student, one who had the privilege and the sheer joy of being friends with Sandra Scheuer and who enjoyed working crossword puzzles in the Hub with Bill Schroeder.

Perhaps because I knew Sandy, remembering her and Bill and the others who lost their lives has always been deeply important to me. And perhaps because I was on this campus in May 1970, I believe it is imperative that the historical integrity of this site be preserved for generations to come. For both these reasons, I am gratified to have been a part of the process that brought us to this day.

During the last three decades—a lifetime ago, it seems—a variety of memorials have been established in remembrance of Allison, Jeffrey, Sandy, and Bill, and to acknowledge the history that happened here.

Of course, there is the May 4 Memorial on the other side of this parking lot. Dedicated in 1990, it stands as a symbol of what happened here and of

Parking lot marker (Source: Brad McKelvey)

the Vietnam era. And it serves as a solemn reminder of the need to inquire, learn, and reflect on the need to respect opposing views and to resolve conflicts peacefully. We need to learn that violence and intolerance toward others is never the answer.

For myself and others, the most moving memorial is the annual candlelight walk and vigil, a tradition established by my colleague and friend, Dr. Jerry Lewis, with the help of students. This tradition has been carried on by members of the May 4 Task Force. Each year since 1971, students, faculty, staff, alumni, and community members from near and far have gathered on the Commons the evening before May 4. With candles illuminating their path, they walk silently around the perimeter of the campus. This moving procession ends right here, as students and others take turns standing vigil throughout the night in the four spots where Kent State students shed their blood. This is sacred ground and it is fitting that we are permanently preserving it now.

On May 4 of every year, classes are recessed from noon to 2:00 P.M. Many students, faculty, and staff use this time to attend the annual commemoration program organized by the students of the May 4 Task Force.

As you've heard, the events of May 1970 moved many faculty members to pursue scholarship focused on nonviolent solutions to conflict and democratic values from public service to civil discourse.

The university established a Center for Peaceful Change, which evolved into the Center for Applied Conflict Management. This commitment to seeking nonviolent solutions is also seen in our interdisciplinary Institute for the Study and Prevention of Violence.

As some faculty redirected their research after 1970, others expressed grief, hope, and renewal artistically—in words, paintings, sculpture, glass, music, and dance.

I'd like to mention one final memorial I think my friend Sandy—as well as Bill, Allison, and Jeff—would approve of the most: scholarships in each of their names for talented, caring, and committed students here at Kent State University. Jeff, Allison, Sandy, and Bill were not able to complete their dreams, but their dreams live on through these students and through all those who follow them. These scholarships are among the most prestigious awards made by the Honors College and they serve as a true living memorial.

The markers we dedicate today stand separate from these and many other existing memorials on this campus. They are an unmistakable physical reminder to all who walk this sacred ground that history was made here. They show us—and will show all who follow us—where four gifted young people lost their lives so senselessly on May 4, 1970.

Thank you. [Pause]

The time has come to formally dedicate the four markers. Very fittingly, this will be done by students—student members of the May 4 Task Force. Their dedication to inquiring, learning, and reflecting on the events of May 4 is significant since none were alive in 1970. I personally would like to thank them for their commitment to understanding.

The B'nai B'rith Hillel marker in the parking lot of Prentice Hall on the Kent State campus (Source: Brad McKelvey)

Preserving the Site and Story of the May 4, 1970, Kent State Shootings

LAURA L. DAVIS

Laura L. Davis is professor emeritus of English at Kent State University and the founding director of Kent State's May 4 Visitors Center. She was a freshman on campus during the 1970 events. Davis was one of the four coauthors of the application to add the May 4 site to the National Register of Historic Places, which was approved in February 2010. This piece was written in 2019.

MAY 4, 1970

At noon on May 4, 1970, I joined three thousand classmates and spectators assembled on and about the Kent State University Commons. Five hundred feet across the field, Ohio National Guardsmen were forming a line that would number 137 enlisted men and officers. Students were continuing a rally begun on Friday, May 1, to protest President Richard Nixon's expansion of the Vietnam War into Cambodia. We also consciously were affirming our First Amendment rights in the presence of the National Guard. We felt that the Guard did not share our right to occupy the Commons and obstructed our efforts to redress the government with our grievances.

In the next few minutes, the Guard ordered students to disperse, launched tear gas from its skirmish line, and moved out while dispensing more tear gas. Much of the gas dissipated in the thirteen-mile-per-hour wind in the large open space. Over the next twenty minutes, there was some chanting, gesturing, and rock-throwing by students. Guardsmen also threw some rocks.

Students retreated as the Guard advanced. Many students and spectators left the area. There was movement, yes, but the scene was not chaotic. Those from campus who had gathered did not imagine that the rifles they saw were loaded. There was no sense of the disaster to come.

After moving off the Commons and reaching the top of Blanket Hill, I went down the slope to the right so that I would get out of the path of the Guard. At the bottom of the hill, on the back side of Lake Hall, I waited, assuming that the Guard would march for a while before returning to their original position. I thought the rally would reconvene and then wind down naturally.

For about ten minutes, the Guardsmen were out of my sight. The line reappeared, marching up Blanket Hill, heading toward the Commons. The way was clear. When the formation reached the top of Blanket Hill, Guardsmen turned in unison, lifted their rifles in unison, and began to fire. They fired down into Prentice Hall parking lot, opposite from where I was standing. I froze in place, curled over, and began screaming, "They're shooting their guns! They're shooting their guns!"

Someone pulled me into Lake Hall. It may have been my friend Linda Wernick, with whom I walked off the Commons. I clung to her in the lobby, sobbing, "Why did they shoot? Why did they shoot?"

Within minutes, a person came in and said people had been shot. As Linda and I left the building, my gaze to the right took in a line of blood drops near the drinking fountain and disappearing down the corridor.

Outside, we walked up the narrow drive to the parking lot, stopping before reaching a boy lying facedown on the roadway. Jeff Miller. All my mind could process was "There is a boy lying still on the ground. I should not go too close and stand over him. That would be gawking. That would be disrespectful."

Linda and I walked on and came to a boy lying on his back. His feet were on the ground and his bent knees were weaving back and forth in slow motion. His legs were clad in orange pinwale corduroy bell-bottoms. Because I also had a pair of orange corduroy bell-bottoms, I would remember and learn that he was Bill Schroeder.

From the slope on which Bill lay, I looked up and surveyed the scene in a slow, panoramic motion. I saw numerous clusters of people standing and looking down at the ground. I realized that they must be standing over others struck down by the bullets.

Linda and I walked back down to the Commons, to the Victory Bell where the rally had begun. People gathered in quiet protest, broken at times by shouts and gestures toward the Guard reassembled at the other end of the field. Bonnie Henry from my dorm came up to me and said, "Allison's been shot." "Allison?" I wondered. I could not think who she meant.

Soon it was made clear to us that the Guard would not permit us to stand gathered at the bell. What was now several hundred people moved to the slope along the Stopher-Johnson edge of the Commons and staged a sit-in in rows as neatly spaced as desk chairs in a classroom. After a time, everyone's beloved geology professor Glenn Frank, who taught the large class I was taking that quarter with Bonnie and Allison Krause, began pacing back and forth before the front row—just as he did in class. But he was pleading with us, crying. I had never seen a grown man cry before. It took a while to convince us that we must leave or we would be shot, too. Those I was sitting among made a plan. We would follow Glenn Frank in a line across the Commons toward the tennis courts. When our feet reached the bordering sidewalk, we would each run in the different direction we had picked. That way, if the Guard started shooting again, someone would be alive to tell the story.

Dispersed, students were ordered to evacuate campus within two hours. At 6:00 P.M., I was home sitting at the kitchen table. My father walked in the back door, looked at me, and said, "They should have shot all of them."

During the twenty-fifth May 4 commemoration in 1995, I sat in the Kiva for a 9:00 A.M. session featuring Todd Gitlin and Scott Bills that would have been the keynote in a schedule less crowded with stellar events. I spotted my East Liverpool colleague Carole Barbato across the room. Carole and I of course knew each other. But neither of us knew the connection the other had to May 4: Carole also was a student at Kent State during the shootings, witnessed the disturbing aftermath that afternoon, and lost friends Sandy Scheuer and Jeff Miller. As some of you reading this know, a marriage was born. We became *Carole and Laura*, the way that Tom Hensley and Jerry Lewis were *Tom and Jerry*. We could finish any sentence the other started. We invariably showed up in coordinating outfits (print jersey dresses, olive-green skirt suits, denim and long necklaces) as though we regularly made the 9:30 P.M. phone check the night before to see what the other was wearing. When our May 4 work was underway, we misbehaved in the Archives searching for Chuck Ayers cartoons, laughing as we tried to shush each other in squeaky mouse voices because we were gasping for air. To ease the tension of innumerable long days with long hours at the tiny worktable in my office in Moulton Hall, we made up our own vocabulary of four letter words so we wouldn't disturb the nun meeting with students in the lobby outside my door. I started it with the epithet *dink*, which Carole often found the need to draw out, inimitably, to *Motherdinker*.

Five years into team-teaching the university's May 4 course and five years closer to a time when Carole and I would retire from Kent State, we began wondering and worrying: "What will happen when no one is around to answer the questions? Who will be there to tell the story?"

MEMORY AND HISTORY

What happened on May 4, 1970, was written on the hearts and minds of generations in the United States and around the world. But the history was not written on the site for years to come. The May 4 Coalition fought hard in the 1970s to preserve the site through recognition from the Department of the Interior so that history could be understood within the place. The time arrived both to renew that effort on behalf of the *place* and to relate the *story* within the site.

In 2006, the first narrative script to be installed within the site was composed by a small group convened by Kathy Stafford, then vice president for university relations, and included Tom Grace, Carole, and me. We drafted text for the Ohio Historical Marker now installed at the Prentice Hall end of Taylor Hall. Leading up to this time, ten years of legal battles had come to an unsatisfactory end. A substantial percentage of the letters sent after the shootings and comments in the newspapers ranged from unsympathetic to venomous. The state governor demanded that a building be erected to cover the site and thereby bury the history. The university changed its name for a time from Kent State to slant *Kent*. Expecting difficulty navigating *any* review body in Columbus, where the marker application would be sent, the group created a sound, but stolid text. For years after, Carole and I delighted in the more vigorous version returned by the reviewer, Eric Schnittke. He arrived for the marker dedication during the 2007 May 4 commemoration seeming wonderfully young to us. Neither he nor his mother exhibited signs of the contested past. After Tom Grace and the new president, Lester Lefton, whose term began July 1, 2006, took the podium, Kathy Stafford concluded the dedication with a sweep of her arm up toward Taylor Hall and the announcement: "This will be the site of the May 4 Visitors Center." She doubled our excitement of the previous evening when Tom Hayden delivered a call to action to the 1960s generation: "It is time for us to write our history."[1] I whispered to Carole, "That is what we are going to do."

In September 2007, David Middleton asked Carole and me to accompany him and a group of his visual communication design students to visit the design firm Gallagher & Associates, creator of a range of museums on historical sites. The students would learn about the opening stage of the designer-client collaborative process. Neither Carole nor I questioned her decision to stay back for the weekend's football games: she was devoted to football. I would be the mouse in the corner, listening and taking notes about museum design. What luck, given what we had ahead of us with the May 4 Visitors Center on the horizon. After a tour of the offices, the Gallagher staff did what was their usual—gather as a firm around a huge conference table with their prospective client. A member of the Gallagher team turned to me and asked me to define the purpose of a May 4 museum. You are wondering how I did not see this coming. All eyes turned on me. I croaked out a couple of sentences. I heard myself say, "The purpose is *to tell the truth.*"

Student visitors jumped in. How do you know what the truth is? There's your truth, and then there's the other person's truth. How about the National Guard? And so on.

The roundtable over, Gallagher's senior graphic designer Shane Allbritton came over to talk to me one on one. She told me how thoughts of Kent State brought back a terrible episode when a family member was murdered in her family's restaurant. She knew what it was like to be close to unexpected, unjust violence.

Over the years, Carole and I would often encourage each other with "Saving the world one person at a time." Shane speaking to me at that moment balanced the scales, and a part of me did appreciate the students' question-everything stance. Still, I rode back to Ohio thinking, "How will it ever be possible to create the museum if what needs to be said can never be said?"

It turned out that Shane and the students at Gallagher that day showed me we never know what someone else's story is. Our job was to tell the May 4 story to the point that it was known at that time with the best, documented facts. One person at a time, visitors would draw their own conclusions from the information.

THE BEGINNINGS OF THE MAY 4 VISITORS CENTER

A new Kent State president could expect to hear from many directions about the May 4, 1970, shootings. When President Lester Lefton arrived, one of his vice presidents was working on the Ohio Historical Marker and Jerry Lewis took the initiative to give him two tours of the site. In November, he received a proposal from Sarah Lund-Goldstein, a Kent State student and member of the May 4 Task Force. The proposal requested a new May 4 Visitors Center to be located in the *Kent Stater* office, to which the Task Force would relocate from the student center. The proposed center was to display artifacts and other items, be staffed by two permanent employees, and have an operating budget. Thus President Lefton soon encountered varying constituencies, each demonstrating continuing interest in honoring the slain students and preserving the history of May 4.

Academic Affairs was notified in 2006 that it could preliminarily plan for a May 4 Visitors Center conceived as a museum—*if* Academic Affairs could secure a space. At that time, my responsibilities as associate provost for planning and academic resource management included budget, strategic planning, academic personnel management, curriculum, reporting, retention initiatives, academic and administrative technologies, distance-learning development, quality improvement, liaison to the Aerospace and Military Science programs—and space planning. In that era of continuous budget cuts, academic units understandably held tight to their space allocations. By the 2007 May 4 commemoration, I was able to develop an academic space plan to make the center feasible. It featured two college deans changing locations; new Architecture classroom and gallery space being created at the gym annex; and space being repurposed for the museum on the second floor, at the corner of Taylor Hall closest to Prentice Hall overlooking the parking lot. In the end, the square footage increased modestly to nineteen-hundred square feet to accommodate the design plan for a professionally designed museum named the Kent State University May 4 Visitors Center in the former *Stater* offices. Advantages included a wide view of the Commons and half of the historic site; easier access to the museum without need for an elevator; and better linkage of the indoor museum with the outdoor Walking Tour and May 4 Memorial. There was no space inside the museum for quiet reflection after viewing the exhibit, but people could easily find that quiet spot at the memorial just steps away. Further, the location paid tribute to the importance of student photographers and journalists in preserving the historical evidence of what happened on May 4, 1970.

The space secured, I was appointed to convene an ad hoc planning committee[2] that brought together members from across the Kent State community interested in discussing the potential features of a May 4 Visitors Center, one that might be externally funded and operate on a self-sufficient basis. Basically, from this point forward, I acted as both coordinator of administrative tasks for various May 4 projects and editor and contributor to their content. Carole and I always felt thankful that we were in positions later in our careers that uniquely allowed us to heed the call we felt had been delivered to us. Because of our ties to May 4, we each wanted to follow that call. At the same time, we felt a responsibility to Allison, Jeff, Bill, and Sandy, the May 4 community, and the historical legacy to do so.

The working group completed its assignment in December 2007. The vision, mission, and objectives statements for the center affirmed that it would be designed to serve all constituencies, be a central source of information about May 4 set in the context of the American Vietnam experience, and promote respect for differing viewpoints. The accompanying May 4 Visitors Center museum proposal from the committee to the president covered a range of issues. It documented public interest in such a museum, the potential for visitors, and historical importance. It looked forward to an extensive consultation process (on which President Lefton would request a report) with a broad range of stakeholders, including the families of those killed and those who had been wounded on May 4. It identified multiple potential sources of funds: pooling scatterings of existing funds, fundraising through the university, the possible sale of locally designed goods during the fortieth commemoration, and specific public and private grant opportunities. It drew an example of a thematic approach for the exhibit that would work well in the size of the allocated space. It promised to strive for historical accuracy and follow the best contemporary methods of museum design. In response, President Lefton approved exploratory planning and asked that, if built, the new May 4 Visitors Center be "first class" and "powerful."[3]

FUNDS AND FOUNDATIONS

As the calendar turned from 2007 to 2008, opportunities needed to be acted on quickly. As the ad hoc working group came to an end, many of its members joined new projects related to the creation of the May 4 Visitors Center. Carole and I decided we had just enough time to meet the January 2008 deadline for a planning grant proposal to the National Endowment for the Humanities (NEH). We provisionally lined up Gallagher & Associates and its affiliate GToo Media to join the team should grant funding materialize, as we had to provide at the time of submission names, bios, and roles, and sample URLs with detailed descriptions (the early grant applications planned on creation of a website).[4] Then, on a dark afternoon in December, Carole and I took our last chance before the holidays to scrutinize the grant guidelines together. The application, we read, must show how significant humanities themes would be reflected in the project and specify humanities scholars on the planning team. We talked about how Paul Fussell's *The*

Great War and Modern Memory could help frame our discussion and used the following quotation in the application: "The Great War was perhaps the last to be conceived as taking place within a seamless, purposeful 'history' involving a coherent stream of time running from past through present to future."[5] We added, "American youth in the sixties would repeat the experience of those during the century's first great war, with the reality of the war experience changing them irrevocably and changing the views of their sisters and brothers at home." As we pondered additional sources of humanities scholarship to use as a frame, I remembered a book review comparing Jay Winter, a current public history expert, to Fussell. The closest library with Winter's books on the shelf was at Youngstown State University, where Carole's daughter was enrolled. We made a list for Alissa Barbato to check out. A week later, any hesitancy I had was dulled by fever and over-the-counter medication for the flu; I left a message on the desk phone of Jay Winter, prolific author and Charles J. Stille professor of history at Yale University. A week after that, he called my cell just as a doctor entered the recovery room where my husband Tom was emerging from anesthesia (the procedure was routine). Stunned that Winter called me back, I excused myself to take the call. Within five minutes Jay was on our team![6] Our entry for an America's Historical and Cultural Organizations grant titled "War and Remembrance in the Vietnam Era: A Public History Visitors Center at Kent State" made it to DC in time.

Making the May 4 Visitors Center a reality by necessity would mean building consensus and making connections. Our cause fit well with the NEH mission: "Because democracy demands wisdom, NEH serves and strengthens our republic by promoting excellence in the humanities and conveying the lessons of history to all Americans."[7] We wanted to convey the lessons of history. To do so, we were asked to find external funds. The organization that could best provide funds required us to engage a broad and strong cadre of scholars in our project. Throughout 2009 and 2010, we built that cadre so that when the time came, we were ready to go. We learned from Jay Winter the nature of *public history,* which confers, he said, the responsibility to build a bridge between history inside the academy and outside and between the state and family experience.[8] We created many opportunities for the Kent State community, town and gown, and many other members of the greater public to be a part of shaping the May 4 Visitors Center content.

In May 2008, people were drawn into 101 Taylor Hall by posters in the windows announcing "Future Site of the May 4 Visitors Center" and encouraging the public to "Help Build the May 4 Visitors Center." The posters' display of the center's Web address *www.kent.edu/May4* added encouragement that the center would become a reality. David Middleton and I created the center's first fundraising brochure. The Kent State University Foundation established the May 4 Visitors Center Fund account for operations and donations, which continued to come in from the public. It joined a KSU Foundation account opened in December 2007 for an endowed internship in memory of Bill Schroeder. Endowed internship accounts followed for Sandra Scheuer and Jeffrey Miller and continue to be sought. Students holding the internship would gain valuable experiential learning and help the public understand the legacy of May 4. In June 2008, Kathy Stafford transferred to the May 4 Visitors Center donated funds in University Relations' foundational account in the amount of $100,000 approved for commencing a design for the center. The charge to raise external funding for the center was making progress.

Carole Barbato, David Middleton, Mark Seeman, and I headed to Washington to open discussion of the design with Gallagher and to meet with a program officer at the NEH, the latter still our best hope for major external funding. Feedback in 2008 from the NEH grant review committee, comprised of a cross-section of citizens, recognized the Vietnam War as an "enduring conflict," and the shootings' relationship to it as a "contributing aspect" of its history. The committee praised the content of the application and consultant scholar and design teams, while calling for more information on the objects in the exhibit and their relation to humanities themes. Karen Miles, NEH senior program officer, added practical advice: broaden the story beyond Kent State, especially by including greater coverage of the war and the changes of the 1960s. She observed that the site's listing on the National Register of Historic Places (National Register) would strengthen our case and recommended adding more scholar consultants from outside the university. The grant application did not succeed in raising federal funds in 2008, but it did expand the concentric rings of collaboration and consultation for the center to help us in our work, connect on a national level to new expertise and affirmation, and make the May 4 Visitors Center stronger in purpose, content, and design and—after three more exhaustive and exhausting submissions—funded.[9]

In each of the four years, the review committees exceeded our expectations with their appreciation of the significance of the May 4 history. That Kent State as a community and institution was resolute in embracing its legacy through ongoing commemorations, symposia, dedication of the May 4 Walking Tour, pursuit of National Register status, and efforts to create the May 4 Visitors Center helped the cause. When we submitted the third and fourth grant applications, NEH senior program adviser David Martz became a sounding board to help us articulate our case as clearly and compellingly as possible. We explained more directly that the museum exhibit would not editorialize; rather, visitors would have context and come to their own conclusions. Martz noted that the museum had an unspoken message: Young people can make a difference. He made us *see* that this is the message of the museum, from the many images of children in gallery I to the comments recorded by seven-year-olds at the end of gallery III. In 2011, our application achieved highest marks possible from the reviewers, he told us, and it was awarded at the maximum level that year, $300,000. To make matters better, just weeks before, the university moved forward with funding the May 4 Visitors Center. Each of Kent State's sixteen college and regional campus deans contributed from their areas to a fund of $667,000. These donations, the university noted, were an expression of "the university's leadership role in promoting nonviolence and other humanities values."[10] The university also invested in an operational budget for the center and created a permanent director position, which I filled in 2012 until my retirement in 2013.

Carole and I had been thinking for some time of proposing to cochair the Symposium on Democracy, which had been founded in honor of Allison, Jeff, Sandy, and Bill for the thirtieth May 4 commemoration. While we had been thinking of the symposium in 2010, we instead recruited participants from the ad hoc Visitors Center committee to form a working group for the 2009 symposium to move along work toward the May 4 Visitors Center.[11] Presentations in 2009 addressed iconography of the civil rights movement; remembrance and history; reconciliation; the role of media in shaping historical content and public opinion; filmmaking as history; and the impact of the Kent State shootings in Canada and asked, "Who controls the story?" Providing the keynote address, Jay Winter concluded his remarks by speaking directly to the audience: "The chance we have is not to transcend injustice, which is an impossibility, but to transform silence about injustice into something active, purposeful, dynamic. . . . To construct a space of meditation, for visitors to this place is one way—in my view an appropriate way—to ensure these events and their meanings are never forgotten."[12]

The 2009 Symposium on Democracy fulfilled its promise as a forum for scholarly discussion and thinking to ground the content development and design process for the May 4 Visitors Center. To help build the library of scholarship on May 4, Carole and I worked with presenters to transform their presentations into essays for publication in *Democratic Narrative, History, and Memory*. To further the mission of expanding the knowledge of the facts of what happened on May 1–4, 1970, a chronology illustrated by ten historic photographs was included in *Democratic Narrative,* published by

Kent State University Press in 2012, the year the doors opened to the Kent State University May 4 Visitors Center.[13] One passage that I carry around in my mind from the book is from Daniel L. Miller and Suzanne Clark's essay, "Wars on Trial in Three Landmark Documentary Films: *Night and Fog, Hearts and Minds,* and *Taxi to the Dark Side.*" The films examine World War II, the Vietnam War, and the US war in Afghanistan during the George W. Bush administration. Connecting to Winter's comments above about remembering May 4 and to other moments in *Democratic Narrative* essays, Miller and Clark describe *Night and Fog*'s closing "image of the ruins of one crematorium . . . emblematic of the broken-down house of mankind" and quote the narrator's voiceover: "'We pretend it all happened only once, at a given time and place.'"[14]

MAY 4 VISITORS CENTER DESIGN AND CONTENT

Activity exploded in 2009. Kent State signed a contract with Gallagher in January 2009 to design the May 4 Visitors Center. With input from Gallagher, we hit the send key on January 28 for "The Meaning of May 4 Then and Now: A Public History Visitors Center at Kent State," our second NEH grant application for the center. Gallagher's first design book proposal submitted in March presented three choices for floor plans on the first floor of Taylor Hall. The university selected the middle-sized plan, which featured an effectively simple three-part design—context, what happened on May 4, reaction and impact. The consultative design process continued to expand, as the content for the Visitors Center was still to be developed.

Extending the scholar base as advised by the NEH, we held three forums in late February and early March. These meetings included faculty from Kent State and other universities (some of whom joined the meetings electronically), several professionals, community members, and students.[15] Administrative assistant Kathy Spicer provided valuable operational support for these forums and others, along with the Democracy Symposium and related book project, the fortieth May 4 commemoration, and design of the Visitors Center and Walking Tour in 2009 and 2010. During the forums period, on February 5, May 4 Task Force members reviewed the basic Visitors Center plan and offered sound advice: consider what happens with the exhibit when more information about May 4 comes out later and gather information from people using a variety of media and methods. Throughout the years of planning, Carole and I would meet regularly with the Task Force and their faculty advisers, first Karen Cunningham and beginning in

2009 Idris Kabir Syed, to discuss the in-progress May 4 history projects and ways to connect more broadly with the May 4 community and the public during annual commemorations.

Forum participants were able to refresh or expand their knowledge of the basic facts of the history via the original version of a chronology of May 1–4, 1970, compiled by Carole from the sources available at that time and given its first review by Mark Seeman, Jerry Lewis, and me. For the scholars forums, Carole added a variety of photo illustrations. Writing this, I see that her doing so was a homage to Peter Davies, author of *The Truth about Kent State: A Challenge to the American Conscience,* which she always recommended as a first read when people asked what was the best May 4 book. (For me at that time it was Joseph Kelner and James Munves's *The Kent State Coverup.*) The chronology's photos also were a sign of what was to come: for the major May 4 projects that followed, Carole acted as photo specialist. Started in 2008, the chronology was seen by many eyes and honed many times over the years, even after Carole left us in 2014. The heart of the May 4 *story,* the chronology lives on in some form in each of the May 4 history projects, up through the National Historic Landmark nomination in 2016.

Discussions during the forums were held in breakout groups and meetings of the whole, with every voice heard. Ideas were generated from the ground up for a foundation document, key themes, and a content outline for the May 4 Visitors Center exhibit. Carole and I were able to actively participate in the discussions, as a court reporter recorded the proceedings. Sharon Barry, whose experience as an exhibit writer included work for the Smithsonian, the Great Lakes Science Center, and the Rock and Roll Hall of Fame and Museum, created the draft synthesis and outline of the discussions, which were shared with participants. She also incorporated discussions from subsequent meetings that included the Kent working team of Vice President for University Relations Iris Harvey, David Middleton, Mark Seeman, and Carole and me and the core Gallagher design team in DC, led by creative director Cybelle Jones. Cybelle first met with the president and executive officers at Kent State on March 31 and continued to do so throughout the Visitors Center project. Sharon kept the files updated through May 2010 with the many revisions Carole and I synthesized from ongoing consultation until the foundation/outline/content documents morphed into the early script for the May 4 Visitors Center's permanent exhibit, from which point Carole and I saw the script through to completion. In general, reviewers were asked for and about additions, corrections, what was most important, specific items to illustrate the ideas, if the script communicated effectively, and which of two or three phrasings for particular items worked the best. As the script developed, I maintained the master copy and wrote/edited the captions and other wording for the exhibit. Carole searched for and gathered files for photos and other graphic-display items.

Our first big gathering of community input began in April 2009, coming from surveys completed by members of the Kent State University Retirees Association and discussion during four public meetings. At each meeting for the campus and public, volunteer recorders gathered comments from groups kept small to encourage any and all ideas. People were enthusiastic that plans were underway to create a museum to tell the May 4 story. Of course, there were flashes of a negativism that was and always will be part of the complex history. Over the years the May 4 history projects were in progress, there was a blog that contained several messages with violent language. And someone left a drawing of a stick figure with a gun in the Visitors Center space. For most, the feeling about the May 4 Visitors Center was "shoulda been done long ago."

Seven major themes emerged in the concept development work and became the skeleton of the exhibit. The themes are listed below on the left (one of the original theme statements is broken in two); on the right appears the corresponding headers/components in the three galleries of the built museum:

Gallery I:
    The Sixties → "The Sixties: A Nation Divided"
    Counterculture and Generation Gap → "Generation Gap"
    From Civil Rights to Human Rights → "Social Justice"
    Dissent in a Time of War → "Vietnam"

Gallery II:
    What Happened and Why: The search for historical accuracy → "May 4, 1970: What Happened"

Gallery III:
    The Impact of May 4 Locally, Nationally, and Internationally → "Impact" and "Reaction"
    May 4, 1970, in American History → three hanging panels featuring lasting effects of May 4
    Why May 4, 1970, Still Matters Today → "What Is the Meaning of May 4 for Today?"

The themes fed into interdependent processes of design of the space and development of the content. The Gallagher team kept working with the evolving ideas, articulating them through design techniques. The right-hand wall immerses you in the colors, icons, causes, and tensions of the

1960s, so that you can better process what you learn about the shootings on May 4 in gallery II. Real 1960s television cabinets with old-school cathode-ray tube monitors show you what the 1960s generation saw growing up. As an example, a vignette on the Social Justice screen shows the little brother of Andrew Goodman, murdered for registering African American voters during Freedom Summer 1964. The boy has tears streaming down his face, yet is singing with the attendees at Andrew's funeral, while from overhead you hear the lyrics "We shall overcome."

All that the right-hand wall expresses in a layered riot of images and information that physically reaches out to pull you in the left-hand wall distills in six huge point-counterpoint images. The last pair of images shows Kent's October 1969 Moratorium March against the Vietnam War, with Allison Krause in the center of the photo helping to carry the protest banner. When Shane Allbritton sent us a cropped version of its planned counterpoint photo, it showed two Middle American women staging a counterprotest. Gone was the figure on the curb at their feet of a boy of about three in jacket and slacks, his blond hair in a Princeton haircut. Photos from the 1960s regularly caused us consternation as they were frequently in a portrait format rather than in the landscape format most often needed for the Visitors Center display. After much lobbying of Shane, we gave up, with sadness. Weeks later, we received a file. There was the little boy on the curb. Shane had found a bit of street scene to patch in on the left-hand side of the photo so that cropping would accommodate the child. Why was it so important to us? John Kennedy was assassinated when we were young. Like all young people, we were home from school on the day of the funeral because of this national event (a first in our lives) and watched the procession on TV. We saw John-John in his short pants and little coat, with his Princeton haircut, lift his hand in a salute as the caisson went by.

Gallery II draws down to a darkened, low-ceilinged space that *encloses* the visitor. You stand in the midst of figures of people close to life size in the huge photos on your left and right and on the wall-sized film screen in front of you. You may be surprised by the facts that you learn. You may reach for the box of tissues on the floor. When designers Cybelle, Shane, and Carl Rhodes came to see the completed museum for the first time, they looked down at the box and said somberly, "We didn't think of that." If Carl were with you, he'd point out as you exit gallery II that the shapes made by the carpet below and the ceiling above subliminally point like arrows to the impact wall in gallery III. The display of news headlines, photos of protests, angry letters, sympathetic telegrams in response to May 4, and artifacts go all the way from the floor to the ceiling and then wrap around the corner to the left. The response to the

Kent State shootings was so broad and so deep that it cannot be contained in the space. In the center of the impact wall is a memorial to Jeff, Sandy, Bill, and Allison, explained by a black-and-white placard: "The newspaper in each home town publishes a front-page story on its resident daughter or son. Leading ordinary lives as college students, Bill, Sandy, Jeff, and Allison did not foresee that their stories would be read around the world."

As work toward the museum progressed, people became drawn to the space—a place where they could share how they remembered and pay respect to those who were lost. At the fortieth May 4 commemoration the next year, I met John and Joanne Rath, Kent State alumni who graduated in 1969. We talked for a long time, standing in front of the large poster with the Visitors Center plan in 101 Taylor Hall, near the windows overlooking the Commons. On May 11, 2010, they became the first external donors to donate funds for a Walking Tour trail marker. They chose marker 1 and asked for the following to be inscribed on their block on the donor wall: "Boston Massacre: 5 dead. Kent State Massacre: 4 dead." Their inscription about marker 1, which describes the national social-political climate in 1970, captures the heart of why the Department of the Interior recognized the site of the shootings as having "national significance." The Raths were soon joined by Dennis and Madeline Block, whose contributions included support of a May 4 Visitors Center internship in remembrance of Bill Schroeder, with whom Madeline had grown up. Other donors, private and corporate, joined the cause.[16] Erica Meuser, one of hundreds of artists who gave expression to the May 4 history, both donated and lent work from her series *In America's Wake* in 2010 and 2011 to draw people into the space for the future May 4 Visitors Center. Meuser's pieces offer moving interpretations of features of the historic landscape, such as Lilac Lane alongside the Commons, combined with figures that suggest timeless narratives of human experience. In another way, alumnus Allen Richardson, journalist, and his partner Karen Curry, faculty member in journalism at Drexel University, offered their expertise for both the fortieth commemoration planning and the evolving May 4 Visitors Center script.[17] Many people contributed in many ways, so wanting the May 4 Visitors Center to happen.

THE MAY 4 WALKING TOUR

People and their communities are said to have a deepened sense of relationship to the past as the forty-year mark of a significant event approaches. In 2009, the university agreed that the May 4 Walking Tour would be a good lasting piece to have in place for the fortieth May 4 commemoration. Groundwork done through the forums and other consultations in the spring generated both major concepts and illustrating details for the May 4 Visitors Center. The Ohio Humanities Council felt very positive about granting funding to help mark the watershed commemoration and provided funds toward scholar participation in creation of the tour. Gallagher transferred attention midyear from the Visitors Center to the Walking Tour. There was just enough time to complete the design, fabrication, and installation of the outdoor exhibit, which features three components: trail markers, educational brochure, and documentary film.

The Walking Tour's seven trail markers are mounted in locations ranging from the far side of the Commons behind Oscar Ritchie Hall to the edge of Blanket Hill overlooking the place where Jeff Miller fell. Carole located photos and I drafted text for the markers and brochure, building on the consultation to that time. We were further advised by Gallagher and scholars and invited experts who reviewed the draft content.[18] Marker 1 provides context: May 4, 1970, immediately became known as "the day the war came home." Marker 2, titled "By Any Means Necessary," quotes Gov. James Rhodes's promise on May 3 "to eradicate the problem" of student protest. Marker 3 displays what I feel is one of the most telling photos of the day. It shows the Guard lined up at the far edge of the Commons behind Oscar Ritchie; demonstrating students five hundred feet across the Common at the Victory Bell; and a student with books under her arm passing through the area between. The Commons was the hub of the campus, and this was the route for foot traffic on every school day. A quote from Joe Lewis on this panel observes: "There was no feeling of danger or impending catastrophe." The remaining trail markers continue the chronology up through the immediate aftermath of students attempting to provide aid to their fallen classmates and Glenn Frank's desperate plea to convince students who staged a sit-in to protest the shootings to leave the Commons.

David Middleton lent his expertise to creating the locator map for the trail markers and all of the graphic design features of the Walking Tour brochure. It is beautifully printed on heavy coated paper and machine folded to a size that he wisely insisted should fit in a jeans pocket. The mood-setting period photo on the cover of the first edition, which sends you back in time, was taken on May 5, 1970, by Alan Canfora. In the foreground you see the tree that served as cover to save his life. To the back stands the Pagoda. When the brochure is folded, the graphic way-finding map on the back identifies the location of the seven trail markers and where each of the thirteen students fell when they were shot. The places where the students fell are underscored when you open the brochure to its full size and view the second map inside.

The interior map is similar in color and tone to the 1970 photo on the cover of the brochure. The tone of the large interior map is explained by its creator's being a children's book illustrator—Chris Sheban, a Kent State grad. We used the map inside the back cover of James A. Michener's *Kent State: What Happened and Why* as a jumping-off place: Michener's bird's-eye view is similar, but we rotated the angle so that you are looking at the site from the Midway Drive end of Prentice Hall parking lot rather than from Memorial Gymnasium. The illustration is *true* in the way an illustration on one page in a children's book is true, conveying the events of a period of time and not just what is on a particular page, giving the essence of mood and character. For instance, the pines and trees stand on Blanket Hill, but they have not been inventoried and painted in one for one. Perhaps you might find yourself thinking of a battlefield like Gettysburg when you look at this map: here is a place where people lived, with buildings and inhabitants and fields and groves through which people walked. And then came a day when soldiers dissected the woods, ascended the slopes, and fired their weapons. The march of the soldiers at Kent State is traced in bright white lines onto the soft tone of the background. The scope of the firing in Michener's map and bullet traces in the original May 4 Memorial brochure are given an updated interpretation here in the position of Jim Russell's shooter. Red lines trace the bullets across the muted background, and the positions of where the students were when they were shot are marked with red badges.

Steve Zapytowski, design and technology expert for theater and dance, was recruited to act as director for an original documentary film for the Walking Tour. Carole worked with Steve to review and sort thousands of photos, selecting the best cropping in the case of duplications and also the best view when photos featured the same moment. Five hundred best-of photos, from many different sources and never before brought together, were selected for the documentary. First, these needed to be put in chronological order. Luckily, Steve had access to a large basement storeroom in the Music and Speech building to lay out the five hundred photos and leave them in place during the many weeks it took to refine placement of each photo for its proper day, hour, minute, and second in the chronology. For the film, this was only the beginning. Steve began the complex and lengthy process of directing and producing a film that in technique compares to Ken Burns's *The Civil War*. Steve chose to name the film *May 4, 1970: Someone to Tell the Story*. The documentary is loaded on iPods that may be checked out by all visitors at the May 4 Visitors Center and used for group visits. The soundtrack of the documentary also is available by phoning 330–672-MAY4 (6294).

While Carole and Steve were sorting photos, I wrote a script for the documentary. It was reviewed by local and external experts and revised with the benefit of feedback from 250 Kent State students, faculty and staff, and community members who came along on practice tours. Feedback helped refine wording and timing in the narrative, as well as the route and placement of the trail markers for the Walking Tour. As for the film, from the beginning, we wanted Julian Bond to be its narrator. I emailed him. He agreed. Late afternoon on frigid January 16, 2010, in Washington, DC, Steve, Carole, and I met Julian Bond in a recording studio. He was wearing a slim dark wool overcoat and a beanie pulled over his ears. Carole and I were smitten. Before we started recording, I observed that relating what happened on May 4 had so much inherent drama that we were not looking to create a sense of rising action that might be conveyed through the narrator's inflection. We believed that adding drama would mislead viewers into believing that students must have known what was coming and that the shootings were inevitable. I asked for a few retakes for one reason or another, but it was different when, near the end of the recording, Julian Bond's voice broke as he spoke Glenn Frank's plea for students to leave the sit-in on the Commons so that they would not be killed too. In the studio, we were moved, as you will be when you hear the recording. Before we wrapped up, Julian kindly recorded a comment to be used within the May 4 Visitors Center. Still starstruck, we were excited that he accepted a ride home on the blizzardy day. Carole entered the address into her GPS as a memento. She left it there forever.

Carole and I did permissions clearances for the Walking Tour in 2009. In 2010, Carole began researching gaps in information about the photographers and working with Cindy Kristof, who managed areas in the University Libraries related to copyright law and fair use and was approved to assist with the extensive permissions clearances for our project. Carole even made a trip to the Yale Archives to turn over photos in the hope that a name was penciled on the back. Sometimes it was. Cindy talked to all manner of archivists and photographers and their heirs. For some, Cindy observed recently, May 4 was an emotional event and they weren't prepared to share their memories or feelings about what happened, even so many years later. Often her conversations were with staffers at places like Getty Images, the largest of the type of company that had attached copyrights and hefty price tags to so many of the photos for which we needed permission. During the projects, I often fretted over how people would be able to understand history and use it as an example to others given the hold such businesses have on the artifacts of our times. But so encouraging was the grace and generosity with which others shared their photos and helped us with access, including John Filo, Howard Ruffner, Paul Tople, Beverly Knowles Burger, John Rowe, Yale University Manuscripts & Archives, *Akron Beacon Journal,* Kent State University Special Collections and Archives, and so many others. People gave so much of their time and themselves because they wanted the May 4 Visitors Center to become a reality.

Yoda. That was our code name for Cybelle Jones, creative director, now principal and executive director at Gallagher & Associates. She guided us through the mysteries of museum design. She imagined fantastic ways of putting our story on the walls of our space: What if people looked in a mirror as they entered the museum and saw *themselves* back in the 1960s? She nurtured our spirits. It is impossible to capture in words on the page the depth to which Cybelle and the entire Gallagher firm committed to working with us as a community to get our history told and our museum built. That we didn't know how to build a museum was the lowest of the obstacles. There had been no process of reconciliation and healing. Some denounced what we were doing. We were not working with a long-accepted set of facts as the Kent State history. We did not begin with an agreed-upon historical site. And yet, from the first moment, Gallagher understood the significance of what had happened at Kent State. The firm stayed with us for four long years, giving so much more of their expertise and their hearts than would ever be paid back in monetary terms. They became part of the May 4 community. At the dedication of the May 4 Visitors Center, Cybelle said that there was never such a big story that needed to be told in such a small space and that this, the smallest exhibit Gallagher had ever created, was the most difficult because of the contested nature of the story, particularly in its own community. Gallagher was "trying to create a dialogue" to show that "America wasn't one thing." Their hope was that the Visitors Center would "carry on that dialogue" and from the exhibit people would learn "how we stand up for our rights."[19]

THE NATIONAL REGISTER OF HISTORIC PLACES

In 1977, the May 4 Coalition was formed to block university attempts to "'bury the history of May 4,'" by "'literally bury[ing] the site of the shootings under a sprawling building.'"[20] Scott Bills noted that differing views of what constituted the site lay at the heart of the struggle. The university considered the site to be where the students fell. Protestors believed the site encompassed all of the ground on which the events on May 4 took place.[21] Mark Seeman, who had served ten years on the Ohio Historic Site Preservation Advisory Board (and chaired 2003–4), reopened efforts to have the May 4 site recognized by the federal government. By the summer of 2007, Carole Barbato, Jerry Lewis, and I had joined him in preparing a nomination to place the site on the National Register of Historic Places.

Mark observed recently that coming to know the history through print sources and being particularly influenced by the original May 4 Memorial brochure map, he didn't realize early on that the site had two halves. There was no question by the time we got together that for context, we would include within the site boundaries all locations of events immediately leading up to the shootings. But, as Mark noted, the National Register criteria required that we *prove* that the site wasn't just the Prentice Hall parking lot side of Taylor Hall. First, we used our historical knowledge to draw in yellow an outline of the site on a base map. On September 27, 2007, we saved that map in our computers as "may4th_1970_battlemap_final.jpg." For the black-and-white base map in this file, Mark engaged with geography graduate student Kevin Surbella to use historic and contemporary aerials from the US Department of Agriculture to create a foundation for definitive mapping of the May 4 site. We were on secure ground there. What about the yellow line? Why was the file called battlemap? The phenomenally helpful officers in the Ohio State Preservation Office, Barbara Powers and Franco Ruffini, suggested applying the principles of Patrick Andrus's *Guidelines for Identifying, Evaluating, and Registering America's Historic Battlefields*.[22] For months Mark, Carole, and Jerry researched photos in the Archives, and the four of us discussed the evidence for the outline of the site. We created the narrative at the same time. I also became keeper of the text files and editor, for which the most important job was to incorporate each individual's contributions into the master file so as to achieve a coherent text and unified voice.

Aware that locally we refer to the history as *May 4*, while the world uses the term *Kent State*, we titled the nomination "May 4, 1970, Kent State Shootings Site." The nomination also needed to prove that the events on the campus on May 4 "made a significant contribution to the broad patterns of our [United States] history" and that its significance was achieved prior to the required waiting period of fifty years.[23] We noted that the historical significance of May 4 was best understood in the context of what historians call the *long sixties* (a term we learned from historian Tom Grace), beginning with the civil rights movement and the antinuclear peace movement and continuing to the end of the Vietnam War, all of which was the backdrop for the national student protest movement. Understanding social changes during this time, exemplified in the generation gap, was equally important. The shootings reverberated on many planes. May 4

- caused the first national student strike and the largest student protest in US history[24]
- further turned America against the Vietnam War,
- affected executive and congressional decision making about the war,
- changed policy in forty-eight states (including Ohio) for dealing with civil disturbances on college campuses,[25]
- hastened the end of Nixon's presidency,
- spurred lowering the voting age to eighteen,
- and created legal precedent in the US Supreme Court.[26]

The killing of Allison Krause, William Schroeder, Jeffrey Miller, and Sandra Scheuer and the wounding of nine other Kent State students—Jim Russell, Robbie Stamps, Joe Lewis, Dean Kahler, Alan Canfora, Doug Wrentmore, Tom Grace, Scott Mackenzie, and John Cleary—instantly and enduringly became a symbol of government confronting protesting citizens with unreasonable deadly force.

There had been some discussion about applying for listing on the National Register in previous years with members of the administration. Still, as the work proceeded, we faced a tactical decision. We decided to wait until we had found our way to a well-developed and well-organized document before sharing a draft with Kent State President Lefton, which took place on January 20, 2009. The president would have preferred to see it earlier in the process. We did not know that he was working on an extensive plan to address the physical plant of the university, long sidelined due to successive state budget cuts. Even without such a plan, many property owners' first question is, "How will historic status affect my ability to provide routine care or make changes to a property?" The simplest answer is that it does not. Meetings with an architecture firm specializing in preservation and the university architect at the University of Virginia resolved all questions about the implications of recognition from the Department of the Interior. From my perspective, the resolution signified President Lefton's quality as a leader to learn more, adjust thinking based on what he learned, and to build consensus with his leadership team. That leadership team, his vice presidents, had arrived at Kent State without hesitations about recognizing the legacy of May 4. The time had come.

President Lefton of course was interested in the parameters of the site. As importantly, he wanted to fully understand the history—precisely what had happened and where it had happened. As you've read above, he had already participated in two tours of the site. Understandably, due to the breadth and topography of the site, the length of time over which events unfolded, and the complexity of movements, he still had questions. Alan Canfora and I gave him a third tour of the site in early March 2009. He was enthusiastic afterward and wanted arrangements made for every member of the university's board of trustees to be given a tour. By mid-April, the trustees also were given a copy of Peter Davies's *The Truth about Kent State,* which was particularly instructive due to its many photographs. In addition, each trustee and executive officer received the current draft of the nomination and the penultimate one. In September 2009, Kent State's board of trustees passed a three-part resolution of support for nominating the site for the National Register of Historic Places, creating the May 4 Walking Tour and the May 4 Visitors Center, so that history could be recounted where it happened and, in turn, be best understood.

For a National Register review process, the major hurdle comes at the state level. We felt we had made a strong case, aided by those who generously served as expert readers: preservation specialist Jeff Brown, external historians Kevin Kern (University of Akron) and Tom Grace (Erie Community College), and faculty member in Pan-African Studies and May 4 Task Force adviser Kabir Syed. Alan Canfora provided exceptional help as well, answering many questions about details during the years of writing for this project and the others you read about here. For the National Register, although we had prepared well, we did not know what the reception would be during the hearing in Columbus. At the hearing, Deputy Historic State Preservation Officer Franco Ruffini took up the Kent State nomination. Within minutes, he was tearful as he made his case. He had been a student at Kent State on May 4. Carole, Mark, Jerry, and I choked up. When Franco finished speaking, other board members around the table spoke with equal feeling about the historic importance of the shootings. Others who had come to provide testimonials—Renee Romano, chair of history at Oberlin University; Leigh Herington, former minority leader of the Ohio State Senate and attorney, as well as a student witness to the shootings; and Kathleen Chandler, Ohio State representative—added their reasoned and heartfelt comments. As the remarks concluded, the audience rose to applaud recommendation of the Kent State shootings site for the National Register. It was the first time I had ever been in a room of strangers who felt as one the inexcusability of the shootings and the rightness that the story be told. The site was placed on the National Register of Historic Places on February 23, 2010, the year of the fortieth commemoration of the shootings. The Ohio Historic State Preservation Office bestowed each of us with a merit award for "preparing exemplary documentation" in our nomination and its contribution to preservation in the state. Mark, as first form preparer, was additionally recognized. Patrick Andrus of the battle-map guidelines and reviewer of our nomination for the National Park Service (NPS) noted elsewhere that the exceptional and *proven* significance of what happened at Kent State made the case for National Register status before the standard fifty years.

During his Democracy Symposium address for the fortieth May 4 commemoration, Rep. John Lewis recognized the place of the Kent State shootings within the long, still necessary struggle for civil rights:

> Allison, William, Jeffrey, and Sandra. And nine other students who were also wounded put aside the comfort of their own lives to get involved in the circumstances of others. They did not have friends or family in Cambodia. But they heard the call . . . of Martin Luther King Jr. and others who had spoken out against the war in Vietnam. . . . They decided to get in the way. It was good trouble. Necessary trouble. But it was dangerous, very dangerous to speak truth to power in those days.[27]

At the dedication of the Walking Tour and National Register plaque on May 4, 2010, Florence Schroeder said of her son, "Bill was a poet and one of his last poems included the line, 'Learning from the past is of prime consideration.' I pray that we have all learned that lesson."

Carole and I had started 2010 with what had become our ritual, submitting what was now our third NEH grant application. Each year, the exhibit script continued to be reviewed by different groups. Every time feedback came in, Carole and I would sit together and analyze it and first tweak the left-hand side of the script. What had been themes and threads in that column in 2010 were labeled *Text*. Then we'd add suggestions for illustrative details to the right-hand side of the script, now labeled *Visuals, Media, & Objects*. A cadre of scholars from inside and outside the university responded to the June 30, 2010, exhibit script and design book. The page of comments to the reviewers at the beginning (yes, I wrote a whole foreword) explained that the script and design still were works in progress and that the reviewers' comments would be applied to these working documents. Requests to the reviewers included the following asks: Are the words and graphic or design details "effective"? Do the "dots connect" so that the whole thing hangs together? Will the material connect with "general and varied audiences"? You'll have to believe me that the next thing was done to make the reviewers' work easier. Reviewers received a questionnaire with seventy-eight questions. This seems excessive, but at this point, every object in the museum design had a number. If people had no comment, they could simply number 1 to 5 to rank an item for effectiveness. Or they could write a comment if they wished. Other questions sought new ideas for illustrations for particular points. Sometimes the reviewer was asked to choose one of several possibilities that had been identified earlier. So, for instance, Clarence Wunderlin, professor of history, looked at the three choices for quotes from Mario Savio's call to students during the Free Speech Movement at Berkeley and voted with an emphatic *XX* for: "There comes a time when the operation of the machine becomes so odious ... And you've got to put your bodies upon the gears." Clarence added a helpful note: "BERKELEY IN THE SIXTIES has footage of him saying those words—extremely effective in that documentary."

In the spring semester, the February 2011 version of the exhibit script and design book current at that time were reviewed by students taking the May 4 class and in the higher education administration courses taught by Susan Iverson. They responded to a revised version of the long questionnaire. Matt G. said of the middle set of large iconic photos for the left wall of gallery I, one featuring a commune bus and the other a nuclear family in a new convertible: "I especially like the Ken Kesey photo in comparison with the oldsmobile [*sic*], it really shows how prevelant [*sic*] the generation gap really was, and Ken Kesey, Neil Cassady and the other merry pranksters are the first family of the hippie generation." Rachel K. offered constructive criticisms for the Vietnam War section of gallery I: "I didn't think that the cartoon was very funny, if you can make it funnier then keep it. I don't think you need the dead Vietnamese guy, seems out of place. All the local stuff is really good." As to whether the Mario Savio quote (settled on as a result of the previous review) "will connect with its audience," student Ricardo N. answered: "Simply profound—Passive ways must cease if change is to come."[28] Eleven scholars reviewed the script updated after this student review.[29] In September, the NEH notified us that our grant was funded!

FABRICATION OF THE MAY 4 VISITORS CENTER

Fabrication is the physical making of the parts for a museum and assembling them to build the exhibit. These parts are pieces displayed in the museum and all of the casework that holds them for display. The iterative process of script development, review, and script revision that you've read about above resulted in 125 photos, graphics, objects, and artifacts at the time of fabrication (not counting elements in the audiovisual pieces). For each, an electronic file or artifact had to be acquired and permissions cleared. From 2011 through early 2012, Carole handled much of this work, with considerable support from Cindy Kristof. Still, there was too much to do. Early in January, an angel came to our rescue in the form of Lori Boes, whom we were approved to hire temporarily for our core Visitors Center fabrication team of two—Carole and me. Lori, who had just graduated with a master's in library science, took over for Carole, who had to get back to teaching, and she and I continued to meet with Cindy regarding permissions. Cindy's file for our project was gigantic and regularly gave us fits. The file wouldn't save pink highlighting to signal items that were complete, it moved so slowly that our meeting times would run out; it couldn't be sent back and forth; was a beast even when put in a Dropbox; and defied regular printing. In the end, Lori transferred the information to a table in Word, which had its own perils, and completed most of the work of the permissions clearances for the film component of the Visitors Center project.

As keeper of the 134-page master script, a single table in Word to facilitate searching, I understood the problems with Cindy's file. Even though my Mac Pro desktop had a tremendous amount of capacity, I had to shut it down after a certain amount of scrolling or it would shut down Word, usually losing the information I was entering. And, no, I didn't want to use Excel—not enough space for words. Words were my province on all of the projects. Leading up to fabrication, I was creating all of the text for the exhibit (headings, explanatory paragraphs, captions), in accordance with strict word-count guidelines. Shane and Carl were designers. They thought all museums had too many words. Carl reluctantly conceded to Iris Harvey's rightful insistence on room to chronicle President Nixon's executive decision making during the Vietnam War. Carl created an upper level to the blue rail at the end of gallery I. Over dashes, Shane and I were headed for couples' therapy. I was confounded by and constantly correcting dashes that were too narrow and/or had spaces on either side of them. In my world, a dash was one-em wide and did not have spaces around it. Designers, it turns out, use a program that employs *kerning* to improve readability and visual appeal, they say. Deeply troubled, I conceded.

The other sphere in which I operated during these years was the administrative. As such, I was the communications hub among the designers, fabricators, architects, university executives, and all manner of administrators, reviewers, AV experts, public relations people, fundraisers, funders, and donors. Lots of emails, mailing lists, matrices, budget plans, work plans, announcements, revised budget plans, contracts, applications, reports, midterm reports, final reports. And interviews, which I would have gladly traded for being at my desk watching the script file crash. Hundreds of functional decisions about colors, carpeting, closet hooks, light bulbs, font size, doors, doorstops, bookshelves, chairs, benches, drawers or no drawers. It was exhausting and completely rewarding, and I always got to work on the creative side, too. Lori helped out in many ways. One interesting assignment was the Polaroids. Lori handled the responses for a call to the public for their photos of everyday life taken between 1950 and 1970 and worked with our fabricating company to print them to look like Polaroid photos. You see these clipped on floor-to-ceiling stringers that range across the front of the layered exhibit on the right-hand wall of gallery I. When student docents give tours of the center, they describe how gallery I captures life during the 1960s on three planes: issues of the national scene in the layered graphic pieces, issues playing out on the local level on the blue rails, and individuals in the Polaroids.

Cybelle connected us to Exhibit Concepts Inc. (ECI), a fabricator from Vandalia, Ohio, with whom she had worked a number of times. Duane Landes, ECI director for our project, convened biweekly conference calls for an invite list that include twenty-eight people at ECI, Gallagher, Kent State, and Karen Curry, whose connections with CBS were helpful to media development during fabrication. Duane's notes for July 19, 2012, represent the typical range of topics in a call: "Narrator selection is underway and initial reaction is #1 is best." The number 1 for the gallery II documentary film was Peter Thomas, whose voice you have often heard on TV. "Carl to arrive Friday 2–27 to review and focus lighting." As fabrication progressed, Carl coordinated the manufacturing and installation of the exhibit with the intended design—to the nth degree, as you see in this note. "Outside of a couple still in the production process, all graphics are complete and ready for delivery next week." Between May 24 and June 21, 2012, Tim Hosler at ECI sent me 217 different graphic approval sheets for every flat surface item to be printed or silk-screened on the walls of the exhibit. Duane refers to the wrap-up of the manufactured items. At the other end of the spectrum of our interaction with ECI, Lori especially appreciated watching the silk screener on site as a Zen experience.

In keeping with the work plan in our funded NEH grant, production of the multimedia components was scheduled during fabrication. Cybelle also had also worked often with GToo media, headed by Mike Buday. In all, twenty-seven multimedia pieces were created for the exhibit: three three-minute montage videos for the three subthemes of gallery I; an eleven-minute documentary film for gallery II; twenty videos for the reaction wall in gallery III; and, at the end of the exhibit, a question-and-response program for the

"Leave Your Voice" stations and a scrolling display of the responses. By this time, many of the scholars had participated over the years in shaping the theme documents and iterations of the script, generously donating their time before NEH grant funding arrived. Some items had changed due to unforeseen reasons. For instance, we represented Woodstock with its iconic poster, a copy of which we bought and hung as an artifact to save money. We used the poster instead of a photo of the dancing crowd at Woodstock because permission for a different photo came with the stipulation that we take two from its photographer. This second photo gave us our dancing crowd with a comparable mood. Other times, we had a better idea, such as moving the drawing by Sandy and Jeff from the right-hand wall in gallery I to the rail of the left-hand wall, where it could be better contemplated.

After news of the grant award came, scholars participating in the funded NEH grant conducted a review in October 2011. They saw first outlines for all the multimedia pieces embedded into the script so that they could think of them in context of the whole exhibit and for which they could suggest revisions and additions. This review also offered help with the previous material in the exhibit script. We were able to fix the error Jeffrey Kimball spotted in a caption about Cambodia: "This is grossly inaccurate. Nixon had secretly begun to bomb (not invade) Cambodia in mid-March 1969." And we did follow Rebecca Klatch's caution about generational point-counterpoint album covers: "only use Sgt. Peppers (not Revolver)." From November to April, Carole and I worked with Mike in the same type of iterative process through which the outline for the media in gallery II became a complete narrative script and sheets into which photos began to be put into place for the documentary *Kent State: A Turning Point*. Scholars reviewed the reworked treatments for galleries I and II in April, with Gallagher's final design book and our exhibit script in hand to use as reference. The media for gallery III was completed at the end, with selections from the treatments the scholars reviewed in October 2011. In September 2012, scholars reviewed final cuts of the gallery I videos. The gallery II documentary continued to be refined through focus-group sessions held in the built gallery. One of the choices settled in these live reviews by people from the campus and public was whether a red or a blue tone should be used during the memorial sequence at the end of the documentary. Each student who died was remembered in a sequence of photos, including a photo taken on May 4 before the shootings. Consensus was that the color blue should be used to highlight each student within the crowd that they were part of. Red seemed too violent at that point in the film where each person is being honored through remembrance. The sequences are heart wrenching as the soundtrack plays "Find the Cost of Freedom."

Throughout the media development process, Kent State AV specialist (and guru who kept us calm) Bryan Molnar collaborated with the designers to find equipment solutions for all that was envisioned. In many cases, there wasn't a readily available product that could be ordered. Bryan located the cathode-ray tubes for Carl's vintage TV cabinets in gallery I, and ordered an extra for just in case. Tablets are prevalent and many-faceted now. They were not then. Carl had designed the kiosks for the gallery III reaction wall without anticipating that the tablet used inside for display would have to be turned sideways, and that in doing so, it would turn the picture sideways. Bryan ordered three possibilities. One worked. Then he jury-rigged it with a piece of coat hanger that peeked out of the top of the case and could be jiggled to turn the thing on and off. Bryan solved his own favorite conundrum by finding the type of software program for the video loop that plays when you are waiting in line at Disney World. For gallery I of the Visitors Center, the software controls a loop of the three three-minute videos in the TV cabinets and a second loop with one ambient soundtrack that plays overhead. The single soundtrack is Mike's solution to having sound for three components in one smallish space. When you spend a couple of minutes in front of one TV, the sound may or may not match up with the video in those moments, but we did some edits for each video so that there are no unseemly clashes. The sound of bombing, for instance, would never be heard when you are seeing a funeral scene.

From the earliest stage, Mike was considering using 3-D in the film to give the viewer a sense of spatial relationships. He brought in an animator. His view was that this medium changes how history can be understood. These elements would come near the end of the film, so that what he called the *ordinariness*—a part of which was the reality that people did not feel a sense of foreboding or expectation of violence—was preserved. He knew the importance of conveying the amounts of space between the students and the Guard. I pointed out to him that we had GIS mapping and contour maps used for the National Register mapping. The animator used these to inform the shape of the hill, which also spoke to the relationship of the students to the Guard at the time of the shooting. The animation segment supplements the archival photos and film footage to graphically reveal the distances in animated lines: 500 feet between the Guard and students on the Commons and from 60 to 750 feet from the shooters at the Pagoda to those they felled. The animation also fills in for film footage that as far as we know does not exist—the Guard's turning point. In 2013, the Council on International Non-Theatrical Events conferred two national awards on *Kent State: A Turning Point.*

One late afternoon, as the thousands of items on the fabrication to-do lists dwindled and Lori and I conferred at the docent desk, Lester Lefton appeared through the exit door of the May 4 Visitors Center. I invited him through to gallery I. He explored the exhibit and departed quietly. From that moment, he became the most vocal and visible advocate for the center. He sent over people after concluding meetings in his office. From podiums, he exhorted all manner of audiences that they must go see the museum. He requested guided tours for those traveling from afar.

A couple of weeks later, more than six hundred people crowded through the May 4 Visitors Center for its two-hour soft opening during Homecoming 2012. Visitors received a copy of *This We Know: A Chronology of the Shootings at Kent State, May 1970*, published that year by Kent State University Press. *This We Know* is a chapbook version of the May 4 chronology with a preface describing the fact-based approach to the history and discussion in the back matter of the impact of the shootings and suggested additional readings. Visual communication design student Amy Crane designed a T-shirt for the opening featuring the quote from Allison Krause, which visitors see at the entry to the Visitors Center: "History must be made relevant to the present to make it useful." The graphic design shows nine white doves arranged on a musical staff to represent the opening of the refrain in Crosby, Stills, Nash, and Young's "Ohio." Above the staff, four white doves fly away.

During the May 4 commemoration in 2013, the May 4 Visitors Center was formally dedicated. Gwen Ifill, coanchor of *Washington Week* and coanchor of the *PBS NewsHour*, concluded panelists' discussion of "The Place of May 4 and the May 4 Visitors Center in American History" by observing: "If there's any place that's turned out to be the trigger point, the reflection point for this [engagement], it's right here at Kent State. . . . And the children that we bring to these memorials and these observances and the way that we tell our story and encourage them to be engaged as well . . . they don't have to do what those students did that day on this campus. But they can do something."[30]

Editors of the *Akron Beacon Journal*, notable for their excellence in reporting on May 4 in 1970 and after, added reflection on the dedication: "The pursuit of enlightened context is what the May 4 Visitors Center at Kent State seeks to bring. . . . The center reflects the welcome evolution of the university in its handling of the tragedy. The moment wouldn't be forgotten, so many refusing to let that happen. So the school opted for a learning experience . . . a coming together to talk about democratic values, and no less the right to assemble in protest of the choices made by our elected government."[31]

NATIONAL HISTORIC LANDMARK

Carole and I last spoke on April 12, 2014. That morning we participated along with Renee Romano on a panel organized by Tom Grace for the Organization of American Historians conference in Atlanta. The first slide in our presentation was:

Institutionalizing History
- 2006: Ohio Historical Marker
- 2007: Tom Hayden, "Kent State: Memories of the Future"
- 2010: National Register of Historic Places
- 2010: May 4 Walking Tour
- 2012–13: May 4 Visitors Center

Carole and I always wanted the history of May 4 to be *institutionalized*. To be visible and accessible to all. To be kept alive as a learning experience. To be embraced by and stewarded in perpetuity by Kent State University. Kent State embraced its history in new and lasting ways. Hundreds of people participated in the effort in the 2000s. Countless others had sustained the effort since May 4, 1970. The federal government confirmed the place of May 4, 1970, in United States history, through funding from the National Endowment of the Humanities, placement of the site on the National Register of Historic Places, and its most distinctive designation—identifying the Kent State Shootings site as a National Historic Landmark (NHL). In 2018, Kent State President Beverly Warren led further institutionalizing of the history of May 4 by presiding over installation of the NHL plaque; addressing the Chautauqua Institute during its week on "The Forgotten: History and Memory in the 21st Century" with her address "Reflections on the Kent State Shootings: From Remembrance to Renewal"; and continuing planning for the fiftieth May 4 commemoration. In November 2018, she announced that "the university will now own its responsibility" to lead both future commemorations and ongoing education about the history of May 4.[32] Presenting alongside Chic Canfora during the May 4 Task Force Fall Forum, President Warren stated that she doesn't want families ever to feel that May 4 will be forgotten and vowed, "Shooting will never again happen on a campus, because we can teach to prevent it."[33]

From February 2014 through November 2016, Mark Seeman and I built and rebuilt the new sections of the narrative for the National Historic Landmark nomination, using as a base the National Register of Historic Places nomination written with Carole and Jerry. Bradley Keefer, associate professor of history, and Mindy Farmer, director of the May 4 Visitors Center, contributed to the framing of the discussion in the nomination and new sections on historical context. Lori Boes, who became assistant director of the Visitors Center in 2013, assisted with bibliographical and detail-level questions, materials acquisition, and source checking. Jeff Brown, Kevin Kern, Tom Grace, and Kabir Syed read drafts of the manuscript during the two years of work that were made extra intense because there was much to do and not much time if we were to make the 2016 deadline for confirmation before the next presidential election. More happily, 2016 also was the one-hundredth anniversary of the National Park Service. The Ohio Preservation Office, where Barbara Powers, deputy state historic preservation officer, was our main contact, championed the cause. The NPS wanted May 4 to be part of its own landmark centennial. In our very first conversation with Patty Henry, she observed of the jubilation over the prospect of a Kent State nomination in the Landmarks office: "All nominations excite us, but this one excites us more!"[34] If not for Patty—guide, editor, cheerleader—who was so calm, clear, and on time with absolutely everything, we never could have gotten the job done. For that job, on November 10, 2018, Mark, Brad, Mindy, Lori, Jerry, Carole, and I were recognized by the State Historic Preservation Office with Public Education and Awareness Awards for our work in preserving the history and site of the May 4 Kent State shootings.

Renee Romano and Tom Grace, who had been there in the struggle for all of the history-making projects, served as anonymous readers for the review of the nomination. After things moved forward and they were identified, Renee sent me a copy of her review, which ends, "At a time in our history when the country is again deeply divided, when we are witnessing protests in the streets and there are growing concerns about privacy and free speech rights, it is imperative that Americans have the opportunity to understand what happened at Kent State in 1970 and to grapple with the broader issues that historic event raises about how our democracy responds to challenges and dissent."

During the decades after the deaths of Bill, Jeff, Allison, and Sandy were deemed by President Nixon's own commission to be "unnecessary, unwarranted, and inexcusable,"[35] many would ask, "Why are you still talking about this?" Renee Romano looks forward to the meaning that May 4, 1970, always will hold for America's citizens who have the resources available to understand the shootings as part of a pattern of excessive government violence against those exercising their First Amendment rights.

You have read here about the work of a recent decade to make the history of the shootings at Kent State available within the place where it can best be understood. When I was asked to say a few words for the dedication of the National Historic Landmark plaque, I felt it was a day to look back:

Having lived through the First World War and two years into World War II, poet T. S. Eliot wrote in *Four Quartets:*

> What we call the beginning is often the end
> And to make an end is to make a beginning.
> The end is where we start from.

Today is a day to remember Jeff Miller, Allison Krause, Sandy Scheuer, and Bill Schroeder, and those wounded on May 4: Robby Stamps, Jim Russell, Joe Lewis, Alan Canfora, John Cleary, Dean Kahler, Doug Wrentmore, Tom Grace, and Scott Mackenzie.

Today also is a day to recognize those who began the work of preserving the memory of the lost and the place where they fell. Some of those beginning this work were among the wounded. Many others were there beside them. Their work is where we start from.

In 1977, the May 4 Coalition pursued a range of tactics to block construction of the gym annex. The Coalition felt that the construction would destroy the ability to understand what had happened in this place. In July, Alan Canfora, Chic Canfora, Dean Kahler, and others took their cause to Washington, where President Jimmy Carter's chief adviser acted as their champion.

While resolution could not be achieved in the ensuing meetings, US Rep. John Seiberling; and US Sen. Howard Metzenbaum and Sen. John Glenn requested that the National Park Service conduct an evaluation of the site of the May 4, 1970, shootings for National Historic Landmark status.[36]

On January 1, 1978, parents of the slain students and the wounded students and their families wrote a letter of support for Landmark status to the secretary of the interior. The study, completed that month, concluded that it was *"too soon* after the events to assess" the following: historical meaning, significance of the student movement, and lasting effect of the Kent State shootings.[37]

Understandably upset, the students and families submitted an appeal, composed by Peter Davies, author of the book *The Truth About Kent State*. He was assisted by Chic Canfora and Elaine Holstein, mother of Jeffrey Miller. Taking issue with the study, they argued a *long* list of supporting points.

Among these, they asserted that the shootings at Kent State did the following:

- led Nixon to withdraw troops from Cambodia earlier than he intended, saving other young lives;
- resulted in a landmark "civil rights and law enforcement negligence case";

- were out of compliance with US Army regulations for responding to civil disturbances;
- happened in a state where the governor called out the Guard more often than the other forty-nine states combined;
- took place in a deeply divided country, led by officials who used harsh rhetoric to characterize student dissent;
- evoked deep "passions" still intense eight years later and which, they said, will remain intense for many years;
- triggered substantial counterprotests;
- deeply affected the nation, as reflected in coverage by media such as *Time* magazine;
- and were as important to our modern history as the Boston Massacre is to our Revolutionary history.[38]

These points would remain the heart of the matter.

Four more levels of review ended with the secretary of the interior agreeing with the study that more time was needed. The study did acknowledge, however, that the shootings may have a symbolism within American history comparable to the Boston Massacre.

Thirty-five years later, in 2013, the Ohio State Preservation Office and National Historic Landmarks Program enthusiastically encouraged the case to be made again.

For the case to be made, the Landmarks Program said that the nomination should show that "Kent State is part of a large arc of . . . tragic moments in American history." They requested that comparisons be made to the Boston Massacre; Wounded Knee; attacks during the labor movement at Ludlow Tent Colony, Haymarket Square, and Matewan; and pivotal moments during the civil rights movement at the University of Mississippi and Edmund Pettus Bridge.

The Landmarks Program further advocated that both periods—May 4, 1970, and the efforts to move the gym in 1977 to 1978—be nominated for national significance. By fast-tracking the nomination, the National Park Service was able to crown its centennial by recognizing the Kent State Shootings site as a National Historic Landmark in December 2016.

The Landmarks Program defines its purpose as recognizing and helping to preserve the sites of events that outstandingly represent the broad national patterns of United States history. These sites provide opportunities for us all to understand and appreciate those patterns.

Near the end of *Four Quartets*, T. S. Eliot says:

> A people without history
> is not redeemed from time, for history is a pattern
> of timeless moments.
>
> The work has always been to preserve those timeless moments so that others may see the pattern.

We look forward. We have upheld our obligation to remember Allison, Bill, Jeff, and Sandy. We have resolved as a community to learn from the past and created paths to hold to that promise. Always, we will want to be able to repeat Jay Winter's words: We have "transform[ed] silence about injustice into something active, purposeful, dynamic." We have "ensure[d] these events and their meanings are never forgotten."

NOTES

Note to readers: Institutionalizing the history of May 4 was a long process that you can think of beginning the day of the shootings. Please know that in addition to the many people mentioned in this piece, hundreds and hundreds more contributed to defining the story and the place, so that we all may learn from the pattern that emerges.

1. "Kent State: Memories of the Future," Symposium on Democracy (lecture, Kent State Univ., Kent, OH, May 2, 2007).

2. My academic area was English. Additional faculty members on the committee included Carole Barbato (communication studies), Karen Cunningham (applied conflict management, May 4 Task Force adviser), Thomas Hensley (political science), Jerry Lewis (sociology), and David Middleton (visual communication design); administrators Donna Carlton (center for student development), Tom Euclide (university architect's office; facilities planning), Steve Paschen (special collections and archives), Diane Ruppelt (development), and Kathy Stafford (univ. relations); and May 4 Task Force members Sarah Lund-Goldstein (student), Roy Skellenger (community member), and Stephanie Vincent (student).

3. Lester Lefton, quoted by Robert G. Frank, provost's update meeting with author, Sept. 12, 2007.

4. External design consultants for the 2008 NEH grant application were Sharon Barry (scriptwriting) and Mike Buday (media) and designers Sara Habich, Cybelle Jones, Sujit Tolat, and Madeline Wan.

5. Paul Fussell, *The Great War and Modern Memory* (New York: Oxford Univ. Press, 1975), 21.

6. External scholar consultants for the 2008 NEH grant application were Diane Britton (history, Univ. of Toledo), Thomas M. Grace (history, Erie Community College), Staughton Lynd (activist), and Jay Winter (history, Yale Univ.). In

addition to Carole and me, Kent State scholars were Stephane Booth (history), Claire Culleton (English), Tom Hensley, Jerry Lewis, David Middleton, Steve Paschen, and Mark Seeman (anthropology). Additional Kent State staff participating in the application were Tom Euclide, Ben Hollis (educational technology), Diane Ruppelt, and Kathy Stafford.

7. Mission and Vision, National Endowment for the Humanities (NEH), https://www.grants.gov/learn-grants/grant-making-agencies/national-endowment-for-the-humanities.html.

8. Jay Winter, discussion by telephone with Carole Barbato and Laura Davis, Aug. 26, 2008.

9. Carole and I served as co-PIs for three additional NEH grant applications, with commitments from the following teams. In 2009, external design consultants continued to be Sharon Barry (scriptwriter), Mike Buday (GToo Media), and Sara Habich (now Pasch) (Gallagher & Associates), Cybelle Jones, Sujit Tolat, and Madeline Wan. Serving again as external scholar and expert consultants were Tom Grace, Staughton Lynd, and Jay Winter, who were joined by Rebecca Klatch (sociology, Univ. of California–San Diego), Renee Romano (history, Oberlin Univ.), and Chris Triffo (filmmaker, Partners in Motion). Continuing to participate as Kent State scholars were Stephane Booth, Claire Culleton, Tom Hensley, Jerry Lewis, David Middleton, Steve Paschen, and Mark Seeman, who were joined by Richard Serpe (sociology). Kent State staff joining Tom Euclide were Michael Bruder (univ. architect's office) and Catherine Hurd (electronic editorial specialist). For the 2010 grant application, Barry, Buday, Habich, and Jones continued as design consultants, joined by designers Shane Allbritton and Carl Rhodes. Gary Stemler (Nordquist Sign Company, Inc.) was chief consultant for fabrication. External scholars and experts Grace, Klatch, Romano, Triffo, and Winter were joined by Mitchell Hall (history, Central Michigan Univ.), Lauren Onkey (education and public programs, Rock and Roll Hall of Fame and Museum), and Franco Ruffini (Ohio Historical Preservation Office). Continuing on the Kent State scholar team were Booth, Hensley, Lewis, Middleton, Seeman, and Serpe; new to the team were Ken Bindas (history), Patrick Coy (applied conflict management), Fran Dorsey (Pan-African studies), David Hussey (social behavioral sciences), Christopher Post (geography), Drew Tiene (instructional technology), Clarence Wunderlin (history), and Steve Zapytowski (theater and dance). For the 2011 grant application, the listed design and fabrication team was Barry, Buday, Habich, Jones, Rhodes, and Stemler. During fabrication, Allbritton rejoined the project and Exhibit Concepts Inc. took over from Nordquist. Grace, Hall, Klatch, Onkey, Romano, Ruffini, Triffo, and Winter remained on the grant and were joined by Christian Appy (history, Univ. of Massachusetts–Amherst) and Jeffrey Kimball (history, Miami Univ., OH). Continuing on the Kent State scholar team were Bindas, Hensley, Lewis, Middleton, Paschen, Post, Seeman, Serpe, Tiene, Wunderlin, and Zapytowski; new to the team was Mwatabu Okantah (Pan-African studies). Joining Kent State staff Bruder and Euclide were Iris Harvey (univ. relations) and Bob Minno (classroom and educational technology).

10. Kent State University, *Find Your Connection to May 4, 1970* (Kent, OH: Kent State Univ. Press, 2010), K3.

11. Carole and I cochaired the planning committee for the 2009 Symposium on Democracy. Participants on the committee included Ken Bindas, Donna Carlton, Fran Dorsey, Paul Haridakis (communication studies), Tom Hensley, Barbara Hipsman Springer (journalism and mass communication), Jerry Lewis, David Odell-Scott (philosophy), Steve Paschen, Drew Tiene, and Sandra Perlman Halem (Kent Historical Society).

12. From Jay Winter's keynote address, published without change as "Remembering Injustice and the Social Construction of Silence," in *Democratic Narrative, History, and Memory,* ed. Carole A. Barbato and Laura L. Davis (Kent, OH: Kent State Univ. Press, 2012), 63.

13. This much revised chronology was written by Carole A. Barbato, Laura L. Davis, and Mark F. Seeman and published first as an appendix: "This We Know: A Chronology of the Shootings at Kent State, May 1970," in *Democratic Narrative,* 194–227. It was then revised and published separately as a book by the same authors: *This We Know: A Chronology of the Shootings at Kent State, May 1970* (Kent, OH: Kent State Univ. Press, 2012).

14. Daniel L. Miller and Suzanne Clark, "Wars on Trial in Three Landmark Documentary Films," in *Democratic Narrative,* 121.

15. In addition to Carole and me, part 1 of the scholars forum on Feb. 28 and 29 included Stephane Booth, Alan Canfora, Patrick Coy, Karen Cunningham, Dan Flannery, Tom Grace, Rebecca Klatch, Alice Lynd, Staughton Lynd, Renee Romano, David Odell-Scott, Lauren Odell-Scott (minister), Richard Serpe, Drew Tiene, and Jay Winter. Part 2 of the scholars forum included Carole and me and Jim Carlton, Patrick Coy, Karen Cunningham, Tom Grace, Sandra Perlman Halem, Paul Haridakis, Iris Harvey, David Hussey, Jerry Lewis, Tim Magaw (student, journalism and mass communication), Renee Romano, Mark Seeman, Richard Serpe, Drew Tiene, Shirley Wajda (history), Jay Winter, and Steve Zapytowski.

16. All donations to the May 4 Visitors Center over the years have signified building lasting support of preserving the legacy of May 4. Through 2018, donors recognized on the donor wall in the center include: National Endowment for the Humanities, Office of the President, Office of the Senior Vice President for Academic Affairs and Provost, College of Architecture and Environmental Design, College of the Arts, College of Arts and Sciences, College of Business Administration, College of Communication and Information, College and Graduate School of Education, Health and Human Services, College of Nursing, College of Public Health, College of Applied Engineering, Sustainability and Engineering, Ashtabula Campus, East Liverpool Campus, Geauga Campus, Salem Campus, Stark Campus, Trumbull Campus, Tuscarawas Campus, Karpinski Engineering, Laura Davis and Tom Clapper, Carole Barbato and Patrick Barbato, Robert J. Gage and Patricia S. Gage, Ohio Humanities Council, John Rath and Joanne Rath, Dan Boes and Lori Boes, Leigh Herrington and Anita Herrington, Dennis Block and Madeline Farkas Block, Paula Slimak, Carol Meyer, and Richard Serpe.

17. For example, Karen Curry and Allen Richardson participated in an internal/external review of the developing May 4 Visitors Center content October 2009, along with Tom Grace, Iris Harvey, Rebecca Klatch, and Drew Tiene.

18. Reviewers for the May 4 Walking Tour included Alan Canfora, Tom Grace, Connie Bodner and William Mahon from Ohio History Connection, Jay Winter,

Renee Romano, Rebecca Klatch, and Jerry Lewis. They completed two reviews of the interpretive panels.

19. Cybelle Jones, participant in "The Place of May 4 and the May 4 Visitors Center in American History," panel discussion moderated by Gwen Ifill (Kent State Univ., May 4, 2013).

20. May 4 Coalition, position paper, quoted in Thomas R. Hensley, "Kent State 1977: The Struggle to Move the Gym," in *Kent State and May 4th: A Social Science Perspective*, 3rd ed., ed. Thomas R. Hensley and Jerry M. Lewis (Kent, OH: Kent State Univ. Press, 2010), 150.

21. Scott L. Bills, "Introduction: The Past in the Present," in *Kent State/May 4: Echoes through a Decade* (Kent, OH: Kent State Univ. Press, 1990), 43.

22. National Park Service, United States Department of the Interior, *National Register Bulletin*, no. 40 (1999).

23. Mark F. Seeman, Carole A. Barbato, Laura L. Davis, and Jerry M. Lewis, "May 4, 1970, Kent State Shootings Site," National Register of Historic Places Registration Form (National Park Service, United States Department of the Interior, Feb. 23, 2010), iii.

24. Urban Research Corporation, *On Strike . . . Shut It Down! A Report on the First National Student Strike in U.S. History, May 1970* (Chicago: Urban Research Corporation, 1970), 1; Todd Gitlin, *The Sixties: Years of Hope, Days of Rage*, rev. ed. (New York: Bantam Books, 1993), 410.

25. Peter Davies, *The Truth about Kent State: A Challenge to the American Conscience*, with The Board of Church and Society of the United Methodist Church (New York: Farrar, Straus, Giroux, 1973), 161, 169.

26. Bills, "Introduction," 37; Sanford Jay Rosen, "The Legal Battle: Finishing Unfinished Business," in *Kent State/May 4*, ed. Scott L. Bills (Kent, OH: Kent State Univ. Press, 1990), 231–38.

27. "Coming Full Circle: Democracy, Engagement and Social Change," Symposium on Democracy (Kent State Univ., Kent, OH, May 3, 2010).

28. Kent State Univ., Special Collections and Archives, May 4 Collection, Box 223, folders 17, 22, 29.

29. Materials for the spring 2011 reviews are located in Kent State Univ., Special Collections and Archives, May 4 Collection, Box 222, folders 2 and 20. Scholars completing the Mar. 15, 2011, exhibit script were Jerry Lewis, Patrick Coy, Rebecca Klatch, Connie Bodner, Renee Romano, Steve Paschen, Christopher Post, student Heidi Summerlin (history), Tom Grace, Mitchell Hall, and Allen Richardson.

30. Carole and I opened dedication programs on the afternoon and evening of May 4. During the afternoon, Senior Vice President for Academic Affairs and Provost Todd Diacon introduced Gwen Ifill as moderator of a panel titled "The Place of May 4 and the May 4 Visitors Center in American History; Chris Appy (professor of history, Univ. of Massachusetts–Amherst); Tom Grace (Erie Community College); Darlene Clark Hine (board of trustees professor of African-American Studies and professor of history at Northwestern); Cybelle Jones (principal and executive director, Gallagher & Associates); Rebecca Klatch (professor of sociology, Univ. of California–San Diego); Edward P. Morgan (Univ. Distinguished Professor of Political Science, Lehigh Univ.); and Renee Romano (associate professor of history, Oberlin College). Speakers President Lester Lefton, Kathleen Clyde

(Ohio House of Representatives), Roger DiPaolo, then editor of the *Kent-Ravenna Record-Courier,* officially dedicated the May 4 Visitors Center, followed by a discussion of "History and Memory in Film" featuring Oliver Stone and moderator Gary Hanson, professor of journalism and mass communication. In the morning, Cybelle Jones, principal and studio director and Carl Rhodes, associate and senior designer, from Gallagher & Associates, along with Shane Allbritton, environmental graphic designer and civic artist, and Mike Buday, executive producer, GToo Media, presented "Meet the Designers of the May 4 Visitors Center."

31. "An Education at Kent State," *Akron Beacon Journal,* May 7, 2013.

32. Beverly Warren, address to May 4 Advisory Committee, ad hoc committee of the fiftieth May 4 Commemoration planning process (Kent State Univ., Kent, OH, Nov. 7, 2018).

33. Beverly Warren, participant in "Building Bridges Across the Generations," May 4 Task Force Fall Forum, moderated by Maddie Camp and Noelle Reese (Kent State Univ., Kent, OH, Nov. 8, 2018).

34. Patricia Henry, Lexie Lord, and Geoffrey Burt, National Historic Landmarks Program, phone conference call with Barbara Powers, Ohio Historic Preservation Office/Ohio History Connection, Mark Seeman, and Laura Davis, Sept. 19, 2013.

35. William W. Scranton et al., *The Report of the President's Commission on Campus Unrest* (Washington, DC: US Government Printing Office, 1970), 289.

36. Bills, "Introduction," 58.

37. James Sheire, "Kent State May 4, 1970 Site," National Register of Historic Places Inventory—Nomination Form (National Park Service, United State Department of the Interior, Jan. 1978), 29–31.

38. "An Appeal to the Secretary of the U.S. Department of Interior to Designate a Portion of the Kent State University Campus in Ohio a National Historic Landmark" (Box 20, folder 31, Jerry M. Lewis Papers, May 4 Collection, Special Collections and Archives, Kent State Univ. Libraries).

PART XI

Lasting Legacies

Why Is It So Cold in Northern Ohio?

MARK RUDD

Mark Rudd was a student activist and organizer in the Students for a Democratic Society (SDS) chapter at Columbia University from 1965 to 1968. He was invited to speak at Kent State University on numerous occasions. This piece was written in 2000.

The first time I ever set foot on the campus of Kent State was the fall of 1968. What struck me most were the trees—huge old elms. I actually thought that the university was located in a grove. I could see the surrounding farmland, but something led me to believe this was the beginning of an upland forest rising toward the east. Perhaps it had been forest before fields.

That was when Terry Robbins, father in heaven, now deceased with two other beloved comrades in an explosion of our own making in 1970, that was when Terry and Lisa Meisel took me down from Cleveland to speak at a big student event, show the Columbia film (just released by Newsreel forty-five days after the events), and especially meet with the SDS chapter. It was that trip, and many others over the next eighteen months, that introduced me to Howie Emmer and Rick and Candy Ericson, and Colin Neiberger, and on and on, these incredibly brave kids—still to this day loyal to the struggle and our heroic ideals (which had the drawback that they were primarily ideals), these determined kids who were always ready—primed—to fight the state no matter what the cost, like jail and expulsion, to fight the university, to fight the jocks, even to fight each other. These were the most accomplished and the most serious of the children of the tire-makers of Akron and the shoe-store owners of Parma and the old commies of Cleveland Heights and Shaker, these were the kids, like me, who were shocked out of their minds when they realized that their country—our country—behaved no better than the Nazis we were raised to hate.

Nineteen or so years pass. Kent State, 1970, has transpired, and Alan Canfora, who was wounded by National Guard gunfire that May 4, and is destined to mine the lessons of that day, I could tell on the phone, destined to spend the next thirty years even to today and beyond, extending on and on into the twenty-first century, not forgetting, not covering anything over, knowing too well the raw wounds of neighbors ostracizing his family for decades in neighboring Ravenna, his father fired because he was the father of a son who was shot at Kent on May 4. Alan Canfora, it's Alan Canfora calling me out of the blue as I'm putting in an early spring garden in Albuquerque, New Mexico, where I'm hiding out as a mild-mannered math teacher in a community college, endlessly teaching people fractions, which they'd rather not think about if they had their choice. "Hey, Bro, we need you here for the nineteenth commemoration of the shootings. We're also doing a twentieth Kent SDS Reunion."

"OK, I'll come if you'll let me say Kaddish."

"Sorry, Mark, it's nondenominational."

"Yeah, but three of the four people who died were Jewish. OK, it's not such a big deal, I'll come anyway."

So it's early May 1989 the next time I set foot on the Kent State campus. We get out of Alan's car near the Student Union, now the headquarters of the May 4 Task Force. A wind rips through me. It's cold and I hadn't even brought a long-sleeve shirt or a jacket, winter having been over long ago in Albuquerque. Is this the same place? No, they must have expanded the campus to a field. I'm completely disoriented. I turn to Alan, "Where are we?"

"In the plaza by the Student Union." He must be used to the change.

"Was I here back in '68 and '69?"

"Same place."

"Oh my god, where are the trees?"

"A blight killed all the elms in the 1970s."

Suddenly I became aware that my throat is subvocalizing the words of the Kaddish, the Mourner's Prayer, recited by Jews continually for the last twenty centuries. Bewitched, befuddled, I'm standing in the plaza at Kent State, reciting a prayer in Aramaic, the language Jesus probably spoke: "Yisgodal, v'yitkadal, sh'may rabah." "Magnified and sanctified is the name of God." In the next four days I can't stop mumbling the Kaddish whenever I walk onto the Kent campus; mourning for the people and the trees.

Six more years pass. Alan Canfora calls again.

"OK, I'll come."

"We'll let you recite Kaddish this time," he tells me.

Mark Rudd speaking at the commemoration in 1995 (Source: Brad McKelvey)

"Too late, I already did it."

In May 1995, the May 4 Task Force sends a young woman student to pick me up from the Cleveland Airport. Alan's too busy with an agent from Hollywood. This is the real thing, he tells me on the phone, some big hotshot director who did something I'd only barely heard of. Finally (Alan thinks), Hollywood will do justice to our history.

My escort brings me to a lecture hall in the Student Union, a forum on the press. We sit down. There are all these middle-age white guys up there on the stage. Paunch city. One appears to be a journalism professor, another a reporter of some sort. The reporter's talking—or maybe he was a reporter-turned-journalism professor: "Yeah, a local SDS boy made good: Terry Robbins blew himself up in a townhouse explosion in New York in March 1970, two months before the Kent shootings." This guy is gleeful. The old chill passes through me.

That night the organizers ask me to lead the memorial procession around the campus. They ask who I want to portray. I don't understand, but I blurt out the name "Allison Krause," not knowing why. Her now-graying boyfriend is facing me. He tells me that Allison was always interested in me, watched my career as it unfolded in the national press from Columbia to SDS to Weatherman in the months before she died. She identified with me, he says. I say nothing. They give me a candle, put me at the head of the line with Allison's mom. I talk to her about her loss as we walk. I look back. There are thousands of people in the line now. Where did they come from?

We're circling the campus. I am out of my body, beyond candles, beyond thought. We come back to the site of the killings. I'm directed to a little square, about six by six, roped off. A young woman, crying, puts a bouquet of flowers in my hands. I stand there. Hundreds are crowded around the spot, as are hundreds more around the other three spots where the students died.

A half hour passes. I put the flowers down, next to the splayed-out figure outlined on the black pavement in white chalk, step out of the square, and someone else steps in, to continue the relay vigil until 12:24 P.M., when the bells are to ring and the memorial rally by the hillside of thousands of daffodils is to begin.

It's the next evening. Most of the events are over. I'm walking across the parking lot where the shootings took place. It's been reclaimed as a parking lot since that afternoon. Let's just forget the whole thing, the big state university machine is telling us. There can't be any memory, it will be wiped out at any cost. I look down. A car's rear tire is sitting on the bouquet I had placed, the night before, next to Allison Krause's chalk body.

The Greater Kent State Era, 1968–70

Personal Transformations and Legacies of Student Rebellions and State Repression

DARLENE CLARK HINE

Darlene Clark Hine is a leading historian of the African American experience. President Barack Obama honored Hine with a 2013 National Humanities Medal for her contributions in black women's history and pioneering the study of the intersection of race, class, and gender. She earned her master's degree from Kent State University in 1970 and her PhD in 1975. This piece was written in 1996.

It is important to situate the Kent State May 4 killings of Allison Krause, Jeff Miller, Sandy Scheuer, and Bill Schroeder between two other, equally significant but often ignored, deadly confrontations between students and state police authorities in 1968 and 1970. The deaths of three unarmed students at South Carolina State College, in Orangeburg, on February 8, 1968, and of two students at Jackson State College, Jackson, Mississippi, ten days after Kent State, comprise a trilogy of tragedies I refer to as "The Greater Kent State Era." Kent State's tragedy is rightly remembered with vigils and symposia, but seldom do we attend gatherings at the other campus killings. As a graduate student at Kent State in May 1970, this lived history exploded my parochial political consciousness. The events shaped the nature of my scholarship and the strategies of resistance I have employed this past quarter of a century. Indeed, it has taken me twenty-five years to break a self-imposed silence about what I experienced, and an equally long period of ivory-tower reflection to articulate the personal, professional, and systemic legacies of Greater Kent State.

On February 8, 1968, South Carolina highway patrolmen killed Delano Middleton, Henry Smith, and Samuel Hammond Jr. following a series of demonstrations to protest racial exclusion and to desegregate the local, white-owned bowling alley. In the only book-length account, *The Orangeburg Massacre* (1984), Jack Bass and Jack Nelson astutely observed, "The real tragedy is that there were lessons to be learned from the Orangeburg incident: lessons in how not to exacerbate a situation of mounting student tension and frustration and in how not to handle student demonstrations. Ohio officials learned nothing from the South Carolina experience."[1] As a consequence of not having learned the lessons of history, administrators at a larger institution in the Midwest repeated the mistakes of their South Carolina counterparts. And ten days later the unthinkable happened again, this time at Jackson State College, where city police shot and killed James Earl Green and Phillip L. Gibbs.[2]

A score and five years have passed. Still, it is necessary that we keep alive the memory of these struggles and rebellions and of sacrifices of all nine students and the scores of wounded. I am persuaded that these tragedies could happen again. There are even more of us who will forever bear psychological scars, invisible and buried. Our healing comes through repeated public affirmations that students are human beings, and as citizens they have a right as guaranteed by the First Amendment to the United States Constitution to speak truth to power and to assemble in dissent, without fear that the awesome power of the state will take their lives.[3]

On May 4, 1970, I stood on the perimeter of the Commons, near Bowman Hall, home of the History Department. Surrounded by other history graduate students and faculty, I anxiously observed the line of armed Ohio National Guardsmen at one end of the grassy expanse and the scores of defiant, unarmed students exercising their right to assemble in dissent. To be sure, I had read about the Orangeburg Massacre in the Nation of Islam's *Muhammad Speaks*. The white media deemed the matter too insignificant to cover. Perhaps black deaths were too common an occurrence to be considered news. Little did I know that four years following the Orangeburg shootings, I would be a faculty member at South Carolina State College and that each day for two years I would walk past the markers that commemorated the dead students. Given the intractable racism that permeates American society and afflicts us all in one way or another, it is telling that I could never have imagined, on that bright sunny May 4 morning, as I looked back and forth from the armed guards to the milling students, that the killings that took place on a black college campus in the Deep South could occur at a large, predominantly white institution in northeastern Ohio.

Perhaps a class analysis combined with my racial one would have had greater predictive accuracy as to which whites had the more expendable lives. After all, students at the University of California at Berkeley and at Columbia University, New York, had dissented, rallied, trespassed, and transgressed for years, but no state police authority had dared to shoot the sons and daughters of the white elite.

A veteran observer of two previous confrontations between citizens and state police authority, I was reminded of the explosions on the west side of Chicago in April 1968 in the wake of the assassination of Martin Luther King Jr. There, armed Illinois National Guardsmen sought to stop friends, neighbors, and others from venting their rage. My mind flashed forward to scenes viewed from the windows of Roosevelt University later in August, of Chicago police bashing the heads of antiwar demonstrators in downtown streets during the Democratic Party's National Convention.[4] Still, these previous conflagrations little prepared me for what I witnessed at Kent State. And when ten days later, police would kill two students on the campus of Jackson State, nothing made sense.

With a hope and idealism born of the civil rights movement, I had believed that America could be made into an open, tolerant society that welcomed different points of view and encouraged dissent. By the end of May 1970, I knew how quickly and with what ease America could become a police state ready to stamp out dissent with force when property was threatened. More chilling still, I now knew that vast numbers of Americans actually sanctioned official violence.[5] The demonstrations at Kent State were in no sense a prelude to the revolutionary overthrow of the US government. But the overreaction of elected state officials and military officers revealed an eagerness to use lethal force. What further bruised an already shattered psyche were the statements I overheard from some white citizens, parents, and even fellow students declaring that the Guardsmen should have shot more protestors. Any fantasies I may have entertained about the efficacy of social activism and overt challenges to authority abruptly evaporated, to be replaced by a silent commitment to engage in day-to-day long-term resistance that would transform scholarship, curriculum, and classrooms, and yes, maybe even minds. I vowed to stay away from grassy knolls and street protests, armed Guardsmen, and inflammatory rhetoric. Figuratively and literally, I, and thousands of others, quietly withdrew into university libraries where we studied, thought, and practiced silence.

Much the same as I had migrated from Chicago's west side to pastoral Kent to escape civil rights strife, I now settled, at least metaphorically, into the library. I studied the US Constitution and researched the strategies and tactics pursued by other generations of resisters. The first result of my "library exile" was *Black Victory: The Rise and Fall of the White Primary in Texas* (1979). In the ensuing years I would concentrate on reclaiming the history of "the silent and silences" and would develop a "dissemblance as resistance" motif, all of which are especially pronounced in my writings on black women's history. After Kent State, my courses and publications aimed to teach students that America's unity is tested but not destroyed by dissent and diversity. It is through an understanding of our differences that we map the road to unity. My work over these past two decades makes entirely unacceptable *Newsweek*'s prophesy that "By the time the history of the 20th century is written, the shootings at Kent State University might not merit more than a footnote."[6]

Powerful historical forces created the political, cultural, racial, and sexual preconditions for the emergence of a host of challenges to the American academy in the wake of Greater Kent State. For the remainder of this essay, I will focus on the legacy of South Carolina/Kent State/Jackson State in the realm of black studies, women's studies, and ethnic studies.[7] I am particularly interested in the agency of excluded and marginalized groups in American society and the strategies they employed to overcome intolerance.

The student and women's movements of the 1970s were remarkably intertwined. The students' call for the development of new areas of study; the hiring of more black, female, and ethnic professors; and the subsequent creation of new knowledge produced by these scholars refuted long-held stereotypes, biases, and assumptions of power and privilege that revolutionized American higher education more effectively than an armed uprising. The culture war that today pivots at the intersections of race, class, and gender had its origins in this era. Allow me to elaborate. Immediately after the Kent State killings, approximately four hundred colleges and universities closed. The American educational enterprise experienced the greatest student and faculty strike in its history. The significance of this strike cannot be overemphasized, yet it is seldom analyzed. The strike punctuated the end of one era and shaped the new one. Some students desired to show solidarity and sympathy with those fallen. Some university administrators, perhaps fearful of possible student rage and potential demonstrations, and even more wary of the violence of unchecked state police power, sent students packing. Photographs in the *New York Times* showed angst-ridden university presidents meeting with President Richard Nixon. Either way you approach or interpret this shutdown, the results were the same—the education industry confronted its weaknesses and admitted vulnerability.

When classes commenced in the fall of 1970, students, faculty, and administrators entered a decadelong negotiation over structures, nature, and content of the curriculum. All parties seemed willing, for diverse reasons, to create an array of new programs and units. The 1970s witnessed a proliferation of black studies, women's studies, and ethnic studies programs, departments, and centers.[8] Many were short-lived, but the more resilient found powerful allies and much-needed external funds in the philanthropic community, especially from the Ford and Rockefeller foundations.

Black studies and women's studies experienced a phenomenal growth. By the 1973–74 academic year, there were an estimated two thousand courses offered concerning the roles, contributions, and treatment of women on campuses across the nation.[9] There were soon more than five hundred black studies programs. What is to be underscored, however, is the rapidity with which demands would shift. Historian John Bracey, director of Afro-American studies at the University of Massachusetts at Amherst, declared in 1975, "Our impact right now should be to infuse the entire arts and sciences curriculum with a black influence." Margaret Walker Alexander of Jackson State believed that the promise of black studies was "to bring a new humanism to American education, to infuse our system with a black perspective."[10] By the end of the decade, black students and faculty and academic feminists were abandoning the inclusionary model of integration of black people or women into traditional disciplines. Now they embraced a model of curriculum transformation. In the early 1990s black students recognized that struggles for freedom and full humanity required concomitant radical transformation of political and economic institutions and changes in cultural and personal values. To elaborate the changes in student consciousness, some black scholars developed and popularized the concept of Afrocentricity as a potent challenge to, and critique of, Eurocentrism's intellectual dominance in the academy.[11]

The fiscal crises of the 1980s triggered the demise of many of the new programs. While some black battle-fatigued faculty and students protested, many administrators resolutely cut funding. Within traditional departments, mounting allegations of erosions of standards led to the denial of tenure and promotion to many black, women, and minority faculty. The tensions on campus grew more heated, and today issues of affirmative action and political correctness spark endless debate. In one arena, however, there was simply no way that the clock could be stopped or reversed. By the 1990s, the scholarship that the Greater Kent State generation had created focused on themes and theories revolving around the social and political constructions of race, class, gender, and sexual orientation as important variables in virtually every traditional field of study. I need only speak of the work of one group of scholars to illustrate this point.

The pioneering generation of black studies and black history scholars who entered the academy in the post–civil rights period amassed an impressive record of scholarship in the area of slavery studies. Because of the pathbreaking and imaginative work of John Blassingame, Leslie Owens, Albert Raboteau, Barbara Fields, and Deborah Gray White, and of such white scholars as Eugene Genovese, Ira Berlin, Herbert Gutman, Peter Wood, Todd Savitt, James Roark, and Michael Johnson, we now know a great deal more about slavery as an institution and about the inner lives of slaves. This scholarship on slave communities, slave religion, slave health, and slave families not only provided more factual information but also deepened our appreciation of nontraditional source materials. We know, thanks to the new social history methodologies, that even the most oppressed and downtrodden people (who do not leave manuscript collections, write diaries, or build monuments) nevertheless created and sustained significant institutions and fashioned a remarkably resilient culture reflected in song, folktales, dance, and decorative crafts. Their essentially humanistic values and belief in the sanctity of life and their worldviews, grounded largely upon a theology of hope, helped to foster an oppositional consciousness that ensured the survival of African Americans in slavery and in freedom.

Universities have historically served a legitimizing function in the larger society. This is most graphically illustrated in the development and establishment of new professions, or the transformations of certain occupations into professions. But universities legitimize also by exclusion. In 1979, I launched a research project on the history of black men in the learned professions, specifically medicine, law, theology, education, and science. At this time, the notion of women as agents and subjects of history was not a significant part of my consciousness and vision.[12] This soon changed as my political, social, and economic thought expanded to incorporate gender as a conceptual category of analysis. Black women became the major focus of my scholarly work, and my study of the nursing profession illustrated the legitimizing power of university.

In the late nineteenth century, nursing was a low-status occupation performed by poor women who acquired training by working long apprenticeships in hospitals and clinics before receiving a diploma. By the early 1900s, nurse activists determined that greater status and respect, higher wages, and increased opportunities were dependent upon moving nursing education from the hospitals into college and university curriculums. They met with massive opposition from the male-dominated medical profession and the doctors and hospital administrators who feared women's autonomy and the loss of women's cheap labor. Nurses persevered, and by following their own parallel course, or duplicating medicine's professionalization process, nursing eventually acquired the legitimacy conferred by the higher education institution.[13]

Those of us who study blacks and women likewise fought for legitimacy within the academy. The results of this long struggle have been mixed. On the one hand, the impact of feminist scholarship in the academy has been substantial although uneven across disciplines. History, English, and psychology departments initially proved more willing than others to develop and offer courses focusing on women.[14] By the 1990s the combined impact of feminist and black scholarship on history was especially pronounced. Today history pays considerable attention not only to women but also to social relationships and the construction of gender systems, to issues of race, to the concerns of the poor, to the structures and experiences of daily life, and to the construction of popular culture. The late historian Nathan Huggins maintained that "The object is not merely to mention and discuss African Americans, women, Hispanic Americans, Asian Americans, white ethnics, and Native Americans—those who have been marginalized in the standard history. Rather, it is to understand the past through them, to see history through their eyes, making them essential witnesses to the events historians discussed."[15]

Today, it is safe to say that feminist paradigms have provided frameworks for understanding what had seemed like anomalous data, offered aid in reinterpreting traditional texts, and facilitated the expansion of canons in virtually all fields to include previously unknown materials.[16] What has been most challenging for women's studies scholars was the need to expose the ideological groundings inherent in "neutral" or "traditional" scholarship while simultaneously demonstrating that to recognize the presence of ideology does not necessarily "leave scholars with only a mindless relativism that disregards evidence and logic."[17] Scholars in both black history and women's history are now developing diasporic, global, and comparative methods and approaches. As a harbinger of where scholars in these areas are headed, Michigan State University established in 1993 the first comparative black history PhD program in the country. Pushing against and beyond the boundaries of the nation-state is the next frontier in this revolutionary scholarship.

Without the grants from the foundations from the National Endowments for Arts and Humanities, much of the progressive, boundary-crossing scholarship produced by the generation emerging out of the Greater Kent State Era would now exist. But even more important than the myriad books produced by those who, like me, retreated to the libraries, is the unshakable conviction that there is tremendous variation in human experiences and that both diversity and unity should be central to historical and, in fact, all educational endeavors. In the current culture war, those who call for the dismantling of the arts and humanities endowments despair of this reality. Gary Nash, president of the Organization of American Historians and director of the National History Standards project, recently wrote:

> The controversy over the standards is part and parcel of a larger, profoundly political, culture war ... We see it now in attempts to abolish or cut back the National Endowment for the Humanities, the National Endowment for the Arts, and the Corporation for Public Broadcasting. All of these controversies involve an assault on curators, artists, and historians who have sought more than a single perspective on the past, have tried to open their work to new voices and different experiences ... Some critics believe that young Americans should not learn that life is bittersweet and that every society's history is full of paradox, ambiguity, and irresolution.[18]

Over two decades ago, the demands of the first generation of idealistic women, minority, and black students on predominantly white campuses calling for the creation of black, women's, and ethnic studies programs, departments, and cultural centers sent shock waves through the academy. Implicit in the demands of these marginalized and excluded groups was a fundamental critique of the underlying assumptions and ideologies of American education. A history of American society—or a canon of great literary works written by privileged elite white males that depicted an American society as a land of equality, freedom, and opportunity for all—was inaccurate and unacceptable.

The events of the Greater Kent State Era merely underscored the distance between the mythical America and the reality. With the traditional curriculum unmediated by race, gender, or class analysis, previously excluded students failed to derive a sense of self-esteem, an understanding of how they came to be—or the roles they could rightly aspire to occupy in the present and future America. As Carole Merritt, a specialist in black material culture, put it, "To know that one's people were present when the nation first developed and that their work and culture have been distinctive, yet integral, elements of American life is to be able to assert one's rights with dignity."[19] And I shall remain silent no longer, for evil triumphs when good women and men do and say nothing.

NOTES

Originally published *in Speak Truth to Power: Black Professional Class in United States History* by Darlene Clark Hine; used here with her permission.

1. Jack Bass and Jack Nelson, *The Orangeburg Massacre* (Atlanta: Mercer Univ. Press, 1984), 235.

2. I. F. Stone, *The Killings at Kent State: How Murder Went Unpunished* (New York: A New York Review Book, 1970). Also see Carol Squiers, "On Kent & Jackson State," *Artforum* (Summer 1991): 14–16.

3. For a different take on this event, see Dwight D. Murphey, "Kent State Revisited," *The Journal of Social, Political and Economic Studies* 18, no. 2 (Summer 1993): 235–55.

4. Terry H. Anderson, *The Movement and the Sixties: Protest in America from Greensboro to Wounded Knee* (New York: Oxford Univ. Press, 1995), 183–238.

5. John Logue, "Official Violence: An American Tradition," in *Kent State/May 4: Echoes through A Decade,* ed. Scott L. Bills (Kent, OH: Kent State Univ. Press, 1982), 143–49.

6. *Newsweek,* May 7, 1990.

7. Kay Boyle, in *The Long Walk at San Francisco State and Other Essays* (New York: Grove Press, 1967), reproduces the list of fifteen strike demands made by the Black Student Union and the Third World Liberation Front. One of the demands stipulated that "fifty faculty positions be appropriated to the School of Ethnic Studies, 20 of which would be for Black Studies Programs." Also see William H. Exum, *Paradoxes of Protest: Black Student Activism in a White University* (Philadelphia: Temple Univ. Press, 1985); Dikran Karagueuzian, *Blow It Up! The Black Student Revolt at San Francisco State College and the Emergence of Dr. Hayakawa* (Boston: Gambit, 1971); DeVere Pentony, Robert Smith, and Richard Axen, *Unfinished Rebellions* (San Francisco: Jossey-Bass, 1971).

8. Beverly T. Watkins, "Rutgers Weighs Moves to Meet Blacks' Demands," *The Chronicle of Higher Education* (hereafter listed as *Chronicle*), Dec. 24, 1973. The percentage of eighteen- to twenty-four-year-old black students increased from 15 percent in 1970 to 18 percent in 1974 (*Chronicle,* Sept. 15, 1975). As the number grew, so did their alienation, estrangement, and rejection of lily-white courses in which black people made an occasional appearance as slave or exotic subaltern. Further, in an unusual move, students argued for greater involvement in community work, offering tutorial assistance to secondary school students, sponsoring cultural affairs, etc., as part of the black studies mission.

9. Cheryl M. Fields, "Women's Studies Gain: 2,000 Courses Offered this Year," *Chronicle,* Dec. 17, 1973; Also see Catharine R. Stimpson with Nina Kressner Cobb, *Women's Studies in the United States: A Report to the Ford Foundation* (New York: Ford Foundation, 1986). Their struggles against racism continue. "Blacks Protest Campus Racism," *Newsweek,* Apr. 6, 1987; Elizabeth Greene, "Racial Incidents at 4 Universities Spark Protests," *Chronicle,* Apr. 20, 1988 (The four universities were Berkeley, Pennsylvania State, Univ. of Kentucky, and Denison Univ.) "Students on the four campuses all charged that their administrations were too complacent about race relations and should take a more active role in improving

people's understanding and appreciation of different cultures. The protesters' demands, which vary from campus to campus, include the creation of black studies requirements for all undergraduates; black, or minority cultural centers; and more black faculty members. At Pennsylvania State, students are asking for a vice-president for minority affairs."

10. Quotes in Karen J. Winkler, "The State of Black Studies," *Chronicle,* Dec. 8, 1975; "Afro-American Studies in the Twenty-First Century: Featuring the Wisconsin Conference on Afro-American Studies, Apr. 18–21, 1971, 1991," *The Black Scholar* 22, no. 3 (Summer 1992).

11. Jerome H. Schiele, "Afrocentricity: Implications for Higher Education," *Journal for Black Studies* 25, no. 2 (Dec. 1994): 150–69; Darlene Clark Hine, "The Black Studies Movement: Afrocentric-Traditionist-Feminist Paradigms for the Next Stage," *The Black Scholar* 22, no. 3 (Summer 1992): 15.

12. See Darlene Clark Hine, "Introduction," in *Hine Sight: Black Women and the Re-Construction of American History* (New York: Carlson Publishing, 1994).

13. Darlene Clark Hine, *Black Women in White: Racial Conflict and Cooperation in the Nursing Profession, 1890–1950* (Bloomington: Indiana Univ. Press, 1980).

14. Margaret L. Andersen, "Changing the Curriculum in Higher Education," *Signs: Journal of Women in Culture and Society* 12, no. 2 (1987): 225–55. Also see Marilyn Schuster and Susan Van Dyne, eds., *Women's Place in the Academy: Transforming the Liberal Arts Curriculum* (Totowa, NJ: Rowan and Allanheld, 1985).

15. My own work included *Black Women in America: An Historical Encyclopedia* (Brooklyn: Carlson Publishing, 1994). For Huggin's remark, see Nathan Irvin Huggins, *Black Odyssey: The African-American Ordeal in Slavery* (New York: Vintage Books, 1990).

16. Susan Hardy Aiken, Karen Anderson, Myra Dinnerstein, Judy Lensink, and Patricia Maccorgquodale, "Trying Transformations: Curriculum Integration and the Problem of Resistance," *Sings: Journal of Women in Culture and Society* 12, no. 2 (1987): 255–75; Kersti Yilo, "Revisions: How the New Scholarship on Women and Gender Transform the College Curriculum," *American Behavioral Scientist* 32, no. 6 (July/Aug. 1989): 658–67; Christie Farham, ed., *The Impact of Feminist Research in the Academy* (Bloomington: Indiana Univ. Press, 1987).

17. Aiken et al., "Trying Transformations," 262.

18. Gary B. Nash, "The History Children Should Study," *Chronicle,* Apr. 21, 1995.

19. Carole Merritt, "The Power of History: Interpreting Black Material Culture," in Darlene Clark Hine, ed., *The State of Afro-American History, Past, Present and Future* (Baton Rouge: Louisiana State Univ. Press, 1986), 213–19. Also see Karen J. Winkler, "Scholars Say Issues of Diversity Have Revolutionized' Field of Chicano Studies," *Chronicle,* Sept. 26, 1990.

Simple Themes and Complex Realities in the Spring of 1970

TOM DIETZ

Tom Dietz is University Distinguished Professor of sociology, environmental science and policy, and animal studies at Michigan State University. He was a charter member of the Kent Legal Defense Fund, which was established after the shootings. This piece was originally written in 1990. The coda was added in 2019.

Each year on May 4, I walk into the forest and spend an hour or two sitting above a valley, reflecting on the spring of 1970 and my life since then. As an ecologist, I know the world and the flow of events in it are too complex to capture directly. Humans mold and structure perceptions and memories to make sense of them. As personal and planetary history moves forward, our vision of the past can become simple and the context of events can disappear. My annual retreat is a way to sustain the complexity of that spring while I try to understand it.

In ecology, there is a tension between complexity and simplicity. Ecologists love the complexity of the biosphere and struggle against the loss of living diversity caused by deforestation, pollution, and other human activities. But ecologists also value abstract models that make sense of the world. For many of us, contemplating how the simple process of Darwinian evolution produced the complex reality of the life on earth is fascinating and rewarding. Ecology is a dialogue between our models and the complex natural history of the planet.

Personal understandings of the world and its history also are conversations between complexity and a simpler view that we can comprehend.

Looking down on a wooded valley I realize that the forest in my mind is a dialogue between me and the forest in the world. In turn, the spring of 1970 in my mind is a dialogue with a complex reality. Reflecting on that time I find some simple themes in a complex, diverse reality. Both the simple and the complex are valuable, each incomplete without the other.

The simple story of Kent is one of dramatic events: the May 1 rally, Water Street that night, the burning of the ROTC building, the shootings, evacuation, continued martial law, indictments, seizing the library, the gym controversy, and so on. These are the first things I think about and usually the first things I'm asked about. But I've found it impossible to make sense of the dramatic events by themselves, and difficult to explain them to others. They lack context and the complexity that comes with it. Without context, the spring of 1970 does not have meaning. It is from the complicated details that the themes and understanding emerge. Over the last twenty years, several themes and details have become important to me.

COMMUNITY

The networks that linked people and organizations at Kent State were extensive and dense. Organizations grew from other organizations: Fellowship of Reconciliation, Kent Free University, Kent Anarchists, Environmental Conservation Organization, Kent Legal Defense Fund, and Kent Community Project were sustained by the same people, and each of these organizations overlapped with many others. This web of relationships, this community, was the movement. It was where we learned from and supported each other. I don't believe the energy and creativity of that period could have existed without it.

GREENS, FEMINISTS, AND GAYS

April 22, 1970, was the first Earth Day, and marked the birth of the new environmental movement. On May 6 "Project Earth" was to have taken place—Kent State's environmental teach-in. During the spring of 1970, the women's liberation movement and the gay liberation movement were also active at Kent State. All were part of the community. For example, the first working groups of the environmental, women's liberation, and gay liberation movements were sponsored by the Free University. Green, feminist, and gay perspectives expanded the concerns of the antiwar movement. These new visions of politics demonstrated the political importance of everyday life and the value of intuitive, personal understanding. And, in turn, the green, feminist, and gay movements benefited from the understanding of structure and power developed in antiwar politics.

ART AND POLITICS

Art was political and politics incorporated the vision and creativity of art. To the list of organizations above I could have added the Needle's Eye, the Tuesday Night Cinema, the Folk Festival, and Gentle Thursday. Art was part of the community and not separate from politics. This made the art more emotionally powerful, while the politics became broader and deeper. Even the Ohio prosecutors seemed to understand this when they included in the Grand Jury Report an attack on the Jefferson Airplane.

PLAYFULNESS AND DISCIPLINE

Simple images of dramatic events filter out both the playfulness of that spring, and the seriousness as well. Fictional accounts seem to have only two kinds of activists: the grim revolutionary and the naive flower child. The flower child might pass out free chili at the Student Union to show that "there is such a thing as a free lunch," or wear a Nixon mask at rallies. The grim activist would work endless hours to raise several hundred thousand dollars as part of the Kent Legal Defense Fund's efforts to fight back against Ohio's prosecution of the Kent 25. But in reality, the same people did both. The playfulness allowed experimentation, relieved tension, and provided the powerful weapon of humor. The discipline got things done.

After a time, my thoughts in the forest turn to the present. Recent changes in Eastern Europe, Latin America, and southern Africa offer some hope of progress on problems of racism, poverty, imperialism, and authoritarian rule. But there is much more that needs to be done. The struggle around these issues remains difficult. And new problems are growing urgent. Over the last twenty years our worst fears about damage to the planetary environment are proving true. Sexism and racism are still prevalent. And weapons of mass destruction threaten millions.

The enormity of these problems is discouraging. But over the last twenty years social movements have persisted and grown, and I believe this decade will see activism flourish. There are lessons for the 1990s in the themes that help me understand the spring of 1970. First, movements have grown too specialized, issue specific, and professional. The networks that make a community should be strengthened so that the community can inform and sustain us. Second, art and playfulness must have a central place in political action because we will need creativity and laughter. Finally, the green and feminist movements offer profound insights not found in other strains of progressive politics and should be at the core of our thinking. But green and feminist thinking must also confront problems of structure and power, and can benefit from the insights of more traditional analyses. The problems we face now cannot be understood or solved by a narrow perspective.

Spring 1970 changes for me each time I think about it. Different parts of that complex time become important as personal and planetary history move forward. The present provides the basis for understanding the past, for finding themes and lessons. Reality is so complex that we can always learn from it as the dialogue between the simple and the complex continues.

CODA

It has been three decades since I wrote this essay, and a half century since the spring of 1970. I still find solace and wisdom in the perspectives of ecology and evolution, in the tangled interconnections of ecosystems, in the arts and in community. Now I sometimes spend May 4 with family and friends appreciating the complexity and diversity they bring to my life. But the landscape still calls me.

Environmental problems, and especially the profound changes we are making to the biosphere through climate and other global changes, species extinctions, and the widespread dispersal of toxic substances threaten both human well-being and the biosphere. Old problems persist: violence, inequality, poverty. Some seem more prevalent or at least more visible than they were even a decade or so ago. The political strategy of creating bias and division was part of the background of 1970, and it persists.

But we have more and deeper perspectives to help us think through these difficult problems. The gay and feminist movements have expanded and diversified, and we are more attentive to many forms of diversity and how they benefit us. We have become much more attentive to the other species with whom we share the planet. Science and the arts continue to help us understand and appreciate the complexity of the world. Our struggles for justice, for peace and for understanding continue. The simple themes of spring 1970 continue to resonate and provide insights into the ongoing, evolving complexity of the twenty-first century. They still reward contemplation.

This piece originally appeared in *Kent & Jackson State 1970–1990*, edited by Susie Erenrich.

Message from a May 4 Baby

(P)reflections on the Fiftieth Commemoration of May 4, 1970

IDRIS KABIR SYED

Idris Kabir Syed is an associate professor in the Department of Pan-African Studies at Kent State University. He served as faculty adviser for the May 4 Task Force from 2009 to 2019. This piece was written in fall 2018.

I was born on March 4, 1971, exactly ten months after the shootings at Kent State University. My parents were both working on their PhDs in English literature at Kent State University then. I grew up in the shadows of the shootings and they follow me continually. On May 4, 1970, at around noon, my parents were on their way to a dentist appointment. Before they got to the office, the National Guard were closing the roads in the city of Kent and they were told they had to return to their apartment quickly. They remained in their Allerton apartment that night, and one of my father's former students, who was in a local Ravenna motorcycle gang, came over for dinner. They talked about the horror of the shootings on campus, and, as my mom remembers, they were all "shocked and frightened." My mother told me my grandmother, who lives in India but happened to be in Washington, DC, at the time, called her that evening to make sure that everything was all right. My parents were unharmed; while no one they knew on campus was shot, nothing was all right.

My parents were not activists but progressive thinkers. My mother remembers befriending "a nice couple," Bill and Marilyn Whitaker, who lived in Allerton and who were involved in Students for a Democratic Society (SDS). My father recalled going to an SDS meeting once in 1968, and in his words "not being impressed." He also remembered encountering SDS protesters at a conference on Asian policy and politics he attended on campus in 1969; the quotation I remember from him about this event is, "They used the word 'fuck' far too often when they spoke."

My mother remembers attending only one commemoration; it was my first, in 1972. She had hazy memories of the event, which was understandable as she was with a fourteen-month-old infant and in her eighth month of pregnancy with my brother. While she did remember parking by Captain Brady's and walking up to the Commons, she did not remember walking by the hundreds of cardboard tombstones placed outside Rockwell Hall that year. The tombstones, thoughtfully inscribed with messages about war, death, and loss, were perhaps one of the most powerful visual tributes to antiwar sentiment on campus. I experienced two other compelling visual tributes to the loss of life, in both cases of veterans, in my commemoration attendances over the years. The first was the planting of 58,175 daffodils (representing US military soldiers who had lost their lives in Vietnam) in 1990 by sculpture professor Brinsley Tyrrell. The second was the Eyes Wide Open display of 3,500 pairs of empty boots (representing US casualties of the Afghanistan and Iraq wars) in May 2008.

My mother did remember being with my father at the Commons on May 4, 1972. She did not remember the South African author Alan Paton reading his poem "Flowers for the Departed" nor the stinging last stanza:

> America, for you these flowers
> Would we could reach out our hands to comfort you
> But we dare not
> We dare not touch those fingers dripping
> With children's blood[1]

She did not remember the keynote speaker, the 1967 Nobel Prize–winning Harvard professor, Dr. George Wald. His speech, "A Call for the Repossession of America," referenced the shootings at Orangeburg in 1968 and at Kent State and Jackson State in 1970. Inspired by black student movements, he spoke, in a way eerily similar to Malcolm X's response to JFK's assassination, about how America was suffering from the chickens coming home to roost in light of the massive casualties from the war in Vietnam. As a fourteen-month-old, I obviously could not remember these facts, but I think I was listening, putting those messages away for a later time. My father went to many more commemorations over the years. I do not know how many, but I remember seeing him at quite a few as an undergraduate and graduate student, and hearing that he attended many more where I did not see him, but he saw me (mixed with pride and prudence for his son).

Both my parents spoke cautiously and ominously about the events of May 4, 1970; it haunted them, albeit in different ways, but haunted them no less. A dark and ominous cloud hovered over Kent State as well. The political activists of the time were becoming more radicalized but also cynical, bitter, and burned out after the killing of so many movement martyrs. It would also be years before the war was over, so that many young veterans were coming home, often a hostile reception, but still bearing the physical and psychological wounds of the horrors they had to perpetrate abroad. Kent, Ohio, had never been a pristine or pure town, but by this time the alcohol abuse became more pronounced and the drug use was harder and more frequent. My mother got a job teaching English at Western Reserve Academy in Hudson, so we moved to Hudson in my brother's first year of life.

The city of Kent was not a frequent destination during my years in Hudson, but every once in a while, my parents' friend, Richard Bernard, would take me to Walter's Bar on North Water Street. He gave me five dollars in quarters and sat me down in front of the pinball machine while he drank beers with his friends. It was a perfect relationship; we both got to do what we wanted and would go back to Hudson after a few hours. I remembered those times fondly, happy that I got to hang out with all the cool older people in this gritty little bar with pool tables and pinball machines. Hudson was much more conservative. Though it was once the home of famous abolitionist John Brown, it was an almost completely white community, not particularly welcoming of people of color. It was in Hudson that identity issues around race would arise for me. These were exacerbated when my mother was fired from Western Reserve Academy under discriminatory practices, which she later proved in court.

Racial identity questions remained an issue through schooling in Cleveland Heights, where we moved. I went to high school as a boarding student on scholarship at Cranbrook/Kingswood in Michigan. Many people associate it with alumni like Ivan Boesky, Alan Simpson, and Mitt Romney; I prefer Daniel Ellsberg, Kathryn Kolbert, and Pero Dagbovie. At Cranbrook, racial, class, and social politics were always in contention. However, it was there that I truly began to open up to a progressive and radical mind-set.

When I returned home to Cleveland Heights that summer, I started to date Shauna Cagan, a student at Cleveland Heights High School. Shauna and her parents, Steve (a professor in photography at Rutgers) and Beth (a professor in social work), were another major influence in my radical politics. Beth and Steve had just finished their book, *This Promised Land: El Salvador,* and had been strongly engaged as antiwar protesters and civil rights activists in New York City in the late 1960s and early 1970s. Shauna was a strong advocate and woman in her own right. At the young age of sixteen, she had already spent time doing public service work in the Dominican Republic. She was, and remains, both a great artist and a profound thinker. Spending time with this family over the summer of 1989 and the next few years was a critical push toward understanding and engaging in mindful social activism.

When I came to Kent State in the fall of 1989, that commitment to social activism was solidified. My first priority was to pursue my degree in Pan-African studies. The Pan-African Studies (PAS) Department has its origins in the November 18, 1968, walkout of African American students following a protest on November 13, led by Black United Students (BUS) and supported by SDS, against the recruitment of criminal justice students by the Oakland Police Department. BUS demanded more institutional representation for their community, which led to the creation of the Institute for African American Affairs (1969), the Center for Pan-African Culture (1970), and finally the Department of Pan-African Studies (1976). The connection and commitment to Pan-African studies have remained with me over the years as I moved from 1989 as undergraduate student and worker, to graduate teaching assistant, to part-time faculty member, to assistant and now associate professor. I owe PAS my political consciousness and, as I often tell my students, every job related to counseling and teaching in my life.

The other seminal event for me that year was attending my first May 4 commemoration as an adult, the twentieth commemoration in 1990. The 1989–90 year was a big one for the university and the May 4 Task Force. The university was in the process of building a memorial on campus to the events of May 4, 1970. The process had already been long in the works and remains contentious, as are all memorials: fundraising was a major problem; arguments about which designs were chosen, how resources were allocated, and who (and what message) was privileged began to arise at that time. The administration convened a committee of faculty to organize a dedication of the memorial. However, because there was little, if any, communication with the students, especially those on the May 4 Task Force (M4TF), students felt the university was trying to control and dilute the message the student organization wanted to put forward.

The president of the M4TF that year was the daughter of that "nice couple," Bill and Marilyn Whitaker, who were friends of my parents. Andrea Whitaker was an anthropology major who was in her sophomore year. The faculty adviser of the Task Force at the beginning of my first year was Dr. Jerry Lewis, but by the spring semester, it was Dr. Michael Lee. The students were preparing for the annual commemoration, but they also organized a two-day student conference after the commemoration. There was a solid crew of about thirty to forty students who engaged in weekly preparation and most were members of both the M4TF and the Progressive Student Network (PSN).

Their hard work paid off on the evening of May 3 with the annual Task Force programs. The evening began with a wounded-student forum. This was the first time that I had heard from those survivors who lived outside the northeast Ohio area. I distinctly remembered the words of Jim Russell: "I was struck down as I was running through the trees, heading for trees for cover. I saw all kinds of pandemonium break loose; everything was out of control. I have never come to grips with that, [as] a matter of fact I left Ohio because it was never resolved correctly here ... I think that this twentieth memorial is time for us to tell the world, 'You don't shoot children for what they think. This is a place to exercise ideas. You don't bring guns onto a campus, you don't bring guns into any civilian situation, you allow people to exercise their right to free thought, assembly, the full constitutional balance of rights. You don't shoot people for what they believe.'"[2] The second panel was equally engaging; from local to international, there were representatives from South Africa and the African National Congress, China, and the Tiananmen Square protest, and there was a Farabundo Marti National Liberation Front representative from El Salvador.

May 4 itself was rainy. The crowds were huge, at least five thousand. I remember that it was so crowded that Shauna and I were standing up above the Commons near Taylor Hall. We were drenched as the May 4 Memorial dedication ceremony began. A few things about the event stood out to me. On this monumental memorial, the names of those shot are tucked away on a small plaque, now covered by foliage. The other is the jagged rock left by the designer of the memorial indicating the incompletion of his original design.

In her announcement of the M4TF silent protest of the memorial dedication, Andrea Whitaker, chairperson of the Task Force, made note of this as well and offered some prescient words as we approach the fiftieth commemoration, stating:

> Also the meaning of the memorial, being dedicated to the events of May 4. The university seems to be absolutely unwilling here to claim the memorial for what it is, not just politically, but the human issue. It is depoliticized, but it is also dehumanized. The names that were put on there are separate. I don't understand. Ten feet or 20 feet, that separation is important to the university because they are unwilling to make the claim of the memorial for what it is. I'd like to read to you what was on the memorial for the students

killed at Jackson State. For Phillip Gibbs: Phillip Gibbs will remain in the memory of all Jacksonians as a martyr who nobly relinquished his life for the cause of human brotherhood. And for James Earl Green, like Gibbs, did not choose to die, but was a victim of death's mandate. He nobly takes the station among other martyrs of the cause. This university was willing to make a statement for what happened on their campus twenty years ago; our university is not. I'd also like to speak to the issue of the message the university is sending out on this twentieth anniversary. This twentieth anniversary that so aptly timed the memorial dedication and for the scholarship dedication. Fifteen years ago the university thought that was enough, the commemoration was enough, and they tried to write the final chapter on May 4. The students then said *no,* that's not going to happen, five years is not enough. This year our president has referred to the twentieth anniversary again as the final chapter; again, concerned students, activists, faculty, and community members said that is not enough. It's not an issue that's going to go away. This isn't about a single remembering issue that you can just forget because it's been long enough. The issue is here—the issues of dissent, the fact that people were killed—are timeless. And they cannot be buried after twenty, thirty, or fifty years.[3]

As the protesters and thousands of others lined the area where the dedication of the memorial was occurring, the words of the administration were drowned out by the silence and the rain. I remember nothing else about this dedication ceremony, nor do I need to.

The commemoration was moved, due to the rain, inside the Student Center Ballroom. This was the first and only time I would see Glenn Frank speak at a commemoration. I did not know about Glenn Frank at the time, but I was struck by his words:

> Four promising young people were snuffed out, and the reason for this act is still not obvious to me today, but, in spite of this, we remember them publicly today. Sandy, Allison, Bill, and Jeff. We remember their loved ones, who must live daily with this mental anguish. The assassination of President John F. Kennedy, the Rev. Martin Luther King, Attorney General Robert F. Kennedy, students at Orangeburg State College in 1968, students at Kent State and Jackson State in 1970, and many, many more, should deepen the criticism regarding the role of government in a democratic society, and each such event diminishes each of us in America. Physical wounds may heal, but psychological wounds may be carried to the grave. Today we also celebrate the lives of those, who by some miracle, were spared, but

spared for what purpose? Those of us left behind for a few more moments of life must seek understanding in our quest for truth. Accept the supreme good of every human being, and allow our faith to overcome all evil and try to establish a democracy of the people, by the people, and for the people.[4]

Of course, I would later learn of Glenn Frank's role after the thirteen seconds and sixty-seven shots. He was a hero as student casualty Tom Grace would so aptly state: "I think the term *hero* is a probably overused, and sometimes much abused word. But if there were a few heroes that emerged throughout that dark day on May 4, 1970, certainly he would be among them."[5]

The year 1990 was also my introduction to Gene Young from Jackson, Mississippi. For the next twenty-one years, Dr. Gene "Jughead" Young was a close friend and mentor. He was the most consistent speaker I remember from the 1990–2010 commemorations. He taught me a great deal about his life in the civil rights struggle, from his first arrest at age twelve to his sustained commitment until the end of his life. I miss Gene every year and was honored to deliver the M4TF tribute to his life at the 2011 commemoration. Gene's friendship, sense of humor, voice, and recitation of Dr. King's speeches are forever burned in my brain; for that, I remain eternally grateful and blessed.

The speaker I was most looking forward to hearing was my favorite civil rights lawyer, William Moses Kunstler. Kunstler was a force to reckon with; he founded the Center for Constitutional Rights and directed the ACLU during the critical years of 1964–72. In addition to clients like Martin Luther King Jr., Malcolm X, Assata Shakur, the Chicago 7, the American Indian Movement, the prisoners at Attica, and the Central Park 5, he represented the students at Kent State in their attempts to get justice. Over the next four years, I took the initiative to drive Bill Kunstler to and from the Cleveland Hopkins Airport when he spoke at commemorations. I distinctly remember how privileged I felt to get that extended time to talk in depth about all of his life experiences. He spoke not only of the movement and his clients but also about his family. On our last trip to Kent State from the airport in 1994, he ran through ideas from his speech with me, quizzing me on my thoughts about the Boston Tea Party. On our way back, we continued the discussion about the American Revolution. I thanked him and wished him safe travels, and he gave me his usual good-bye—"Power to people, my brother, see you again!"—with his fist in the air. I cannot ask for a better last memory of him in this world. An African proverb says that we stand on the shoulders of our ancestors. I stand on Dr. Frank's, Dr. Young's, and William Moses Kunstler's shoulders, tall, with strength and pride.

The twentieth annual commemoration obviously had a great impact on me. I did not, however, join the leadership of the Task Force; rather, in the fall of 1991, I became the chair of the Middle East Committee of the Progressive Student Network (PSN) and the assistant to Keita Sa'ad, the African Affairs chair of BUS. I still attended Task Force meetings weekly, and all M4TF members were active in PSN and vice versa. August 1991 was the beginning of the first Gulf War, Operation Desert Shield/Storm, and both PSN and M4TF were actively engaged in protesting the war.

I had the task of approaching BUS to support our antiwar efforts. BUS students had their own specific agenda and were understandably wary of working with their liberal, white peers. I was unaware of the intricacies of intersectional work, unaware of the history on the Kent State campus between SDS and BUS. When students from the BUS board challenged me about why they should support PSN and what the war had to do with them, they pointed out that they were catching hell in their own neighborhood; they were the targets of war in their own communities, the drug war, police brutality, and a war of poverty. Even if I was working with a BUS board member, these students were not going to give me a pass. I must have been floundering because the PAS department chair, Dr. Edward Crosby, stepped in. He told the crowd to give me a chance. He reminded them that in Vietnam, and likely with this war, the people who would be most likely to lose their lives were African Americans and Latinos. He told them that the problems of racism, poverty, police brutality, and often drugs were interrelated with war. He referenced the book *Bloods: Black Veterans: An Oral History* and encouraged us all to think critically about what was happening, especially politically, around us.

As the war ramped up through the fall, PSN mobilized to join the national antiwar march in Washington, DC, that January. We sent a contingent of about fifty students to DC. Leslie Cagan, Shauna's aunt, coordinated the DC national antiwar march. The march took place on a warm winter day. The estimated crowd numbered five hundred thousand yet received little press coverage. The Kent State contingent did make the news, however, as I was interviewed on CNN; I reiterated the history of KSU students' antiwar struggle from Vietnam to the Gulf War and spoke of our duty to voice our dissent nationally. Upon our return to Kent State, I worked with the Task Force chairperson, first-year student Lara Bauer, to invite Leslie Cagan to be our keynote speaker for the 1991 commemoration.

The war and the media blackout of the antiwar response to it greatly affected my motivation (or lack thereof) over the summer and fall semester of 1991. I was burned out, frustrated, and wondered what the purpose of social activism was if it could be effectively marginalized and discounted with such ease. I realized over the next six months that getting involved with the movement was a marathon, not a sprint. This idea was reinforced when I met Kwame Ture (Stokely Carmichael), whom BUS brought to Kent State in February 1992.

Meeting Ture was inspirational and essential to my development. He validated the work I had done over my first few years at Kent and recruited a number of us from BUS to organize a student cadre of the All-African People's Revolutionary Party (AAPRP). We engaged, over the next few years, in a weekly study group in Akron and Kent, where we were taught socialism from an African context. We read and dissected the approaches of Kwame Nkrumah in Ghana and Sekou Toure in Guinea. This supplemented the history I learned in my Pan-African studies courses. When Ture came back in 1993, I was amazed he remembered meeting me the year before. I was astonished that a civil rights leader of his stature was able to recall specific details from a conversation he had with me a year earlier. He was so incredibly sharp that it was as if he knew where I was in my development and where I would go. I sat down for an hour-long interview with him in 1993 and discussed the rebellions that had taken place in Los Angeles in 1992; this interview served as the basis for an article I wrote for the spring 1993 issue of *Uhuru* magazine, the official publication of BUS.

By the fall of 1993, Shauna and I had broken up, and I started a relationship with former Task Force chair Lara Bauer. I was also finishing my undergraduate degree and had become the editor for *Uhuru* magazine. Life was full and busy. I graduated in spring 1994 with my BA in Pan-African studies and English. I was not sure what I wanted to pursue for graduate school; with the assistance of Dr. Crosby, I started a liberal studies master's program in the fall of 1994. Lara, who had also graduated in 1994, moved to South Korea to teach English. It was not long before I joined her. By the fall of 1995, I was living in South Korea; the spring 1996 commemoration would be the only one I would miss in my adult life.

The students who worked with the Task Force after the mid-1990s were capable and diverse in their political orientations. As a graduate student (I had transferred into the community counseling program that year), I still went to meetings but took a backseat role. The one exception was in 1998.

That year the Task Force had worked toward closing and cordoning off the parking spaces where the four students were killed in the Prentice Hall parking lot. The group had secured signatures of support by all four families and tried to present their letter to then president Dr. Carol Cartwright at the vigil on May 3. Dr. Cartwright felt that it was inappropriate to be approached by the Task Force students at the vigil and refused to take the letter. As we met that night to discuss how to proceed, there was debate even among the wounded students. Some, like Robbie Stamps, felt that we were wrong to approach Dr. Cartwright in that setting; others, like Alan Canfora, supported the students and echoed the support of Task Force students from parents like Doris Krause, thankful that students, not even born when her daughter Allison was killed, were still standing up to honor her memory.

Interestingly, Dr. Cartwright remembers the situation very differently than I do. She wrote of the experience: "A group from the May 4th Task Force approached me at the vigil in 1999 [sic] and told me that permanent markers were now desired. With a deep sense of respect for their loss, I took time to gain assurance that the families were ready. They were and we moved forward."[6] This memory, while administratively convenient, is not accurate either in date or in spirit. While this memory marks what many believe to be a turning point in the administrative response to May 4 at Kent State, it is fabricated and disempowers the self-determination and struggle of the students. History and facts, however, corroborate my memory of the experience and show how all movements for progress with the May 4 Movement have been bottom-up (i.e., student-led) rather than top-down (i.e., promoted by the administration).

After the commemoration on May 4, 1998, Ron Kovic, in his wheelchair, led 250 people on a march from the Commons to the administrative offices at the library. Dr. Cartwright and her staff agreed to meet with a group of representatives from the Task Force and the students asked me to speak as an alumnus and graduate representative. We presented the letter from the families and over the next two hours put forth our reasoning for closing off the spaces. Dr. Cartwright and her staff were amenable to accepting the letter from the families after our pleas and over the next year worked diligently to meet our demands. I still think of the cordoned-off parking spaces as one of the most tangible victories of the Task Force. There are no longer oil stains where Jeff, Allison, Sandy, and Bill fell from the National Guard's bullets, and families, students, and community members can commemorate with optics that dignify the memory of their loss.

The thirtieth commemoration in 2000 was perhaps one of the most powerful I attended. Students from Anti-Racist Action were integrally involved in planning the commemoration that year. Gloria Green McCrae, sister of James Green, and Demetrius Gibbs, son of Phillip Gibbs, along with Gene Young, represented Jackson State. Their personal reflections of the Jackson State martyrs were particularly profound. Wa Bun Inini (Vernon Bellecourt) represented the American Indian Movement. Julia Butterfly Hill gave an inspiring account of her year living with Luna, the name she gave to the great Redwood tree she was trying to protect from logging. Her decidedly ecofeminist message was insightful and challenging for all who heard it. Noam Chomsky was also prescient, reminding us of the international challenges of militarism throughout the world, and warning of continued trouble in the Middle East. A year and a half later, I was haunted by this message as I watched the planes fly into the Twin Towers.

The two speakers who had the greatest impact, however, were Mumia Abu Jamal and Ramona Africa. Mumia, sitting in a jail cell, managed to get an audiotape out to the students from the Task Force. The Commons was silent, save for Mumia's booming bass voice:

> Kent State teaches that a so-called free society will slaughter students who are exercising their alleged constitutional right of demonstrating for peace and give awards to the killers, and do so with impunity. The passions that drove over a quarter of a million people into the streets against the Vietnam War have cooled in thirty years, but for many—for the poor, for radical dissidents, for prisoners and increasingly for Black youth—that war has come home. Kent State was indeed a vile and bloody marker, but as Amadou Diallo shows us, the blood spilled by the state continues to run. It also teaches us the very real limits of the law. When it is the state itself that commits criminal acts, all these absolutely awesome examples scream to us from the charnel house of history. And none of these vicious, premeditated mass murderers spent a single hour in a jail cell. What does this tell you of the nature of things? In truth, weren't those four kids at Kent State in fact liquidated because they were exercising their alleged constitutional rights? What does this reveal about the true nature of the state? Of America? Of the Constitution?[7]

These questions were probing but equally prosecutorial.

Ramona Africa, the lone adult survivor of the 1980 MOVE bombing in Philadelphia, had lived through a horrifying and unimaginable experience. I was aware of the bombing and had studied her writings. After suffering this state-sponsored terrorism, she spent seven years in jail; I expected her to present her righteously angry story. Instead, she was solemn and reverential and gave this progressive charge to the crowd:

> The thing is, right here at Kent State, thirty years ago, people were attacked by the National Guard. Four people were shot down, nine others injured. And I think that Jeffrey Miller, Sandra Scheuer, William Schroeder, and Allison Krause would agree with me when I say that empty words are not enough

to pay homage to them. We must pay homage to these victims of state-sponsored terrorism through our action, through our dedication and our commitment to stop the system that caused their deaths, that caused injury.

It has now been thirty years, but nothing has changed. We have to fight that much harder. We have to be that much more serious. We have to come at these people as hard as we possibly can to stop their terrorism. Right now things are not getting better for people. They're getting worse. Cops feel like they have a license to shoot people down in the street, beat people down in the street, to lock people up at will despite their innocence. And I'm saying we have to stop that—we as a people coming together. Not just black people, not just poor whites, not just indigenous people or Latino people in this country, but all of us. Because the one thing that those running this country fear the most is unity, is the people coming together realizing who the real enemy is.

We are not each other's enemy. We have to be clear on who the real enemy is and come together, work together. We cannot afford to have the mentality of "I can't work with that person because they did this twenty years ago." We don't have the time for that. We can't afford that. We all have to come together, work together, to end this insanity.[8]

Of course, we did not come together; in fact, there has been increased polarization over the past twenty years. The election of George Bush in 2000 was chaos and marked contentious presidential elections, which have plagued us in the new millennium. The attacks of 9/11 shocked the world. Terror of this scale was terrifying. Those of us engaged in antiwar activism knew the precedents for this attack; colonial policies in the Middle East, primarily carried out by Britain and the United States over the past 150 years (but also supported by much of the world), had eventual consequences. If only we had listened to Malcolm X and Dr. George Wald, thought about our chickens coming home to roost, but alas, we did not. Instead, we went straight to war in Afghanistan, which has now become the United States' longest foreign war. Even worse, two years later we would unwisely expand our military operations to include overthrowing Saddam Hussein in Iraq.

The attacks of 9/11 fundamentally changed American society. Since then governmental power, especially that of the executive branch, has greatly expanded, often subjugating individual rights. The Patriot Act and renewals and expansions of the National Defense Authorization Act have led to extraordinary renditions, torture, and extrajudicial killings. These realities had a chilling and silencing effect on my political engagement and involvement for a number of years. I rarely talked about politics with friends or coworkers. I kept to myself.

When, in 2003, students and community members approached me about getting involved in an antiwar march after the annual commemoration, I passed. I had a bad feeling about the atmosphere surrounding the march. My wariness was not without reason. As two hundred students and community members marched down Main Street, the police (including local Kent city police, SWAT, and the Portage County Drug Task Force) cordoned off the street and closed in on the marchers on three sides, forcing them into the street. With a helicopter hovering above, the police targeted specific marchers and as they entered the street, some were attacked and thirteen were arrested. The brutal and militaristic response of the police toward peaceful protesters was a frightening reminder of how much we still need to learn when engaging those expressing their First Amendment rights to redress their government.

Dr. Michael Lee served as M4TF faculty adviser for fifteen years, the longest to date, but left the university in the 2004–5 year. Karen Cunningham took over the role from Dr. Michael Lee. The other notable point of Cunningham's new role as adviser was that, as a professor in what is now the School of Peace and Conflict Studies, a faculty member from a department created because of the shootings on May 4, 1970, she was now advising the group that led the yearly commemorations.

Over the next five years, M4TF continued in their commitment to honoring the wounded students and the families of Jeffrey, Allison, Sandra, and Bill. They also fulfilled their mission to examine the antiwar, civil rights, and social justice issues that were important to the students who created the M4TF in 1975. Notable speakers over that time were Tom Hayden, Cindy Sheehan, John Filo, and Mary Ann Vecchio.

I became faculty adviser in the 2009–10 academic year, right before a major commemoration, this time the fortieth. I have the unique distinction of being the first faculty adviser born after the events of May 4, 1970. Over my ten years in this position, I have had many moments where I have been personally challenged. I have not always been proud of my behavior and reactions, but I have tried to learn from my mistakes, heal open wounds (some which I created), and remain a faithful advocate for the students in the M4TF. I will not provide a comprehensive list of speakers we have had over the last ten years, but rather, I will highlight some of the moments that have been significant to me.

On the fortieth commemoration, I was honored to work with many local people who had been involved with the movement at Kent State University. The M4TF sponsored programs, including a forum on student activism featuring Robert Pickett, former vice president of student government and one of the founders of BUS. This was important to me because the program was jointly sponsored by BUS and the M4TF. Students were exposed to an incredible student leader–turned-attorney (and now judge), who spoke truth to the power of Vice President Hubert Humphrey, challenged the Oakland Police Department, and, even when warned to stay away, risked his life as he stood with his white comrades on the Commons on May 4, 1970. The Task Force also invited Dr. Daniel Miller, alumnus of Kent State University, who screened his documentary film, *Fire in the Heartland.* BUS and M4TF students were so impressed by the film that they wrote a letter asking that it be shown in all First-Year Experience classes to give incoming students an orientation to the importance of the civil rights and antiwar struggles here at Kent State University. Students from M4TF also wrote to the administration demanding the removal of three trees, planted by President Glen Olds after the shooting, which were in the line of the Guardsmen's fire into Prentice Hall parking lot; this goal was achieved in the fall 2017/spring 2018. The other demands, not yet met by the administration, included the establishment of thirteen scholarships in honor of the thirteen students shot and full funding and completion of the memorial. I was also honored to meet and interact personally with Mark Rudd, Bernardine Dohrn, members of the SDS and cofounders of the Weather Underground, and Bobby Seale, cofounder of the Black Panther Party for Self Defense. All three were so steadfast and genuine with their engagement with the students that I could not help but be humbled and inspired.

Another inspirational moment was working with local Vietnam veterans from Warriors Journey Home. After engaging with the veterans' organization over the 2011–12 school year, members of the M4TF were so impressed with their work that they decided to put their money where their hearts were. The Task Force decided in May 2012 to donate $1,000 to the organization for their work in building school libraries in Vietnam.

In 2013, M4TF brought Bill Ayers—or as many conservatives call him, Obama's terrorist—as one of their keynote speakers. My experience with both Bill and Bernardine was as wholly committed humanists, far from my idea of terrorists. Bernardine has spent her entire adult life fighting for children's rights, not to mention the rights of women and people of color throughout the world. Bill, likewise, has never stopped his dedication to the liberation struggle for African Americans and others as he spent many years as a professor of education. Bill, to his credit, spoke of the profound cost of the choices of militant resistance with the loss of life for Diana Oughton, Terry Robbins, and Ted Gold. He stated that he regretted their loss. He also reminded us that the true terrorism were the violence perpetrated by the state in Vietnam,

Cambodia, and Laos and the racism perpetrated in and outside of the United States since its inception. The year 2013 also marked the first year that the May 4 Visitors Center was open for the commemoration.

The year 2014 was particularly powerful for three speakers—Chris Butler, Dean Kahler, and Robin Jackson. Robin was a current student from Jackson State. It was incredible to see the connection between M4TF students and a student from Jackson State, both honoring students who had lost their lives before these students were even born. Dean Kahler had to have his wheelchair lifted on and off the stage in the Student Center Ballroom. He started his speech poignantly by pointing out that it is always depressing to him as a person with mobility challenges that in the forty-four years he has been at Kent State University, there are still campus facilities not easily accessible to mobility-challenged people. Chris Butler gave one of the most moving speeches I have ever heard for his close friend Jeff Miller. In it, he had an imaginary conversation with his therapist, and it cut to the core.

While 2014 was a successful commemoration, it was saddened by the sudden loss of communication studies professor Dr. Carole Barbato, who had unexpectedly died on April 30, shortly after retiring from Kent State University. Carole, who was integral in the creation of the May 4 Visitors Center and getting Kent State University on the National Register of Historic Places, along with Lori Boes and Laura Davis, was a strong, longtime supporter of M4TF and me personally.

After fall 2014, students from the M4TF became concerned with the militarization of police forces across the country. Also notable was the rise of the Black Lives Matter (BLM) movement and the killing of Tamir Rice in Cleveland. The students of the Task Force became increasingly supportive of this cause. As it was the forty-fifth year, students wanted to both honor May 4 history and represent the civil rights struggle, so they invited Dick Gregory to speak on campus again. It was the last time Gregory would come to campus and it was a real honor to meet him. During breakfast, we talked about his early comedy days, and about Bill Cosby, Malcolm X, and John Brown. I realized he was practicing his speech with me, just as Bill Kunstler had done twenty years earlier.

It was also the first year that our new university president, Dr. Beverly Warren, spoke at a commemoration. During that academic year, she had attended more than one Task Force meeting; she spoke of her decision to take the job as she walked through the May 4 Visitors Center, which was still under construction, in the spring of 2014 during a visit to campus. She also spoke compellingly of her memories of civil rights and antiwar protests, as well as her affinity toward both when she was a college student. The Task

Force mistakenly introduced her as the first Kent State University president to speak at a M4TF commemoration; Dr. Carol Cartwright had introduced Jackson State University president Dr. John A. Peoples at a prior commemoration.

This concern with extrajudicial killing by police and BLM culminated in the invitation of Samaria Rice, Tamir Rice's mother, to be the keynote speaker for the 2016 commemoration. On April 25 of that year, the City of Cleveland settled a wrongful death lawsuit with the Rice family. The award was $6 million, with $5.5 million going to the estate of Tamir Rice and $250,000 each going to Samaria and Tamir's sister Tajai, with whom I had worked at an arts program at Cudell Rec Center the previous summer. All hell broke loose, and the backlash—or blacklash as I like to call it—toward our speaker was particularly vitriolic and violent. The only other speaker I can remember as being the target of more anger was Mumia Abu Jamal. People from all over the country were calling the university to express their anger at the Task Force's invitation. The press barraged us with interview requests, which I handed to students whenever I could. The administration, which publicly supported the M4TF choice of Rice as keynote speaker, still had phone calls from alumni and donors routed to my office to explain the M4TF decision to invite Samaria. I happily obliged, pointing out the historical connections between Orangeburg State, Kent State, and Jackson State and the M4TF's consistent commitment to human rights for all. I could not understand the callousness of people toward someone who had lost her child; they would say horrible things like, "She definitely got rich off of his death, how much are you paying her?" I told them we would pay her $3,000, which is less than half of what she received to speak at other universities. I would then go home, spend time with my son, and think that no amount of money could ever replace him. I was quite sure Samaria felt the same way about Tamir. The outright racism and hatred in some of those calls brought me to tears. I reminded the haters that like the Krause, Scheuer, Schroeder, and Miller parents, Samaria also lost her son to a shooting perpetrated by governmental authority.

As she so simply but eloquently stated during her address, "Once again I was just thrown into this; I was cooking lasagna for my children when all of this happened. So I am just a mom at the end of the day, but also in honoring my son I want to be able to change the laws and create some change across America, period . . . I didn't realize we're still wanting justice for these four babies that was killed, 'cause at the end of the day, they still somebody's baby, you know what I am saying? I was just blown away that they haven't received justice yet. I don't understand. I'm having a hard time understanding that. When you talking about the National Guard shooting into a crowd of unarmed civilians, and some college students at that? America should be ashamed of itself, period."[9]

The fortieth anniversary of the Tent City protest and all of the commemoration events were organized around that theme in 2017. Students and community members made up the speakers list that year and spoke of their protracted struggle from 1977 to 2017. Many students and community members kept up their demands in a public forum held by the administration that Blanket Hill be restored to its original state, removing the now-defunct Memorial Gym Annex.

The commemoration in 2018 was the fiftieth anniversary of the shootings at Orangeburg State. The invited keynote speaker, Dr. William Hine, was present on both the Orangeburg and Kent campuses when their respective shootings occurred. I was honored to give a tour of the campus to Dr. Hine and his ex-wife, Kent State alumnus Darlene Clark-Hine. During that walk we discussed their time on campus and the need to write about Orangeburg, Kent State, and Jackson State. In our conversation and in his speech Dr. Hine spoke eloquently of the lack of attention the shootings at Orangeburg received, even today. He spoke of the need to remember Orangeburg, Kent State, and Jackson State and their historical relevance. In light of hundreds of shooting incidents occurring at schools since Jackson State, his words and witness are incredibly important.

As I write this chapter in the fall of 2018, our campus still struggles with the issue of the shooting on campus and we always will. This time, however, the threats come from our own student ranks. Over the past few years conservative student groups and one particular conservative student (now alumnus), Kaitlin Bennett, has been pushing for an expansion of gun rights on the KSU campus. Groups like hers, Liberty Hangout, have been emboldened, and often funded, by right-wing political action committees and Trump's brand of white nationalistic Republicans. Groups she supports, like the Three Percenters, who provided security at her most recent rally on September 29, 2018, have also provided "security" in violent right-wing protests like those of Malheur National Wildlife Refuge Occupation in Oregon and the Unite the Right rally in Charlottesville.

These groups claim they are not racist, but they are often linked to white nationalist groups and violence. Kaitlin Bennett, the infamous alumna whom current students call "bumpstock Barbie," said that BUS members were "probably welfare babies." The gun-rights advocates were surrounded by police officers. Interestingly, one of the Three Percenters, Skylar Steward, broke out of this protection and charged—by his own admission, but before his flag was grabbed by a counterprotester—into Antifa, BLM, and student counterprotesters with his hand on his (presumably) loaded weapon. He was grabbed by a state trooper and pulled back, but he was not arrested. Four arrests were made; none of those arrested were affiliated with Kaitlin Bennett's supporters. Skylar Steward's behavior, as witnessed in the videos posted online, certainly seems to be worthy of arrest. I cannot help but wonder what his fate would have been if he was an armed BLM member; experience has shown he would have probably been killed, or at the very least arrested. My mind goes back to May 4, 2003, the beginning of the war in Iraq. I remember the brutal and vicious police response to the peaceful antiwar protesters. (I was not there because I knew I would be targeted.) I saw no violence from BLM or Antifa protestors as I observed the protest between Bowman and Lake Halls. I am not saying it did not occur, but I did not see any. What I did see from them was proactive, organized, nonviolent protest utilizing the tactics of civil disobedience and noncompliance. Skylar Steward was another story; it seems like he was shielded and privileged by police.

This most recent rally is troubling and speaks to continued trouble we face, both as a university and as a society. The M4TF has agreed to work with the administration to organize the fiftieth commemoration. However, we are historically wary of this decision; we still need to find a balance. We have to learn the lessons of May 4, 1970, and its aftermath, and those lessons are hard, not easy. The Task Force struggles with the decision to work with the administration. The students want to move the relationship with the administration forward, but only if that means the administration's commitment, input, and an honest and holistic view of the shooting, its precursors, and repercussions. Too often in our history as a university, the administration has wanted to bury the story, viewing it as a liability. The M4TF, while recognizing there is a new administrative support for what they do, is rightfully guarded; they want to make sure their message will not be diluted and their voices and choices will be heard, respected, and honored in the preparation and presentation of the fiftieth commemoration.

Indeed, May 4, 1970, should not be sanitized as has often been done with the struggle for freedom and human rights for African Americans. It is disingenuous and dangerous. The truth must be told, even if, and especially when, it is painful and uncomfortable. We must listen to voices that may be difficult for us to hear. We have to engage with the trauma of others who are, like us, traumatized, albeit in different ways. We have to find ways to protect freedom of speech without the use of governmental force. We must honor the lives lost, but also the student struggles against war, racism, governmental corruption, and lies. We have to find ways to move beyond dehumanizing and demonizing the other. While we stand up for our own beliefs, we must also listen to, and try to understand, those we disagree with. We must always try to find ways to disagree without resorting to or accepting violence.

My last year as faculty adviser to the M4TF will be 2019–20, if I make it to that point. Ten years is more than enough. I will continue to support this group as long as I live. I owe much to the M4TF; it has allowed me to work intimately with a community of students, activists, scholars, artists, hippies, Yippies, veterans, people of all walks of life. I have been extremely proud to have done this work over the years and hope I can forever honor the spirit of Orangeburg, Kent State, and Jackson State.

NOTES

1. https://omeka.library.kent.edu/special-collections/items/show/3252?search=Alan%20Paton.
2. James Russell, May 3, 1990, Wounded Student Panel, Kent State University, Kiva; transcribed from videotape, courtesy of Michael Pacifico.
3. Andrea Whitaker, May 4, 1990, Commemoration Student Commons; transcribed from videotape, courtesy of Michael Pacifico.
4. Glenn Frank, May 4, 1990, Commemoration, Kent State University Center Ballroom; transcribed from videotape, courtesy of Michael Pacifico.
5. Thomas Grace, May 4, 1990, Commemoration, Kent State University Student Center Ballroom; transcribed from videotape courtesy of Michael Pacifico.
6. C. Cartwright, "The Duty to Remember: The Privilege to Inspire Change," in *Managing the Unthinkable: Crisis Preparation and Response for Campus Leaders,* ed. G. M. Bataille and D. I. Cordova (Sterling, VA: Stylus, 2014), 189.
7. *May 4, 1970,* http://may41970.com/.
8. *May 4, 1970,* http://may41970.com/.
9. Samaria Rice, 2016 commemoration, https://boxcast.tv/view/46th-annual-may-4th-commemoration-525282.

Appendix

May 4, 1970, the Struggle for History and the Internet

MICHAEL PACIFICO

Michael Pacifico graduated from Kent State in 1974. He has helped organize more than twenty-five May 4 commemorations and organizes the annual May 4 vigil. He is beginning to organize, digitize, and catalog his collection of May 4–related photographs, videos, multimedia creations, and papers collected or created since May 1970.

ADDENDUM TO 2002 ARTICLE:

When I first wrote this piece in 2002, the internet had just begun a massive explosion in information and usage. This piece outlines the contention that the struggle for truth in history would benefit exponentially through the use of the internet and that it would allow for a more personal rendition of history and a forum for debating history. History would no longer be the sole property of an elite with an agenda to dictate and interpret that history, and would provide an inexpensive and efficient means for individuals to partake in this debate on a national and international scale.

In retrospect, my contention seems less than earth shattering, yet true in its scope. The number of internet users has increased from 960 million in 2004 to 4 billion in 2018. Facebook and the advent of Web 2.0 had just emerged in 2004. The internet has become more personal and more expansive. There are well over 2 billion Facebook users today and the instantaneous recording of history is a reality. The realization of justice around the Kent State shootings is within our grasp. Annual May 4, 1970, commemorations by the May 4

Task Force and its mission have worldwide exposure. Kent State University, once antagonistic to the struggle for truth and justice, has had no choice but to accept its role in the tragedy that was May 4, 1970, and embrace the truth. History is the struggle for truth and justice and we all are a part of it.

Notes and statistics have been updated where possible.

Michael Pacifico
February 8, 2019
Kent, Ohio

Throughout the twentieth century, progressives on the left have been confronted with the problem of disseminating factual information about unfolding social and political events. The overwhelming control and ownership of the means of communication by a dominant corporate media has often led to a skewed historical reality in sharp contrast to actual historical facts. As John Wilcock, former *New York Times* correspondent, wrote in 1968: "There is a credibility gap between the press and the people, because newspaper owners are plain and simple liars."[1] The murders of four students and the wounding of nine others by the Ohio National Guard at Kent State on May 4, 1970, presents an excellent case study of media manipulation of information and its effect on historical understanding.

The need to control popular perceptions about the shootings and to set the tone for subsequent misinformation was no more evident than in the *Kent-Ravenna Record-Courier* headline of May 4, 1970, which blared out at Portage County residents: 2 GUARDSMEN, 1 STUDENT DEAD IN KSU VIOLENCE. An accompanying front-page editorial headlined UNIVERSITIES MUST OUST HOOLIGANS had this in its opening paragraph: "Ohio will no longer tolerate its state universities being used as sanctuaries by lawbreaking hooligans who destroy, terrorize and burn." Subsequent coverage by the *Record-Courier* attempted to offer numerous excuses for the Guards' behavior as evidenced by these page 3 headlines on May 5: [OHIO NATIONAL GUARD GENERAL] DEL CORSO SAYS SNIPER FIRED BEFORE GUARD and COLONEL: GUARD HAS RIGHT TO SELF-DEFENSE. Federal investigations would later conclude that there was no sniper and that the Guards' lives were not in danger at the time they took aim and fired on the unarmed students.

Yet, media portrayals of student demonstrators as violent and deserving of such punishment continued to permeate our culture. Such stereotyping by the mainstream press and politicians was commonplace throughout the antiwar movement. Such was the case that any politician wishing to gain favor with the electorate could, without shame, make inflammatory and false statements about antiwar demonstrators and be assured of press coverage. On the eve of May 4, 1970, while commenting on demonstrations at Kent State in response to the invasion of Cambodia, James Rhodes, then governor of Ohio and campaigning for the Republican nomination to the US Senate, uttered these choice words at a press conference in Kent:

> The scene here that the city of Kent is facing is probably the most vicious form of campus-oriented violence yet perpetuated by dissident groups and their allies in the state of Ohio . . . Now we're going to put a stop to this . . . when they start taking over communities, this is when we're going to use every weapon of the law enforcement agencies of Ohio . . . They're worse than the brownshirts and the Communist elements and also the night riders and the vigilantes . . . We are going to eradicate the problem, we're not going to treat the symptoms.[2]

This message was broadcast throughout Ohio and to the Ohio National Guard's bivouac area on the Kent State campus. The next day four students were eradicated.

The mainstream press and politicians attempting to excuse their complicity in the shootings often referred to the events of May 4 as a riot. In a Harris poll taken in August 1970 among persons sixteen and older, this question was asked:

QUESTION 9

I am going to remind you of some incidents and episodes that have taken place in this country over the past couple of years. For each, tell me if you think the action was necessary and justified, or whether it was unjustified and repressive? (READ EACH STATEMENT AND RECORD BELOW)

Item: The National Guard shooting at *rioting* [my emphasis] students at Kent State University which resulted in four deaths

Responses: Necessary and justified/Unjustified and repressive/Not sure[3]

Exactly three years later, the same question[4] was asked again among persons eighteen years and older. Both these surveys were so worded despite a Justice Department memo, released in July 1970, that summarized an FBI investigation stating that the shootings were not necessary, that the Guardsmen were not surrounded, and that no student had posed a threat to the lives of the

Guardsmen.[5] Facts would not be allowed to get in the way of such self-serving mainstream "history."

Despite heavy popular opposition to the Vietnam War, information in the press was predominantly antistudent and prowar. The antiwar movement's ability to disseminate its message was hampered by a powerful and adverse press that dominated America's cultural landscape. The richness and diversity of the antiwar movement was kept hidden from the vast majority of the public and portrayed as a threat to every decent American's way of life.

Despite America's humiliating retreat from Vietnam and the ensuing national self-reflection on our nation's foreign policy in the middle and late 1970s, America's perceptions of the events at Kent State on May 4, 1970, and the image of the anti–Vietnam War demonstrator changed very little. Annual student commemorations at Kent State were often obscured by media coverage that reduced this historical event to a mere case study on violence while ignoring its complex political and cultural roots. Those commemorating the events of May 1970 were repeatedly counseled not to take any actions that could precipitate more violence. The underlying assumption was that the students on May 4 were responsible for their own deaths. Examining the events so as to determine the truth in order to secure a just conclusion was just not on the media's agenda. Even twenty-five years after the event, opinions had changed very little. In a 1995 survey of Kent State students conducted by doctoral students at Kent State, it was concluded that:

> There were predominantly two responses to the question of who was to blame for the event. Some students responded that every party involved should be blamed equally. Others said there was no blame to be given—it just happened ... The second disturbing response regards property. Property is a central concern of the students. A typical response focused not on free speech rights, not on the reason why people were involved in the demonstrations on May 4th, but on the destruction done to the town of Kent and the ROTC building.[6]

The authors of the survey concluded that "the community in which this incident occurred still seems scared by it. There is a fundamental lack of knowledge in students' attitudes about the protesters and Guardsmen as well as a general lack of awareness of the incident." How could this happen despite all the scholarly evidence, investigations, and books published that concretely show the National Guard fired on unarmed students whose distances from the Guard ranged from 71 feet to 730 feet? Foremost has been the unrelenting onslaught of media misinformation.

In 1984 NBC released a made-for-TV movie about the events of May 4, 1970. According to Jeff Goldstein, the producer of the movie, "The network representatives said that in order for the film to be *believable* [my emphasis], we had to show that the National Guardsmen were harassed by students." Commenting on the actual photographic evidence available on the shootings, Goldstein continues, "Ask them if those photos are lying. The photos show hundreds of feet of distance between the Guards and the students. This film creates a mediated reality that is inaccurate."[7]

Annual May 4 commemorations on the Kent State campus continue until this day. Since 1975 they have been sponsored by the May 4 Task Force, a student group on the Kent campus whose mission has proved to be a valuable counterbalance to the popular misperceptions about the anti–Vietnam War movement and the events at Kent State. Yet, despite their sometimes heroic efforts, misperceptions continue to prevail. Media coverage of the commemorations, both local and national, while generous, tend to focus on closure and reveal little factual information about the events being commemorated and are devoid of any serious analysis. The public is urged to move on and if we are to learn any lessons from this tragedy, it is the simplistic notion that violence is bad. The notion that a repressive government, intolerant of dissent, could willfully murder those who disagree with it is "unbelievable" and not to be broached.

Student textbook descriptions of the events of May 4, 1970, fared no better in their dedication to historical accuracy. From *The American Pageant:* "Restless students nationwide responded to the Cambodian invasion with rock throwing, window smashing, and arson. At Kent State University, in Ohio, members of the National Guard fired into an angry crowd, killing four and wounding many more.... The nation fell prey to turmoil as rioters and arsonists convulsed the land."[8] And from *The American Adventure:* "At Kent State University, the ROTC building was burned down. Later, members of the Ohio National Guard fired on demonstrators. Four students were killed."[9]

Not only are these descriptions brief and inadequate but they erroneously connect prior violent events (either from May 2 at Kent State or from other campuses) to the actual events that preceded the shootings on May 4. The overall effect is to create a false historical reality that the shooting of students at Kent State was either justified or understandable.

The technology of information exchange, whether it be the invention of the printing press, wireless communication, or even the ballpoint pen, has always offered new and challenging opportunities for social activists and progressive historians to espouse their views and advance their causes. The digital revolution and the meteoric rise of the internet in the 1990s to the present is no exception. The World Wide Web is full of sites that deal with every imaginable social cause and numerous historical events. It offers a unique challenge to activists and progressive historians in that, unlike previous forms of information exchange, it is dynamic, instantaneous, and universal, providing a level playing field for the dissemination of information. Content can be added or deleted selectively in a timely fashion without having to radically alter the whole. Readership can access this content instantaneously on computers with a click of a mouse and potential readership is global.

Additionally, the internet has effectively challenged and arguably surpassed print media's dominance as the major source of information for the public. In 2000, when I first wrote this article, internet usage worldwide was only 361 million individuals.[10] In 2018 the internet reached over 4 billion individuals, a meteoric rise of over 1,000 percent.[11] Internet usage by Americans has grown over 121 million in 2000 to 287 million in 2016.[12] Ninety-seven percent of adults ages eighteen to twenty-nine have access to the internet, up from 72 percent in 2000, constituting the highest percentage of any age demographic.[13] More telling is the following conclusion reached by a study detailing internet usage among youth ages twelve to seventeen in a 2005 study.[14]

> The most recent Pew Internet Project survey finds that 87% of all youth between the ages of 12 and 17 use the internet. That translates into about 21 million people. Of those 21 million online teens, 78% (or about 16 million students) say they use the internet at school. Put another way, this means that 68% of all teenagers have used the internet at school.
>
> This represents growth of roughly 45% over the past four years from about 11 million teens who used the internet in schools in late 2000. In the Pew Internet Project survey in late 2000, we found that 73% of those ages 12 to 17 used the internet and that 47% of those in that age cohort used the internet at school.

When valuable new tools such as the internet become available, it is imperative that they be used to advance the cause of social justice and historic truth. Fortunately, online resources abound for those seeking information about May 4, 1970. Most are written by individuals whose knowledge of the events is intimate, thoughtful, and accurate. These sources complement some of the excellent books written on the event and supplement them with updates and very rigorous analysis. This is living history at one's fingertips, not the one-dimensional, self-serving blather of a media constrained by ratings and convenient historical amnesia.

As the author of one website on May 4, 1970 (see website descriptions below), I have responded to numerous requests for assistance from students engaged in a variety of May 4–related projects. A high school student wrote: "The 3rd period world history class would like to thank you for your help in the research of our play. You were a great help to us and our play. Thank you!!!

Sincerely.

'Right to be informed'"[15]

Julia, a college student wrote: "I want to thank you for all of your help with my research. I ended up with a 96%!!! and my professor was very impressed at the fact that I had dug so deeply to get my information. That couldn't have been done without your quick responses and suggestions . . . I found myself very caught up in learning about the shootings and the Task Force, and in informing those in my class and my family and friends."[16]

Alan Canfora, wounded at Kent on May 4, 1970, has spearheaded two websites on May 4. He offers the unique perspective of both victim and eyewitness to the shootings and responds to numerous Web inquiries about his experiences. Alan also utilizes his Web presence to arrange for speaking engagements on college campuses throughout the country.

As the above examples suggest, it is not enough to merely publish information on the internet. Social activists and progressive historians must take advantage of the Web's interactive and dynamic nature. Communicating with one's readership is imperative and Web authors must construct a user-friendly Web environment that can be readily adapted to reflect the ever-changing nature of historical understanding. History teaches valuable lessons and offers insight into social movements and events many years into the future. The internet offers progressive activists a unique opportunity to level the playing field in the struggle for historical truth and to counterbalance the ever-present onslaught of misleading and revisionist history.

Below is a list of May 4, 1970, websites along with details of the major areas of coverage of each. There are many areas of overlap between sites, but each site has its own character reflecting the unique experiences and perspectives of the authors. Those who would use the list below for research are urged to take advantage of the vast wealth of information available outside the digital realm, including books, personal interviews, and visiting Kent State and taking advantage of its archival holdings in its May 4 Collection. The selection below is not meant to exclude other excellent Web sources on May 4, 1970, and its aftermath.

Kent May 4 Center
URL: http://www.may4.org/
From the website:
> Kent May 4 Center, based in Kent, Ohio, is the leading national & international organization seeking truth & justice regarding the Kent State massacre of May 4, 1970.
>
> Four students were killed and nine students were wounded when the Ohio National Guard fired 67 gunshots at 12:24 P.M. during an anti-war confrontation on the Kent State University campus.
>
> We also seek to provide the best educational information for students, researchers, historians, scholars, news media and all others seeking evidence, facts, eyewitness quotations, investigative reports, photographs and more about the Kent State tragedy of 1970.
>
> Our longstanding Kent May 4 Center Director is Alan Canfora—the recognized leader of the May 4 Movement for Kent State truth and justice based in Kent, Ohio. Alan Canfora was a leader of the 1970 Kent State students' anti-war revolt, an eyewitness injured by a bullet during the shooting incident and the acknowledged leading expert about the Kent State tragedy of May 4, 1970.

Alan Canfora's Home Page
URL: http://alancanfora.com/
Alan Canfora's home page includes a wealth of data on May 4, 1970, and subsequent related events. His site navigation tool lists the following headings: About Alan, Announcements, Books on May 4, Book Project, Commemorations, Guestbook, Legal Cases, May 4 Chronology, May 4 Links, Organization, Photos, Shooting Victims and Speaking Engagements. It is an excellent site for those doing research and reports.

Kent State University, Special Collections and Archives,
May 4 Collection
URL: https://www.library.kent.edu/special-collections-and-archives/kent-state-shootings-may-4-collection
From the website:
> Kent State University was placed into the international spotlight on May 4, 1970, after 13 students were shot by members of the Ohio National Guard at a student demonstration. Four students were killed and nine others were wounded, including one who was permanently paralyzed from his injury. The May 4 Collection, established by the Kent State University Libraries in 1970, includes over 300 cubic feet of primary sources related to the Kent

State shootings and their aftermath. The collection is open to the public and is used by researchers from around the world.

Mike and Kendra's Kent State, May 4, 1970, website
URL: http://www.may41970.com/

Originally conceived to be a vehicle for my and my wife's personal reflections and experiences, this evolved into a general gateway site for May 4 information and concentrated on events subsequent to and related to May 4, 1970, until the site ceased to be updated in 2003. Despite that, it contains a wealth of information on May 4 and subsequent related events.

Some major features of this site are:
1. Information on the struggles to construct an appropriate May 4 memorial on the Kent State campus and to close off the parking lot where the four slain students fell.
2. Chronologies for the Kent State shootings in May 1970 (with photos) and the Jackson State shootings of May 1970.
3. An extensive section with numerous articles and photos from the gym struggle and tent city in the late 1970s, which saw students occupy a site where the shootings occurred in an attempt to prevent the construction of a gymnasium that would obscure this historic site.
4. A photographic archive on many of the annual May 4, 1970, commemorations.
5. A section on books and resources related to the Kent State, Jackson State, and Orangeburg shootings.
6. Extensive coverage, including photos and transcripts of speeches, from the thirtieth annual May 4 commemoration.

Mike and Kendra's Flickr Links for May 4, 1970, Commemoration Photos
URL: https://www.flickr.com/photos/michaelpacifco/collections/72157629793859603/

Photos I took of annual May 4 commemorations from 1987 to 2013 are organized by year. They are not inclusive of every commemoration in the date range.

Mike and Kendra's Flickr Links for Author's Archive
URL: https://www.flickr.com/photos/michaelpacifco/collections/72157666712383187/

This is a continuing project to digitize and publish the massive amount of data collected by Michael and Kendra Pacifico over the past forty-five-plus years related to the aftermath of May 4, 1970, and the struggles to preserve and memorialize the truth about the murders. Hundreds of documents and artifacts, including videos, will eventually be cataloged, digitized, and published online. This is year one of a five-year project. In addition to publishing the collection online for research, the collection will be available for display when requested.

Some of the websites mentioned above have email links to their website authors. Make your investigation and research of Kent State, May 4, 1970, an interactive and personal adventure.

Peace,
Michael G. Pacifico
Kent, Ohio
January 2002 (updated February 2019)

NOTES

1. Roger Lewis, *Outlaws of America: The Underground Press and Its Context: Notes on a Cultural Revolution* (Harmondsworth, UK: Penguin/Pelican, 1972), 14.
2. Peter Davies and the Board of Church and Society of the United Methodist Church, *The Truth about Kent State: A Challenge to the American Conscience* (New York: Farrar Strauss Giroux, 1973), 21–22. For the complete text of Governor Rhodes's speech at the press conference, go to: https://www.library.kent.edu/ksu-may-4-rhodes-speech-may-3-1970.
3. Louis Harris Poll, Howard W. Odum Institute for Research in Social Science Public Opinion Poll Question Database, the Univ. of North Carolina at Chapel Hill, https://nevermore.irss.unc.edu/ddi-explorer/?fileId=23218&siteUrl=https://dataverse.unc.edu#?selected=@_id%3Dv318611%26type%3Drow&view=chart.
4. Louis Harris Poll.
5. Davies and the Board of Church and Society of the United Methodist Church, *The Truth about Kent State*, 5.
6. Grant Cos and Stephanie Westmyer, "Attitudes and Opinions: 1970–1995," in *25 Year Retrospective of Kent State and Jackson State*, ed. Center for Ethics in Political and Health Communications, Emerson College (Boston: Center for Ethics in Political and Health Communications, Emerson College, Apr. 23–24, 1995), 36.
7. Cos and Westmyer, "Attitudes and Opinions: 1970–1995," 57.
8. Thomas A. Bailey and David M Kennedy, *The American Pageant* (Lexington, MA: D. C. Heath, 1994), 961.
9. Social Science Staff of the Educational Research Council of America, *The American Adventure* (Boston: Allyn and Bacon, Inc., 1975), 149.

The above two textbook references are courtesy of email correspondence from Dr. James W. Loewen. Dr. Loewen has written two books dealing with historical misinformation. For further information about his work, go to http://www.uvm.edu/~jloewen/.

10. https://www.internetworldstats.com/stats.htm.

11. https://royal.pingdom.com/incredible-growth-of-the-internet-since-2000/.

12. http://www.internetlivestats.com/internet-users/us/.

13. https://www.statista.com/statistics/184389/adult-internet-users-in-the-us-by-age-since-2000/.

14. http://www.pewinternet.org/2005/08/02/the-internet-at-school/.

15. Correspondence to Mike and Kendra's Kent State, May 4, 1970, website, previously unpublished.

16. Correspondence to Mike and Kendra's Kent State, May 4, 1970, website, previously unpublished.

Index

Page references in *italics* refer to illustrations.

Abraham and Isaac (Segal) sculpture plans (1980s), 26, 166
Abu Jamal, Mumia, 289, 294
Adams, John, 2, 7, 106, 148, 151, 153, 165, 181
Africa, Ramona, 289
Agnew, Spiro, 32, 39, 120, 124, 153
Akron Beacon Journal: on May 4/Kent State Shootings, 112, 120, 135; on May 4 Visitors Center, 247
Alexander, Margaret Walker, 269
All-African People's Revolutionary Party (AAPRP), 287
Allbritton, Shane, 225, 234, 245
Allie (student), 37
Altgeld, John Peter, 129
American Civil Liberties Union (ACLU), 35, 141–44, 285. *See also* Kunstler, William Moses; Rosen, Sanford Jay
American University, 72, 82–83
America's Historical and Cultural Organizations grant, 228
Andrus, Patrick, 240, 243
Antifa, 295–96
anti-Semitism, Rosen on, 145–47, 150, 154, 165
art, legacy of May 4/Kent State Shootings and, 277
Arthrell, William G. "Bill": May Day protest (May 3, 1971), 84; napalm protest, 43; on Tent City protest (1977), 101–10; at Washington protest (1971), 72, 86

Artzner, Greg: "In my dream" (Artzner and Leonino), 197–99; "You Carried Us" (Artzner and Leonino), 203–4
AT&T, 31
Auld, Jeff, 209
Ayers, Bill, 292

Backus, Nate, 34
Baez, Joan, 2, 106, *114*
Baker, Robert, 149
Balyeat, Robert, 134
Barbato, Alissa, 228
Barbato, Carole A.: death of, 293; May 4 Visitors Center role of, 172; parking lot dedication, 217; *This We Know* (Barbato and Davis), 217, 249, 256n13. *See also* May 4 Visitors Center
Barry, Sharon, 232
"Battle of Washington, The" (Riddle), 65–86; explanation of, 65–67, 86; and Griffiths, 66–67, 86; Kent State students' travel to, 67–71; May Day protest (May 3, 1971), 78–85; motivation and plans of demonstrators, 71–77; Theodore Roosevelt Bridge location of, 74, 76
Bauer, Lara, 286, 287
Bellecourt, Vernon (Wa Bun Inini), 101, 288
Bennett, Kaitlin, 295–96
Berlin, Ira, 270
Bernard, Richard, 281
Bevan, Alex, 54
"Big Chill" generation, 164
Bills, Scott, 223, 239

Black Lives Matter (BLM), 293–96
Black Panther Party, 31, 83, 93, 165, 292
Black Student Union, 273n7
Black United Students (BUS), 59–61, *60*, 282, 286–87, 292, 295
Blanket Hill. *See* Tent City protest (gymnasium plans, 1977)
Blassingame, John, 270
Block, Dennis, 235
Block, Madeline, 235
"Blood Brothers," 174, 178. *See also* testimonials of victims
Boes, Lori, 245, 246, 249, 251, 293
Bond, Julian, 238
Boswell, John, 112
Boudin, Leonard, 124
Boyle, Kay, 273n7
Bracey, John, 269
Brock, Barbara, 29
Brown, Charlie, 180–81
Brown, Jeff, 242, 251
Brown, John, 293
Brown, Michael, 182
Brown, Paul, 134
Brown, R. Jess, 94
Brown, Rolly, 53–58, *58*, 204
Brown, William, 127
"Bucket of Blood, The," 93
Buday, Mike, 246, 247, 248
Burger, Beverly Knowles, 239
Bush, George W., 290
Butler, Chris, 293

Cagan, Beth, 281
Cagan, Leslie, 286
Cagan, Shauna, 281–82, 283, 287
Cagan, Steve, 281
"Call for the Repossession of America, A" (Wald), 280
Cambodia, invasion of, 4, 32, 47, 60, 102, 163–64, 247
Campus Camera, 34
Candlelight Walk and Vigil, 207–16, *212–15*
Canfora, Alan: and Kent 25 case, 119, 121, 122; on Krause family, 10; and Kunstler's address (1976), 131; and legacy of May 4/Kent State Shootings, 262–64; and May 4 Task Force, 288; and May 4 Visitors Center, 236, 241, 242, 252; Rosen on legal cases, 147; and Tent City protest, 102, 106, 114; victims' testimonials about, *160*, 177, 178, 180, 181
Canfora, Albert, 102, *108*
Canfora, Ann, 102, *108*
Canfora, Roseann "Chic," "Chickie," "Chicken": on legal issues, 35, 119–27, *126*; at May Day protest (May 3, 1971), 71, 78, 83, 86; and May 4 Visitors Center, 250, 252; Tent City protest, 105–6
Canterbury, Robert, 167
Carlton, Donna, 254n2
Carmichael, Stokely (Kwame Ture), 287
Carr, Jerry, 106
Carter, Jimmy, 252
Cartwright, Carol, 217, 287–88, 294
Case Western Reserve University, 32–33, 56
Cassady, Neil, 244
Castro, Fidel, 38
Cathy (student), 68–71, 78–79, 80–84
CBS News, on May 4/Kent State Shootings, 175
Center for Constitutional Rights, 125, 285
Center for Peaceful Change (Center for Applied Conflict Management, Kent State University), 208–10, 219
Chandler, Kathleen, 242
Chicago: Chicago Commons Association, 92–93; civil rights movement in, 91–93; Haymarket Square (1886), 129
Child, Barbara, 141–44
Chomsky, Noam, 289
Christensen, Lars, 38–39, 42–44
Chronicle of Higher Education, The, 273n8
Church, Frank, 163
City of Jackson v. John R. Salter, Jr. et al., 94
civil rights movement. *See* race issues and civil rights movement
Clark, Mark, 93
Clark, Suzanne, 231
Clark-Hine, Darlene, 295
Cleary, Andy, 172
Cleary, John, 146, 168–73, 178, 241, 252
Cleary, Kathy, 170, 172
Cleary, Lizzy, 172
Cleveland Police Department, 31
Cochrane, Julia, 107, 109
COINTELPRO (Counter Intelligence Program, FBI), 31, 179
COLLAGE (literary magazine), 30
Collins, Judy, 193
Congress on Racial Equality, 30
Cooley, Charles, 214
Cooper, Sherman, 163
Cosby, Bill, 293
Costanza, Midge, 105
Crane, Amy, 249
Cronkite, Walter, 175
Crosby, Edward, 286, 287
Cullum, Joe, 171
Cunningham, Karen, 231, 254n2, 291
Curry, Karen, 235, 246

Daley, Richard, 93
Dane, Barbara, 189–92
Darrow, Clarence, 129
Davies, Peter, 7, 140, 143, 165, 232, 242, 252
Davis, Laura L.: and May 4 Task Force, 293; on May 4 Visitors Center, 221–58; *This We Know* (Barbato and Davis), 217, 249, 256n13. *See also* May 4 Visitors Center
Davis, Rebel, 39
Davis, Rees, 149, 151, 153
Davis, Tom, 228
Del Corso, Sylvester, 32, 52, 167
Democratic Narrative, History, and Memory, 216, 230–31, 256n13
Department of Justice, 120, 121, 125, 136, 165, 179
Dershowitz, Alan, 124
Detroit Free Press, on May 4/Kent State Shootings, 135
Diamondstein, Al, 29
Dietz, Tom, 275–78
Dix, David, 104, 107
Dodge, Carter, 107, 115
"dog napalm" protest, 37–44, 43
Dohrn, Bernardine, 292
DO IT, 80
Duin, Steve, 174

Eagle, Bill, 184
Eliot, T. S., 252–54
Ellsberg, Dan, 193
Emmer, Howie, 30, 261
"Emotional Pain for Those Who Remember" (Lewis), 213–14
Engdahl, David, 149
Environmental Conservation Organization, 276
Ericson, Candy, 261
Ericson, Rick, 261
ethics of remembering, 212–14
Euclide, Tom, 254n2
Evers, Medgar, 92
Exhibit Concepts Inc. (ECI), 246, 255n9

Fargo (Ibrahim Al-Kafiz), 59
Farmer, Mindy, 250, 251
FBI (Federal Bureau of Investigation): COINTELPRO (Counter Intelligence Program), 31, 179; and Kent 25 case, 120, 121, 133–35, 137; photographs of Kent State protest by, 29; students' film confiscated by, 34; victims' testimonials about, 170, 179
Fellowship of Reconciliation, 276
feminism, legacy of May 4/Kent State Shootings and, 276–78

Fields, Barbara, 270
Fields, Cheryl M., 273–74n9
Filo, John, 239, 291
Finn, Natalie, 33–34
Fire in the Heartland (Miller), 292
"Flowers for the Departed" (Paton), 280
Fonda, Jane, 124, 193
Ford, Seabury, 120, 134–35, 137
Four Quartets (Eliot), 252–54
Frank, Glenn, 52, 201, 203–4, 223, 236, 238, 284, 285
Franklin, Bobby, 30
Franklin, Doris, 29
Free Press, on May 4/Kent State Shootings, 135
Free Speech Movement, 244
Fuldheim, Dorothy, 33, 35, 107, 109, 201
Fussell, Paul, 227–28

Gallagher & Associates, 224–25, 227, 229, 231–33, 236, 239, 246–47, 255n9, 257n30, 258n30
Gandhi, 76
Garland, Jim, 189–92
gay perspective, legacy of May 4/Kent State Shootings and, 276–78
Geltner, Michael, 148
Genovese, Eugene, 270
Georgetown University, 84
Gibbs, Demetrius, 288
Gibbs, Phillip, 190, 266, 288
Gibson, Sue, 30
Gitlin, Todd, 223
Glenn, John, 252
Glenville uprising (Ohio, 1968), 32
Goffman, Erving, 210
Gold, Ted, 292
Goldblatt, Ellen Sue, 149
Golding, Brage, 109–10, 166
Gonzales, Jesse Rodriguez, 67–71, 73, 77, 78, 83–84
González, Emma, 174
Goodman, Andrew, 234
Goodrich, Tim, 185
Grace, Tom: injuries of, 178; and Kent 25 case, 122; on Krause family, 9; and Kunstler's address (1976), 128; *The Long Sixties*, 178, 240; at May Day protest (Washington), 71, 78, 84–85; and May 4 Task Force, 285; and May 4 Visitors Center, 224, 240–42, 250, 251, 252; Rosen on legal cases, 146–47; victim testimonial of, 162–67, 167
Gray, Eldri, 92
Gray, John Hunter, 90–96
Great War and Modern Memory, The (Fussell), 227–28

INDEX 311

Green, James Earl, 190, 266, 288
Gregory, Dick, 59, 293
Griffiths, Jeff "Grif," 66–67, 86. *See also* "Battle of Washington, The" (Riddle)
Grudsky, Aida, 145
Guidelines for Identifying, Evaluating, and Registering America's Historic Battlefields (Andrus), 240
Gutman, Herbert, 270

Haldeman, H. R., 119, 165
hallowed ground. *See* memorials and tributes
Hammond, Samuel, Jr., 189, 266
Hammond v. Brown, 138, 140, 141
Hampton, Fred, 93
Hanrahan, Ed, 93
Hart, Gary, 164
Hartzler, Jeff, 122
Harvard University, 123–24
Harvey, Iris, 232, 245
Hastie, Michael, 185
Hastings, Robert, 134
Hayden, Tom, 116, 224, 291
Haymarket Square (1886), 129
Hearts and Minds (documentary), 231
Henry, Bonnie, 222, 223
Henry, Patty, 251
Hensley, Thomas "Tom," 223, 254n2
Herington, Leigh, 242
Higgins, Jerry, 179
Higgins, Kevin, 179
Hill, Julia Butterfly, 288
Hine, Darlene Clark, 195, 265–74
Hine, William C., 295
Hipp, Sus Marie, 30
Hogg, David, 174
Hogle, Jim, 138
Holstein, Artie, 181
Holstein, Elaine, 3–5, 7, 8, 181, 211, 252
Hosler, Tim, 246
Huebner, James, 111
Huggins, Nathan, 271
Humboldt State University, 184
Humphrey, Hubert, 292
Hussein, Saddam, 290

Ifill, Gwen, 249
I Hate the Capitalist System (Dane), 192
In America's Wake (Meuser), 235
Inglee, Roy, 29
"In my dream" (Artzner and Leonino), 197–99
"inquire, learn, and reflect," 216n3
Institute for the Study and Prevention of Violence (Kent State University), 219
Institute of African American Affairs (IAAA), 61
Iverson, Susan, 244

Jackson, Aunt Molly, 190
Jackson, Clara, 29
Jackson, Jesse, 164, 165
Jackson, Mim, 106
Jackson, Robin, 293
Jackson, Sid, 29
Jackson Movement of 1962–63, 92
Jackson State College/University (Mississippi): *City of Jackson v. John R. Salter, Jr. et al.*, 94; Jackson Movement of 1962–63, 92; Kent State victims' testimonials about, 163–65, 167, 179; and legacy of May 4/Kent State Shootings, 265–74; Scranton Commission on, 133; shootings at, 36, 95–96, 120; tributes to, 190, 193–96, 280, 284–85, 288, 293–94
Janik, George, 104, 105, 113
Johnson, Michael, 270
Johnson, Walter Giles, 150
Jonathan (professor), 39–41
Jones, Cybelle, 232, 234, 239, 246
Jones, Edwin, 134

Kaddish (Jewish prayer of mourning), 210, 262–63
Kafiz, Ibrahim Al- (Fargo), 59
Kahler, Dean: injuries of, 130, 142; on Krause family, 9; Lewis's testimonial about, 178, 182; and May 4 Task Force, 293; and May 4 Visitors Center, 241, 252; Miller's mother on, 3, 5; Rosen on legal cases, 147, 149, 153; victim testimonial of, 157–61, 160
Keefer, Bradley, 250, 251
Keller, Barney, 141, 142–43
Keller, Galen (Lewis), 141–44, 179, 183
Keller, Steven, 149
Kelner, Joseph, 180, 232
Kennedy, John F. (president), 146, 234, 280
Kennedy, John F., Jr. (president's son), 234
Kennedy, Robert, 36, 146
Kent (town): citizen activism in, 87–89; May 1, 1970, protest, 47–48, 54–55; mayor of (Satrom), 14, 32, 48–49, 129, 175
Kent Anarchists, 276
Kent Community Project, 276
Kent Free University, 276
Kent in Exile, 56
Kent Legal Defense Fund, 35, 275–78
Kent State: A Turning Point (documentary film), 247
Kent State Coverup, The (Kelner and Munves), 232

"Kent State Massacre, The" (Warshaw, Dane, and Garland), 189–92
"Kent State Revisited" (Kunstler), 131
Kent State Shootings (May 4, 1970). *See* May 4/Kent State Shootings
Kent State University: Athletic Department on May 4, 1970, events, 60; Center for Peaceful Change (Center for Applied Conflict Management), 208–10, 219; *COLLAGE* (literary magazine), 30; Foundation, 229; Institute for the Study and Prevention of Violence, 219; protest prior to May 4, 1970, events, 27–32, 37–44, *43*, 47; students' education at, 26–27, 56; "Who Killed Allison? Why? What Had She Done?" (Levine), 13–14. *See also* Kent (town); Kent State University, buildings and layout; May 4/Kent State Shootings; May 4 Task Force (M4TF); May 4 Visitors Center; Tent City protest (gymnasium plans, 1977)
Kent State University, buildings and layout: Blanket Hill (May 4, 1970), 159; May 4, 1970, rally location, 60–61; Music and Speech building, 31–32, 39, 47, 237; ROTC building, 48–49, 55, 138, 169, 175–76; Taylor Hall, 158–59, 177; Tri-Towers, 38, 57
Kent State: What Happened and Why (Michener), 237
Kent 25: Arthrell at Washington protest (1971), 72; Federal Court case overview, 35; Kunstler on, 129; Whitaker on stifling effect of, 132–40. *See also* Arthrell, William G. "Bill"
Kern, Kevin, 242, 251
Kerry, John, 88
Kesey, Ken, 244
Kielar, Neil, *109*
Kimball, Jeffrey, 247
King, Coretta Scott, 88
King, Ed, 94
King, Martin Luther, Jr., 31, 76, 146, 243, 267, 284–85
Kissinger, Henry, 119
Klatch, Rebecca, 247
Klein, Michelle, 209
Kleindienst, Richard, 165
Koneybeare, Chris, 106
Kovic, Ron, 102, *114*, 130, 193, 288
Kozlowsky, Albert (and family), 179
Krause, Allison B., *22*; annual rituals and historic markers for, 210–12, 217, 219, 220, 235–39; boyfriend's tribute to, 11–15; building named for, 107; daisy put in rifle by, 49; legacy of May 4/Kent State Shootings, 264, 265; and May 4 Task Force, 288, 294; and May 4 Visitors Center, 222, 223, 227, 230, 234, 235, 241, 249, 252; Miller's mother on, 3; Rosen on legal cases, 146, 153; tribute to father of, 6–10, *9;* victims' testimonials about, 163, 174
Krause, Arthur, 6–10, *9*, 181, 212
Krause, Doris, 9, 181, 288
Krause, Laurel, 181
Kristen, Beverly, 29
Kristof, Cindy, 238, 245
Ku Klux Klan, 165
Kunstler, William Moses: commemoration speeches by, 285, 293; and gymnasium plans, 103, 116, 128–31, *130;* and Kent 25 case, 35, 106, 107, 124

Lambros, Thomas, 106
Landes, Duane, 246
Lane, Mark, 124
Lapham, Lewis, 132
law enforcement: Chicago police, 91; at May Day protest (1971, Washington, DC), 78–85. *See also* legal maneuvering and the courts; National Guard; Tent City protest (gymnasium plans, 1977)
Lee, Michael, 282, 291
Lefton, Lester, 224–27, 241–42, 249, 257–58n30
legal maneuvering and the courts: Adams's role in, 7; Federal Court case, 35–36; *Hammond v. Brown*, 138, 140, 141; Kent 25 case, 35, 72, 106, 107, 119–27, *126*, 129, 132–40; Krause's (Arthur) role in, 6–10; Kunstler's address (1976), 128–31, *130;* Lewis's (Galen) contributions to, 141–44; May 4/Kent State Shootings legacy of, 275–78; and Miller family, 4–5; Ohio Supreme Court, 180; Rosen on cases of 1975–1977, 145–54, *154*; stifling effect of official response to Kent State shootings, 132–40; US Supreme Court, 7, 148, 180, 241; victims' testimonials about, 165, 170–71, 179–84. *See also* May 4 Visitors Center; Tent City protest (gymnasium plans, 1977)
Leonino, Terry, 197–99, 200–202, 203–4
Levine, Barry, 11–15
Lewis, Christopher John Adams, 143, 181, 183
Lewis, Galen Keller, 141–44, 179, 183
Lewis, Jerry M.: on Candlelight Walk and Vigil, 207–16, *212–15*, 218; Hensley's work with, 223; and May 4 Task Force, 282; and May 4 Visitors Center, 232, 240, 242, 250, 251. *See also* May 4 Visitors Center
Lewis, John, 243

INDEX 313

Lewis, Joseph: Cleary's testimonial about, 170; injuries of, 134; and May 4 Visitors Center, 236, 241, 252; victim testimonial of, 174–85; and wife's contributions to legal cases, 142–44, 146
Lewis, Lisa, 182
LGBTQ rights, legacy of May 4/Kent State Shootings and, 276–78
Libana, 143, 144
Liberty Hangout, 295
Life magazine, on May 4/Kent State Shootings, 121, 171
Lincoln, Jim, 30
Liteky, Charlie, 184
Lively, Pierce, 152
Lodi (student), 39
Long Sixties, The (Grace), 178, 240
Long Walk at San Francisco State and Other Essays, The (Boyle), 273n7
Lund-Goldstein, Sarah, 225, 254n2

MacKenzie, Scott (Donald), 147, *167*, 178, 241, 252
Magpie (musical duo), *58*, 197, *204*
Malcolm X, 146, 280, 285, 290, 293
Malheur National Wildlife Refuge Occupation, 295
Mann, Ellen, 177
markers on campus (May 4 Walking Tour), 211–16, 217–20, *218*, 220, 235–39. *See also* memorials and tributes
Martin, George, 138
Martz, David, 229–30
May Day protest (1971). *See* "Battle of Washington, The" (Riddle)
May 4, 1970: Someone to Tell the Story (documentary film), 237–38
May 4 Coalition: and gymnasium protest, 102, 111, 114–15; and May 4 Visitors Center, 224, 239, 252. *See also* Tent City protest (gymnasium plans, 1977)
May 4/Kent State Shootings, 45–61; activism by Kent citizens as response to, 87–89; activism prior to, 25–36, 37–44, *43*; bayonet injuries (May 3, 1970), 50; civil rights activism as response to, 90–96; legacy of, 261–64, *263*, 265–74, 275–78; May 1 (Friday) protest, 47–48, 54–55; May 2 (Saturday), ROTC building fire, 48–49, 55, 138, 169, 175–76; May 3 (Sunday) events, 49–50; May 4 (Monday), protest plans, 50–51, 55, 59–60; "May 4" term for events, 240; violence and aftermath of, 51–52, *52*, 53–58, *58*, 60, 60–61; Walsh on unfolding of, 32–35. *See also* "Battle of Washington, The" (Riddle); legal maneuvering and the courts; memorials and tributes; testimonials of victims; *and individual names of victims*
May 4 Memorial (monument), 214–17, 237, 240, 283
May 4 Task Force (M4TF), 279–97; and antiwar efforts (2003), 291, 296; commemoration (1990, 20th anniversary), 282–88; commemoration (2000, 30th anniversary), 288–90; commemoration (2010, 40th anniversary), 291–92; commemoration (2012, Vietnam veterans project), 292; commemoration (2013), 292–93; commemoration (2014), 293–95; commemoration (2017, 40th anniversary, Tent City protest), 295; commemoration (2018), 295–96; ongoing struggles recognized by, 296–97; and race identity, 281–82; Task Force advisor's background, 279–87
May 4 Visitors Center, 221–58; concept and inception of, 223–27; *Democratic Narrative, History, and Memory*, 216, 230–31, 256n13; design and content, 231–35; events and legal battles remembered by, 221–25; fabrication of, 244–49; faculty committee and external consultants, 254n2, 254n4, 254–55n6, 255n9, 256n11, 256–57nn15–19, 257–58nn29–30; funding for, 227–31, 244, 246–47, 250, 254n4, 255n9, 256n16, 271–72; as institutionalization of history, 250, 254n; *Kent State: A Turning Point* (documentary film), 247; *May 4, 1970: Someone to Tell the Story* (documentary film), 237–38; "May 4" term for events, 240; May 4 Walking Tour, 235–39; National Register of Historic Places recognition of, 232, 239–44, 250–53; opening and dedication, 249–54, 257–58n30
McCrae, Gloria Green, 288
McDonald, Joe, 110
McGehee, Edward, 29
McGovern, George, 164
Mechler, Ted, 106
Meisel, Lisa, 261
Mejia, Camillo, 185
memorials and tributes, 1–15, 187–204; "A Call for the Repossession of America" (Wald), 280; Candlelight Walk and Vigil, 207–16, *212–15*; commemoration (1974), 113; commemoration (1976), *97, 126*; commemoration (1980), 116; ethics of remembering, 212–14; 50th anniversary, 173; "Flowers for the Departed" (Paton), 280; "In my dream" (Artzner and

memorials and tributes (*cont.*)
Leonino), 197–99; "inquire, learn, and reflect," 216n3; "The Kent State Massacre" (Warshaw, Dane, and Garland), 189–92; to Krause (Allison), 11–15; to Krause (Arthur), 6–10, *9;* Leonino's recollection, 200–202; markers on campus (May 4 Walking Tour), 211–16, 217, *218,* 235–39; May 4 Memorial (monument), 214–17, 237, 240, 283; to Miller, 3–5; reunion (1985), 57, *58;* Segal sculpture plans (1980s), 26, 166; "Students in our country, at Kent and Jackson State" (Near), 193–96; "Who Killed Allison? Why? What Had She Done?" (Levine), 13–15; "You Carried Us" (Artzner and Leonino), 203–4. *See also* "Battle of Washington, The" (Riddle); May 4 Task Force (M4TF); May 4 Visitors Center; Tent City protest (gymnasium plans, 1977); *and individual names of speakers*
Merritt, Carole, 272
Metzenbaum, Howard, 105, 252
Meuser, Erica, 235
Michener, James A., 237
Mickey (student), 41
Middleton, David, 224, 229, 232, 236, 254n2
Middleton, Delano, 189, 266
Mildred Andrews Fund of Cleveland, 26
Miles, Karen, 229
Millay, Edna St. Vincent, 131
Miller, Daniel, 292
Miller, Daniel L., 231
Miller, Jeffrey G., *22;* annual rituals and historic markers for, 210, 211, 217, 219, *220;* Brown on, 57; building named for, 107; and Kent 25 case, 122; Krause's boyfriend on, 12; legacy of May 4/Kent State Shootings, 265; and May 4 Task Force, 288, 293, 294; and May 4 Visitors Center, 222, 223, 227, 229, 230, 235, 236, 241, 252; mother's description of Krause (Arthur), 7; mother's tribute to, 3–5; Rosen on legal cases, 146, 153; victims' testimonials about, 163, 172, 181
Miller, Russ, 5
Miller, Tom "Aquinas," 121–22
Mississippi, civil rights movement in, 91–96. *See also* Jackson State College/University (Mississippi)
Mitchell, John, 86, 120, 165
Molnar, Bryan, 248
Morgan, Craig, 148
Moseley, Patricia, 87–89
Moseley, Scott, 87, 89
Moynihan, Daniel, 36

Muhammad Speaks (Nation of Islam), 266
Munves, James, 232
"Murder of Harry Simms, The" (Garland), 190

"napalm" protest, 37–44, *43*
Nash, Gary, 272
National Endowment for the Humanities (NEH), 227–29, 231, 244, 246–47, 250, 254n4, 255n9, 256n16, 271–72
National Guard: bayonet injuries by (May 3, 1970), 50; Glenville uprising (1968), 32; and gym plans (1977), 109–10; martial law imposed on campus, 59–61, 135, 276; May 4, 1970, shootings by, 50–51, 55, 59–60; Rhodes's order for, 103; and ROTC building fire, 48–49, 55, 138, 169, 175–76; tear gas used by, 87–89; "Who Killed Allison? Why? What Had She Done?" (Levine), 15. *See also* legal maneuvering and the courts; testimonials of victims
National History Standards project, 272
National Lawyers Guild, 31, 103
National Park Service (NPS), 243, 251
National Register of Historic Places, 232, 239–44, 250–53
Nation of Islam, 266
Nazi Germany, Kent State analogy to, 145–47, 165
Near, Holly, 193–96
Neiberger, Colin, 261
Neier, Aryeh, 148
Newsweek, on May 4/Kent State Shootings, 268
New York Times, on May 4/Kent State Shootings, 268
Night and Fog (documentary), 231
Nixon, Richard: Cambodia invasion by, 4, 32, 47, 60, 102, 163–64, 247; draft ended by, 112; Haldeman on May 4/Kent State Shootings and Watergate, 119, 165; and Kent 25 case, 119, 120, 124–25; legacy of May 4/Kent State Shootings, 268; on May 4/Kent State Shootings, 11; and May 4 Visitors Center, 221, 241, 245, 251, 252; President's Commission on Campus Unrest (Scranton Commission), 120, 133, 179, 251, 258; protesters criticized by administration of, 39; resignation of, 5; Rosen on legal cases, 153; victims' testimonials about Kent State, 163, 165, 175, 179, 180; Washington protest (1971), 72; "Who Killed Allison? Why? What Had She Done?" (Levine), 14. *See also* Vietnam War
Nkrumah, Kwame, 287

Noll, Dolores, 29
Nowakowski, Constance, 47–52, *52*

Ohio: Attorney General of, 127; sovereign immunity law, 7; State Historic Preservation Office, 242, 251; Supreme Court, 180. *See also* Kent 25; Rhodes, James A.
Ohio National Guard. *See* National Guard
Olds, Glenn, 113, 292
Orangeburg (South Carolina) massacre: events of, 265–66, 268, 273, 280; and legacy of May 4/Kent State Shootings, 265–74; *The Orangeburg Massacre* (Bass and Nelson), 266; tributes to, 189, 201, 280, 284, 294–95, 297
Oregonian, on May 4/Kent State Shootings, 174
Organization of American Historians, 272
Oughton, Diana, 292
Owens, Leslie, 270

Pacifico, Kendra Lee Hicks, on Krause (Arthur), 6–10
Pacifico, Michael, *212*
parking lot markers on campus (May 4 Walking Tour), 211–16, 217, *218*, 235–39. *See also* memorials and tributes
Paschen, Steve, 254n2
Paton, Alan, 280
Peach, Leroy, 30
Pelosi, Nelda, 183
Peoples, John A., 294
People's Coalition for Peace and Justice, 67. *See also* "Battle of Washington, The" (Riddle)
Persky, Jerry, 30, 68, 85
Pickett, Robert, 291
Pittman, Curtis Lee (Jeter), on May 4, 1970, events, 59–61, *60*
police. *See* law enforcement; May 4/Kent State Shootings
Portage County. *See* Kent 25
Powers, Barbara, 240, 251
President's Commission on Campus Unrest (Scranton Commission), 120, 133, 179, 251, 258
Progressive Student Network (PSN), 283, 286
Progressive Workers Movement, 116
Pyles, Dixon, 94

Quirk, Joyce, 104, 105, 107

Raboteau, Albert, 270
race issues and civil rights movement: African American students and May 4, 1970, events, 59–61, *60;* civil rights in Chicago (1970), 90–93; civil rights in Glenville (1968), 32; civil rights in Mississippi (1970), 91–96; Kent State victims' testimonials about, 165; King on, 31, 76, 146, 243, 267, 284–85; and legacy of May 4, 265–74; race identity, 281–82. *See also* Jackson State College/University (Mississippi); Orangeburg (South Carolina) massacre; *and individual names of organizations*
Rath, Joanne, 235
Rath, John, 235
Ravenna (Ohio): as county seat, 37; Kent State victims treated at, 170
Ravenna Record Courier, Krause (Arthur) interviewed by, 9
Rawlings, Charles, 107
Reagan, Ronald, 124
Real, Mark, 30
Reid, Scott, 210
Rhodes, Carl, 234, 245, 246, 248
Rhodes, James A.: actions leading up to May 4, 1970, events, 49, 50; Del Corso and, 32; events leading up to May 4, 1970, 49, 50; and Kent 25 case, 120, 124, 127, 133, 134; and May 4 Visitors Center, 236; National Guard ordered by, 103; Rosen on legal cases, 148, 153; victims' testimonials about, 157, 163, 167, 176, 180; "Who Killed Allison? Why? What Had She Done?" (Levine), 15
Rice, Samaria, 294
Rice, Tajai, 294
Rice, Tamir, 293, 294
Richardson, Allen, 235
Rickel, Alice, 106
Riddle, Tom, 65–86. *See also* "Battle of Washington, The" (Riddle)
Riggs, Jimmy, 121
Ritchie, Oscar, 236
rituals. *See* May 4 Visitors Center; memorials and tributes
Roark, James, 270
Robbins, Terry, 261, 264, 292
Romano, Rence, 242, 250, 251
Rosen, Catherine, 145–46
Rosen, Sanford Jay, 7, 145–54, *154*, 182
Roskens, Ronald, 33
ROTC building, burning of, 48–49, 55, 138, 169, 175–76
Rowe, John, 2, 106, 239
Rubin, Jerry, 80
Rudd, Mark, 261–64, *263*, 292
Ruffini, Franco, 240, 242
Ruffner, Howard, 239
Rupe, Jerry, 138

Ruppelt, Diane, 254n2
Russell, Becca, 183
Russell, Jim: and May 4 Task Force, 283; and May 4 Visitors Center, 237, 241, 252; Rosen on legal cases, 147, 153; victims' testimonials about, 172, 174–85
"Rutgers Weighs Moves to Meet Blacks' Demands" (Watkins), 273n8

Sa'ad, Keita, 286
Sacco (Nicola) and Vanzetti (Bartolomeo) case, 131
Salter, John, Jr. (Gray), 90–96
Santayana, George, 213
Satrom, Leroy (Kent mayor), 14, 32, 48–49, 129, 175
Savio, Mario, 30, 244
Savitt, Todd, 270
Scheuer, Martin, 2, 102, *108*, 116, 147, 181, 210, 212
Scheuer, Sandra L., 22; annual rituals and historic markers for, 208, 211, 212, 215, 217, 219, *220*; Brown on, 57; building named for, 107; and Kent 25 case, 122; Krause's boyfriend on, 12; legacy of May 4/Kent State Shootings, 265; and May 4 Task Force, 288, 294; and May 4 Visitors Center, 223, 227, 229, 230, 235, 241, 252; Miller's mother on, 3; Rosen on legal cases, 146, 153; and Tent City protest, 102; victims' testimonials about, 163, 166, 181
Scheuer, Sarah, 2, 102, *108*, 181, 212
Schmidt, William, 134–35
Schnittke, Eric, 224
Schroeder, Florence, 107, 181, 212, 243
Schroeder, Lou, 181
Schroeder, William K., 22; annual rituals and historic markers for, 211, 212, 217, 219, *220*; Brown on, 58; building named for, 107; and Kent 25 case, 122; Krause's boyfriend on, 12; legacy of May 4/Kent State Shootings, 265; and May 4 Task Force, 288, 294; and May 4 Visitors Center, 222, 227, 229, 230, 235, 241, 243, 252; Miller's mother on, 3; Rosen on legal cases, 146, 153; victims' testimonials about, 163, 181
Schultz, Bill, 102
Schwartz, Michael, 166, 216n3
Schwartzmiller, Arnold, 34
Scranton, William, 133
Scranton Commission. *See* President's Commission on Campus Unrest (Scranton Commission)
Scribner, David, 35, 125–26, 127, 138
Seale, Bobby, 292
Seeger, Peggy, 189

Seeger, Pete, 88
Seeman, Mark, 229, 232, 240, 242, 243, 250, 251
Segal, George, 26, 166
Seiberling, John, 252
Shaffer, Lawrence, 134
Shakur, Assata, 285
Sheban, Chris, 237
Sheehan, Cindy, 291
Sheerer, Benjamin, 35, 138
Simmons, Marvin, 185
Simms, Harry, 190
Skellenger, Roy, 254n2
Smith, Burt, 183
Smith, Henry, 190, 266
South Carolina State College. *See* Orangeburg (South Carolina) massacre
Spartacus Youth League ("Sparts"), 115
Spicer, Kathy, 231
Stafford, Kathy, 224, 229, 254n2
Stamps, Robert, 37–44; on earlier protest, 37–44, *43*; and May 4 Task Force, 288; and May 4 Visitors Center, 241, 252; Rosen on legal cases, 147, 153; victims' testimonials about, 178
Stanley, Chris, 106
Steward, Skylar, 295–96
Stone, I. F., 133
Stringer, Bonny, 106
Student Nonviolent Coordinating Committee, 91
Students for a Democratic Society (SDS), 30–31, 116, 261–64, 279
"Students in our country, at Kent and Jackson State" (Near), 193–96
Surbella, Kevin, 240
Syed, Idris Kabir, 232, 242, 279–97. *See also* May 4 Task Force (M4TF)

Taxi to the Dark Side (documentary), 231
"Teach-in for Peace" (Humboldt State University), 184
Teamsters strike (Ohio, 1970), 32, 49
Tenenbaum, Irene, 33
Tent City protest (gymnasium plans, 1977): Blanket Hill location of May 4, 1970, events, 159; events of, 26, *97*, *100*, 101–10, *108*, *109*, 113–16, *114*, *115*; 40th anniversary of, 295; Kunstler's address about, 128–31, *130*
testimonials of victims, 155–85; by Cleary, 168–73; by Grace, 162–67, *167*; by Kahler, 157–61, *160*; by Lewis, 174–85
Third World Liberation Front, 273n7
"This is the way we spray the freaks" (chant), 80

INDEX 317

This Promised Land (Cagan and Cagan), 281
This We Know (Barbato and Davis), 217, 249, 256n13
Thomas, Peter, 246
Thomas, William K., 35, 125, 138–39, 149–53
Thompson, Roy, 124
Thompson, Tommy, 175
Three Percenters, 295
"Tiny" (student), 68–70
Tople, Paul, 239
Toure, Sekou, 287
Trump, Donald, 295
Truth about Kent State, The (Davies), 7, 140, 143, 165, 232, 242, 252
"Truth-Seeking and Remembering" (Lewis), 213–14
Ture, Kwame (Stokely Carmichael), 287
Tyrrell, Brinsley, 280

Uhuru (BUS), on Ture, 287
Unite the Right, 295
University of California at Berkeley, 30, 91, 244, 267, 273–74n9
University of Massachusetts at Amherst, 269
US Supreme Court, 7, 148, 180, 241

Vanzetti (Bartolomeo) (Sacco and Vanzetti case), 131
Vecchio, Mary Ann, 211, 291
victims of shootings. *See* Canfora, Alan; Cleary, John; Grace, Tom; Kahler, Dean; Kovic, Ron; Krause, Allison B.; Lewis, Joseph; MacKenzie, Scott (Donald); Miller, Jeffrey G.; Russell, Jim; Scheuer, Sandra L.; Schroeder, William, K.; Stamps, Robert; testimonials of victims; Wrentmore, Douglas
Vietnam War: Cambodia invasion, 4, 32, 47, 60, 102, 163–64, 247; Free Speech Movement, 244; Huebner's service in, 111–13; Kent State protest, prior to May 4, 1970, 27–32, 37–44, 43; "long sixties," 240; public's perception of, 54; veterans' protest against, 88; Vietnam Syndrome, 164; War Powers Act, 163–64; Warriors Journey Home, 292. *See also* "Battle of Washington, The" (Riddle)
Vincent, Stephanie, 254n2
Visitors Center. *See* May 4 Visitors Center

Wa Bun Inini (Vernon Bellecourt), 288
Wald, George, 280, 290
Walsh, Anthony, 25–36; on difficulty of memories, 25–26; on events of May 4, 1970, 32–35; on Kent State students' education, 26–27; and legal issues of May 4, 35–36, 103, 106, 110; on Vietnam War draft and protest, 27–32
Walsh, Mary, 26
"War and Remembrance in the Vietnam Era" (America's Historical and Cultural Organizations grant), 228
War Powers Act, 163–64
Warren, Beverly, 173, 250, 293
Warriors Journey Home, 292
Warshaw, Jack, 189–92
"Wars on Trial in Three Landmark Documentary Films" (Miller and Clark), 231
Watergate, May 4/Kent State Shootings and, 119, 165
Watkins, Beverly T., 273n8
Weather Underground, 30–31
Wernick, Linda, 222
Whitaker, Andrea, 282, 283
Whitaker, Marilyn, 279, 282
Whitaker, William, 106, 132–40, 279, 282
White, Deborah Gray, 270
White, Robert, 30, 32, 50, 85–86, 158, 209
"Who Killed Allison? Why? What Had She Done?" (Levine), 13–15
Wilson, Brian, 184–85
Winter, Jay, 228, 230, 231, 254
Winter Soldiers' Investigation, 124
Wittmaack, Ron, 29
"Women's Studies Gain" (Fields), 273–74n9
Wood, Peter, 270
Woodrum, Kenny, 28–29
Wrentmore, Douglas, 147, *167*, 178, 241, 252
Wulf, Mel, 147
Wunderlin, Clarence, 244

"You Carried Us" (Artzner and Leonino), 203–4
Young, Don J., 149, 180
Young, Gene, 285, 288
Young Socialist Alliance and Socialist Workers Party, 31

Zapytowski, Steve, 237–38
Zimmerman, Robert, 13